CAMUS

A COLLECTION OF CRITICAL ESSAYS

Edited by

Germaine Brée

A SPECTRUM BOOK

Prentice-Hall, Inc., *Englewood Cliffs, N.J.*

Current printing (last digit):
16

LIBRARY OF CONGRESS CATALOG NO.: 62-9305

Printed in the United States of America

11270-C

Acknowledgments

Certainly no book has benefited more than this one from the immediate, sympathetic response of all whom the editor approached—doubtless a testimony to the high esteem and affection which the personality and work of Albert Camus have elicited. My thanks go to the authors, translators, magazine editors, and publishers who gave their kind permission to print these articles. More particularly, I wish to mention the graduate students of the University of Wisconsin: Jeanne Strauss, who translated Spanish articles for my research, and Sondra Mueller, Emmet Parker, Eric Schoenfeld, Jean-Marc Vary, Josephine Valenza, whose names appear in the volume. I am particularly grateful to Ellen Conroy Kennedy for the unflagging patience and thoroughness with which she traced innumerable articles, for her perception in evaluating them, for her translations of several essays, and for her care in editing the manuscript.

Germaine Brée

Table of Contents

INTRODUCTION—*Germaine Brée* 1

ALBERT CAMUS: IN MEMORIAM—*Nicola Chiaromonte* 11

CAMUS IN AMERICA—*Serge Doubrovsky* 16

ALBERT CAMUS: MILITANT—*Justin O'Brien* 20

A SOBER CONSCIENCE—*Wilfrid Sheed* 26

SARTRE VERSUS CAMUS: A POLITICAL QUARREL—*Nicola Chiaromonte* 31

ALBERT CAMUS'S ALGERIA—*Roger Quilliot* 38

ALBERT CAMUS AND THE CHRISTIAN FAITH—*Thomas L. Hanna* 48

ALBERT CAMUS: THE DARK NIGHT BEFORE THE COMING OF GRACE?—*Bernard C. Murchland, C.S.C.* 59

CAMUS THE PAGAN—*Henri Peyre* 65

THE ETHICS OF ALBERT CAMUS—*Serge Doubrovsky* 71

ALBERT CAMUS: A BRITISH VIEW—*S. Beynon John* 85

THE WORLD OF THE MAN CONDEMNED TO DEATH —*Rachel Bespaloff* 92

AN EXPLICATION OF *THE STRANGER*—*Jean-Paul Sartre* 108

ETHICS AND AESTHETICS IN *THE STRANGER*—*Robert Champigny* 122

IMAGE AND SYMBOL IN THE WORK OF ALBERT CAMUS —*S. Beynon John* 132

NOTES ON *THE PLAGUE*—*Gaëtan Picon* 145

EXILE AND THE KINGDOM—*Gaëtan Picon* 152

AN AMBIGUOUS WORLD—*Roger Quilliot* 157

CAMUS AS DRAMATIST—*Henry Popkin* 170

TRIBUTE TO ALBERT CAMUS—*Jean-Paul Sartre* 173

Chronology of Important Dates 177

Notes on the Editor and Contributors 179

Bibliography 181

CAMUS

Introduction

by Germaine Brée

It is natural that a collection of critical essays of Albert Camus should differ from collections devoted to writers like Dostoevsky, Joyce, or Proust. *The Stranger* appeared a scant twenty years ago. All Camus's published work falls within the brief and recent span of years between 1942, date of *The Stranger*—his first and most widely acclaimed book—and 1960, the date of his death. It is more than likely that as yet no critical point of view can be considered as more than preliminary and tentative. In the next few years Camus's "Notebooks" may be published, and perhaps also some of the preliminary drafts of his works. Certainly, as a writer, he will then appear to us in a new light.

The essays in this collection, however, though perhaps none except Sartre's study of *The Stranger* can be considered as definitive, have other vivid qualities. Like Sartre's, they are often contemporaneous or almost so with the works with which they deal, which they approach with all the freshness and immediacy of discovery. Some of the essays included here were written ten years ago; Sartre's dates from 1943. They appraise Camus's work as it appeared to the eyes of critics at certain stages in its evolution; they even sometimes speculate, rightly and wrongly, about its future orientation. Camus can never again be read in quite that light, nor will any work of his impose itself again, as did *The Stranger,* by its authentic quality and tone.

In contrast to these articles of discovery, as we might call them, stand the few essays written just after Camus's death: Chiaromonte's "In Memoriam," as well as Doubrovsky's essay on Camus's ethics and its relation to Sartre's, Malraux's, and Gide's. Here perspectives have changed dramatically. Criticism no longer cautiously anticipates the future. Now set in the past, Camus's work is brusquely seen in a new perspective, as a unified whole situated in relation to the broader patterns of literature and the history of ideas. It is rare for so crucial a turning point in the life of literary works to be so immediately and clearly distinguished. The historian of literature is now ready to take over. A detailed, scholarly biography of Camus by Professor Carl Viggiani is already in the making and will be welcome.

The two decades during which Camus's name became increasingly famous cut our century in two in its very middle, with neat precision. In many ways the 1930's now seem to us thoroughly remote; they belong to a closed era. The mid-century uncovered fundamental changes in our understanding of most things of vital concern to our lives, stimulating radical and dangerous conflicts within our thought as well as within political organisms. Inevitably, even if he had wanted to, a man like Camus could not avoid the remorseless inner and outer pressures which, during those years, made writing a rather strenuous affair. Camus's readers and, a fortiori, his critics shared his concern with the ambient problems, political, ethical, or philosophical. There were no bulwarks to insulate literature in a neat little compartment. The terrain covered by critical studies of Camus's work is consequently very broad, and often reflects the strains and stresses of a particular historical moment. Many articles are in fact implicit dialogues, or, rather, debates. Rachel Bespaloff's article on that most fundamental of Camus's characters—the man condemned to death—can be fully grasped only in the light of the then still recent revelation of the concentration camp world. Chiaromonte's succinct summation of the controversy that centered around *The Rebel* is written from within the very heart of the discussion. Quilliot's two essays likewise carry on what is essentially a running argument with unconvinced opponents—those opponents of Camus whose articles we could not include but who are thus not excluded from our book.

Certainly, almost any essay about Camus written in this first period raises issues which were fundamental during those mid-century years: existentialism, Marxism, Christianity; political opportunism and political action; individual and collective moral responsibility. Some of these issues are no doubt perennial, though raised afresh in new circumstances; some are perhaps temporary. As Sartre would say, they "situate" Camus and his commentators in time. A new generation presumably will not be concerned with them in quite the same way. The common concern linking writer and critic is therefore in itself of considerable interest, defining, as it does, those elements in Camus's writings belonging to an epoch, upon which an artist must place the stamp of his own originality if he is to transcend the limits of his own generation.

Through many of these essays, underlying other issues, runs a basic comparison: the contrast and controversy between Sartre and Camus. It may well be that the never-interrupted dialogue between the two men will eventually appear as the ideological centerpiece of our time, at least insofar as Western Europe is concerned. Inevitably, a book of essays about Camus today turns out to be a book about Sartre, also. It is interesting to distinguish here, with S. John, one characteristic of contemporary British criticism, which is as ill at ease with that segment of Camus's work dealing in ideological controversy as is modern British philosophy when confronted with existential trends.

It may seem that literary criticism itself takes only second place in this volume. This is more apparent than real—and perhaps unavoidable, since Camus's first readers often found it necessary to clarify for themselves the intellectual vision needed in order to grasp the nature of Camus's fictional world. Champigny's article on "Ethics and Esthetics in *The Stranger*" and Doubrovsky's on Camus's ethics show how inextricably Camus's imagery is fused with awareness, and how inseparable are his coherently elaborated literary form and the questioning mental view that fashioned it.

Debate, dialogue, controversy—varied estimates widely differing in methods of evaluation and argumentation—these are the characteristics of a criticism of actuality and personal involvement. In order to encompass its vitality better, I adopted a deliberate policy in my selection of essays. I left aside the four or five book-size critical studies of Camus's work, for they have been easily available for some years now, almost all of them in paperback. They are listed, along with the original and translated versions of Camus's published works, in the bibliography. This in no way reflects on their value, however. Given the limits of one volume, I wanted to present articles which would bear on different facets of Camus's work, as well as reflect a characteristically wide diversity in points of view—always, of course, within the limits of relevancy and honest appraisal. I attempted to group the articles loosely according to centers of interest, moving closer and closer to the core of the work with analyses of the properly "literary" concern with image and language.

The opening article, written by Chiaromonte, one of Camus's closest friends, recalls the living person and situates Camus's thought vis-à-vis that most fundamental of contemporary problems: the nature of our relation to history. Sartre's "Tribute to Albert Camus," which ends the volume, brings us back full circle to the point of departure.

In the long history of intellectual exchanges between France and the United States, Camus's position is unique. No French writer before him reached so wide an American public. The first short essays in the volume touch upon this popularity.[1] These are followed by three articles bearing upon Camus's political activity. They contain more factual information than is usually available. Facts here seemed more relevant and useful than controversial judgments. The article on Algeria, because of its painstaking accuracy, is a case in point. From this article, readers can draw their own conclusions on a very hotly-debated issue.

More subtle, though still perhaps more marginal than it has commonly

[1] We had planned to include two essays, "Camus and the American novel" by Harry R. Garvin (*Comparative Literature,* Summer, 1956) and "Camus's Dramatic Adaptations and Translations" by John Philip Couch (*French Review,* October 1959), which, for lack of space, we were obliged, regretfully, to omit.

been thought, is the question of Camus's religious beliefs. The debate here is wide open. Father Murchland, Hanna, and Peyre approach the question from very different angles, but with a truly dispassionate and pleasing objectivity. Together they do away with much of a confusion which Camus might have likened to those mists that in *The Fall* roll over the skies of Amsterdam. From religion to ethics to aesthetics the path is straight. I then turned to some of the best among contemporary critics, Gaëtan Picon in particular, for evaluations of particular works—Camus's novels, short stories, and plays—or of the images and symbols in his essays and fiction.

The articles here gathered—raising as many questions perhaps as they answer—originating in Britain, France, Italy, and the United States, written by people holding widely differing political and religious beliefs, are only a very small fraction of the innumerable articles written about Camus. But they are, I think, a highly representative fraction. They cannot, to be sure, and should not fully encompass Camus's work in its richness and strength. But they will clear the path toward a fuller understanding of the value, limitations, and greatness of an aesthetically sensitive, deeply committed, and honest man.

Camus's rapid rise to celebrity between 1942 and 1945 is unparalleled in the history of French literature: *The Stranger, The Myth of Sisyphus,* the two plays *Caligula* and *The Misunderstanding,* together with Camus's role in the Resistance and the widespread interest in his *Combat* editorials, started his career in meteoric fashion. This sudden fame was not easy for the young writer, and there were many in the clannish and often supercilious world of Paris letters who, as long as he lived, reproached Camus for something he had neither sought nor wanted. With the publication of *The Rebel* (1951), barely a decade after his brilliant debut, Camus touched off one of the major controversies of the time, at least among Western European intellectuals. In an open letter to Camus, Sartre recalled those days:

> You were almost exemplary. For you bore within yourself all the conflicts of our time and went beyond them because of the ardor with which you lived them. You were a real *person,* the most complex and the richest, the last and the most gifted of the heirs of Chateaubriand and the scrupulous defender of a social cause. You had all the luck and all the merits, bringing to a sense of greatness a passionate love of beauty, to the joy of living, the sense of death . . . How we loved you then.[2]

Sartre's "then" tells a whole story: the story of Camus's struggle against the temptation to yield tacitly to the pressures of adulation and attack, and lose himself in the febrile activity of Paris; of his refusal to be de-

[2] Jean-Paul Sartre, "Réponse à Albert Camus," *Les Temps modernes,* VIII, No. [illegible] (August, 1952), 345, 346.

flected from a course he could maintain only through a strict inner and outer discipline.

"Each artist," Camus wrote, "preserves deep down a unique spring which, throughout his life, feeds what he is and what he says. I know that, for me, this spring is in the world of poverty and light I lived in for a long time." Throughout his spectacular career, culminating in the award of the Nobel prize in 1957 when he was forty-four, Camus never allowed himself to forget that he had once been a lonely child, defenseless against himself and against a paradoxical and often shockingly brutal world. This early unhappiness was the source of much of his strength and even, sometimes, of his inflexibility.

Another of the motivating forces behind both Camus's actions and his work was a violent and apparently never resolved struggle of opposing character traits. Like his Caligula, Camus had a drive toward self-affirmation, which, unchecked, might have turned into a cruel form of self-indulgence that he seemed to identify with the amorality, indifference, and serenity of the cosmos. But Camus also had a passionate need for self-denial, for a kind of effacement within the "world of poverty" that was his as a child. Each one of these powerful inner forces could have led to forms of self-destruction, which the act of writing seems to have held in check. The climate of Camus's work is inseparable from his struggles to maintain a sane equilibrium. At all times Camus refused the romantic delectation of thinking of himself as an individual apart from all others, marked by fate for a singular career.

Yet, even to his unflinching eyes, something like fate seems to have been at work in the career of the Algerian boy from a destitute working-class home, who almost from his first attempts at writing appeared as "the most gifted of the heirs" to the great prose of Chateaubriand.

"I think of a child who lived in that poor section," (of Algiers) he wrote in his first work, *L'Envers et l'endroit* (Betwixt and Between), "that section, that house. There were only two floors and the stairs weren't lighted. Even now, after many long years, he could find his way there in complete darkness . . . His body is impregnated with that house. His legs preserve the exact measure of the height of the steps. His hand the instinctive, never vanquished horror of the banisters. Because of the roaches." In this barrenness, the silent uncomplaining figure of his deaf mother seems to have created in the child an overwhelming sense of compassion, all the harder to bear because of his helplessness. She was the inspiration for one of the essential figures in many of his later plays and novels and suggested a fundamental symbol: the silent mother, the land of Africa, the earth, death.

The silence that both separated and united the mother and son, born as much of her endless labor as of her deafness, was later to influence the young writer's thought deeply concerning the problems of communication and expression. He was often to define the writer's "commitment" as the obligation to speak for those who are silent, either because, like his mother, they are unused to the manipulation of words, or because they are silenced by various forms of oppression. Speaking not long before his death of the novel he wanted to write, and which he was never to write, Camus said that he would have achieved nothing until he had placed "at the center" of his work "the admirable silence of a mother and the effort of a man to find some form of justice or love which could counterbalance this silence." A major source of Camus's work, which from the very start carried it beyond the frontiers of social satire or recrimination, is Camus's understanding of and sensitivity to that part of all lives which is spent in solitude and silence. He, too, struggled with that almost intolerable compassion which rings in the words of his youthful Caligula: "Men die and they are not happy." It was from this depth of compassion that Camus drew a sense of solidarity with human beings so profound that he could accept them in their fundamental nudity—an acceptance certain doctors come to experience, such as Camus's Dr. Rieux in *The Plague.*

To this basic experience of sadness, Africa added an experience of joy. No one has spoken of the glory of the Mediterranean landscape better than Camus. As a boy he roamed over its beaches and hills. The landscape of North Africa appears in all his writing, carrying with it the sense of freedom and life through his essential symbols: the sun, the sea, and many different sorts of light. "There is a solitude in poverty" he wrote, "but a solitude which gives its proper rank to all things. At a certain level of wealth the sky itself and a night full of stars seem natural possessions. But at the bottom of the ladder the sky takes on all its meaning: a grace without price."

To lose either the sense of one's human vulnerability and therefore solidarity with others, or the sense of one's participation in the grandeur of the cosmos is in Camus's language to move into the "desert" of exile. One can accept a drastic simplification which Camus himself made when he said that he was born in a country—North Africa—which, unlike Europe, taught no lesson other than that "there is on the one hand man, in his essential poverty and vulnerability; on the other, the glory of the cosmos in which he moves."

The few other facts of concern to those who wish to understand the work of Albert Camus more fully are well-known: the brilliant scholastic record which, with the help of his grade-school teacher, won him entrance to the lycée, then to the university; the tuberculosis which struck him at seventeen, of which he was never entirely cured. Camus began to keep "Notebooks" almost immediately after his first encounter with tuberculosis, and it is probably the reaction to his illness that made a writer of the passionate young Algerian. Young Camus, rather like his character Meursault in *The Stranger,* seems to have had an infinite capacity for living fully in the sensuous plenitude of each passing minute. If death is the essential discovery and the beginning of lucidity in Camus's first works, this awareness seems to be due partly to his confrontation with a problem he might not otherwise have envisaged in the same way. His reaction was first one of revulsion, then of refusal and of a passionate commitment to fight this personal form of "the plague."

The word "revolt" is not used by Camus in any generally accepted sense, and that is where the arguments and admonishments of some of his more highly abstract commentators have failed to reckon with Camus's meaning. His revolt is not directed against the romantic aspiration to transcend and destroy the limitations of the human being. It is directed against all that conspires to lessen any man's capacity for functioning with the greatest chance for happiness within these limitations. The enemies Camus detected and relentlessly fought were all the forces that stifle human beings—another of his basic symbols—whether these forces be mental, individual, or institutional; stemming from somnolence, insensitivity, or the myriad ideologies and systems, the complacent "godless theologies," of our time.

It is in this very personal context, rather than in abstract intellectual formulas, that one must seek the genesis of Camus's work and its freshness. The full flavor of the personality, sensitivity, and imagination of the man has often been lost in unnecessarily complex analyses. If, as seems likely, *The Stranger* continues to be one of the significant works in twentieth-century literature, it is not merely because of the new qualities of tone and energy in the writing.

Camus may have felt he was "a son of the Greeks"; nonetheless he brought a new resonance to French literature. Before him, the only great voice in recent French letters that seemed to come directly from "le peuple" and not from the middle class, whether "petty" or privileged, was that of Charles Péguy. But Péguy felt he was the inheritor of a medieval world, to which he clung and which served him both as a bulwark and as a justification, while Camus came from a country "without memory," which was at that time still untrammeled by traditional realities or myths. In a much broader sense than is the case with Péguy, Camus did belong to "le peuple."

He was never hampered by the grinding and obsessive sense of limitation and guilt that Sartre seems to feel as a "petit-bourgeois" in the era of "the Masses." That is perhaps why Sartre, who speaks so often of "commitment," has never been able decisively to make the practical choices involved in action—forever postponing that crucial moment where action limits thought and challenges its conclusion. Sartre settles with his conscience through speech and writing, whereas Camus took positions and acted directly in the political issues of concern to him, whether with or against the point of view prevalent in his entourage. The football player and lightweight boxing champion of Algiers that he had once been never mistook a battle of words for a real battle with all the physical risks, violence, and dangers it involved. Both what he had to say and the way he said it stood out with startling distinctness against the complex and often nebulous background of a literature richer at that time in literary *savoir-faire* than in authentic literary creativeness.

In many ways, Camus was a typical Algerian, with the Algerian propensity for improvisation and parody in every phase of daily living. This aspect of his personality escaped many of his critics, all the more since those years of war and occupation during which he became known were not conducive to light-hearted mockery. His natural Mediterranean flair for drama and mystification found an outlet in his passion for the theater—all facets of the theater. In the years just before World War II, with surprising persistency and patience, Camus directed a small amateur theatrical group—performing, adapting, producing. He came back to the theater as a stage director in the last years of his life, a little by chance, but with a sense of exhilaration that no other activity ever gave him. A feeling of the stage, of the voice speaking directly to an audience, of dialogue projected across the footlights to link audience and actor is present everywhere in his work. Camus was immensely sensitive to the quality of the human voice. It is one of his major tools of creation and establishes with the reader a certain carefully calculated rapport. Whatever the work, there is always a dialogue implicit in Camus's fictional universe: between himself and his main characters; between them and the reader; between the reader and the author. He and his characters address themselves to an audience.

Camus's unusual capacity for "dead-pan" impersonation, satire, and hoax is one of the highroads to the understanding of the peculiar, paradoxical form of imagination most obviously at work in *The Stranger, Caligula,* and *The Fall.* Emmanuel Roblès, an Algerian like Camus and a novelist in his own right, has recalled the amusing strategy that Camus, as a young journalist, employed with the censors, two cavalry officers allotted the surveillance of the daily *Alger Républicain.*[3] Camus took to sprinkling his articles with innocuous phrases, purportedly quotations from the most unquestionable writers: "When a man is on a horse, the horse is always the more intelligent of the two," signed André Maurois. Or, he might insert unsigned quotations, which the censors invariably removed. " 'Gentlemen,' " he would say with devastating courtesy, " 'It's by Montaigne. We omitted the name. Is it still censored?' " This playfulness and sometimes grim irony have no small part in the genesis of much of Camus's early work and in his favorite method of fictional creation: impersonation. Of *The Fall* Camus explicitly said, "Here I used techniques of the theater, the dramatic monologue and the implied dialogue, in order to describe a tragic comedian." Perhaps *The Stranger* and *The Fall* prove so disturbing to many readers precisely because they are as deliberately

[3] Emmanuel Roblès, "Hommage à Camus," *La Nouvelle revue française,* IX, No. 87 (March 1, 1960).

intended to disrupt the reader's tranquillity, as Camus's tricks were to provoke the censors. "Is there an aspect of your work important in your eyes and which seems to you neglected by your commentators?" Camus once was asked. "Humor," he answered. And certainly it is a fact that few critics have remarked upon the ferocious humor everywhere evident in *Caligula* and the more apparent but even more devastating humor pervading *The Fall.* Some of the confusion concerning Camus's ideas arises from a tendency to equate them with the points of view of his fictional characters. A dramatic monologue, obviously, is not the same thing as a personal confession. The aesthetic intents in these two forms of writing are basically opposed. Clamence, the Satanic impersonator, is Albert Camus's creation, only ironically his mouthpiece, and never Albert Camus himself. In a sense Clamence is a very modern version of Diderot's *Rameau's Nephew,* although no "philosopher," unless it be the reader himself, is there to maintain the dialogue. Camus asks a great deal of his reader.

There is of course, in Camus's work a pattern of thought and an evolution, both of which have often been discussed. First, Camus himself noted that his work was evolving around certain successive themes: at the beginning, the theme of Sisyphus: absurdity; then the theme of Prometheus: revolt; later, the theme of Nemesis: measure; and finally, the theme of love, which, because of Camus's sudden death, seems to have been left undeveloped, though suggested perhaps in some of the short stories of *Exile and the Kingdom.*

Much less discussed so far are Camus's experiments with form, in both drama and the novel. These experiments, though planned beforehand, were nevertheless worked out by trial and error, as Camus's "Notebooks" show:

> I used very different types of aesthetics and styles in my successive books. As an artist I feel cruelly limited by my gifts and faults, but I have never felt limited by aesthetics of any kind. For me styles are only means put at the disposal of a special purpose which I barely discern.[4]

And again: "I write on different planes to avoid mixing different forms. So I wrote plays in the language of action, essays in a rational form, novels on the obscurity of the human heart." [5] In the very last of the interviews he gave, the *Venture* interview from which I have just quoted, Camus was asked, "Which of your works do you look upon as the most satisfying? Can you explain why it lingers with you in that way?" He answered, "I do not reread my books. I want to do something else . . ." This is the very essence of the man, and perhaps of the artist. Camus's work is a search, a search for a truth felt, which he was atttempting to clarify and communicate through literature. He was far from believing

[4] "Albert Camus (1913-1960): A Final Interview," *Venture,* III, No. 4 (Spring-Summer, 1960), 25-39.

[5] *Ibid.,* 35.

that he had "arrived" either intellectually or as an artist, and he spoke and wrote of only a few hard-won certainties. That the impact of his work in his own time was great, the essays included in this collection clearly show. Perhaps more than anything else, it is the stubbornly committed artist Albert Camus never ceased to be that will carry his name into the future as one of the two or three major writers produced by the Western world during the momentous years of the mid-twentieth century.

Albert Camus: In Memoriam

by Nicola Chiaromonte

A man is dead: you think of his living face, of his gestures, his actions, and of moments you shared, trying to recapture an image that is dissolved forever. A writer is dead: you reflect upon his work, upon each book, upon the thread that ran through them all, upon their vital movement toward a deeper meaning; and you seek to form a judgment which takes account of the secret source from which they sprang, and which is now stilled. But the picture of the man is not made up of the sum of your memories; nor the figure of the writer of the sum of his works. And one cannot discover the man through the writer, or the writer through the man. Everything is fragmentary, everything is incomplete, everything is prey to mortality even when destiny seems to have granted both man and writer the gift of living to the limit of his forces, and of giving everything humanly possible, as in the case of Tolstoy. The story of a man is always incomplete; it is sufficient to think of what could have been different—almost everything—to know that his story can never contain the meaning of a human life, but only what that existence was permitted to be and to give. The truth was the living presence, and nothing can replace it. Immortality is an illusion for thought and art, as for man. They are nothing but relics mutely surviving time's erosion and history's disasters, like monuments of stone. But it is in this very fragility—that equates the humblest existence with one we falsely call "great," and is simply one that had the luck to express itself—that there lies the meaning and value of human life. And that value is eternal.

Albert Camus appeared in my life in April, 1941, in Algiers, where I had come as a refugee from France. I met him soon after my arrival, for in Algeria he was famous: the leader of a group of young journalists, aspiring writers, students, friends of the Arabs, enemies of the local

"Albert Camus: In Memoriam." From *Dissent,* VII, No. 3 (Summer, 1960), 266-270. Translated by Miriam Chiaromonte.

bourgeoisie and Pétain. They lived together, passed the days on the seashore or hillside, and the evening playing records and dancing, hoping for the victory of England and giving vent to their disgust with what had happened to France and to Europe. They also put on plays, and in that period were preparing a production of *Hamlet* in which Camus, in addition to directing, played the leading role opposite the Ophelia of his wife, Francine.

He had published a volume of prose poems entitled *Noces* (Nuptials), they told me. I did not read it, because in those days I was not in the mood for prose poems, but chiefly because the company of him and his friends was enough. In their midst I found the France I loved and the pure clear warmth of French friendship. I attended the rehearsals of *Hamlet,* went to the beach with them, took walks with them, talking about what was happening in the world. Hitler had just occupied Greece, and the swastika waved over the Acropolis. I suffered continual nausea and solitude in the face of these events. But solitary and shut off as I was, I was the guest of those young people. To know the value of hospitality one must have been alone and homeless.

I try to recall details, as if through them I could relive those days and learn something more about the young writer with whom I actually spoke little, since he felt no more like talking than I. I remember being totally obsessed by a single thought: we had arrived at humanity's zero hour and history was senseless; the only thing that made sense was that part of man which remained outside of history, alien and impervious to the whirlwind of events. If, indeed, such a part existed. This thought I considered my exclusive privilege. I felt that no one else could be so possessed by it; yet I yearned for someone to share it with. But there was no one. It was not an idea compatible with normal life, let alone with literature—or so it seemed to me.

However, I did have something in common with this twenty-eight-year old writer—love of the sea, joy of the sea, ecstatic admiration of the sea. I discovered this one day when I was his guest at Oran and we went by bicycle beyond Mers-el-Kebir to a deserted beach. We spoke little even then, but we praised the sea, which does not have to be understood, which is inexhaustible and which never palls. All other beauty does, we agreed. This agreement sealed our friendship. Camus told me then that he was writing a tragedy about Caligula, and I tried to understand what could attract a modern writer to such a subject. Unfettered tyranny? But contemporary tyranny did not seem to me to have much in common with Caligula's.

From Oran I continued my journey to Casablanca from where I had been told I could embark for New York. I said good-bye to Camus and his wife, knowing that we had exchanged the gift of friendship. At the core of this friendship was something very precious, something unspoken and impersonal that made itself felt in the way they received me and in our way of being together. We had recognized in each other the mark of fate—which was, I believe, the ancient meaning of the encounter between stranger and host. I was being chased from Europe; they remained, exposed to the violence that had driven me out. I carried away with me the impression of a man who could be almost tenderly warm one moment and coolly reserved the next, and yet was constantly longing for friendship.

I saw him again in New York in 1946 on the pier where I had gone to meet his ship. In my eyes he seemed to me like a man coming straight from the battlefield bearing its marks, pride and sorrow. By that time I had read *The Stranger, The Myth of Sisyphus,* and *Caligula.* In those black years the young man from Algeria had fought and conquered. He had become, together with Jean-Paul Sartre, the symbol of a defeated France, which because of them had imposed itself victoriously in its chosen domain—intelligence. He had won his position on the stage of the world; he was famous; his books were brilliant. But to me he had conquered in a more important sense. He had faced the question which I considered crucial and which had so absorbed me during the days that I first met him. He had mastered it and carried it to extreme and lucid conclusions. He had succeeded in saying, in his fevered way and in an argument as taut as a bow, why, despite the fury and horror of history, man is an absolute; and he had indicated precisely where, according to him, this absolute lay: in the conscience, even if mute and stilled; in remaining true to one's self even when condemned by the gods to repeat over and over the same vain task. In this lay the value of *The Stranger* and *The Myth of Sisyphus* for me.

With an almost monstrous richness of ideas and vigor of reasoning Sartre had said something similar. But when he arrived at the question of the connection between man and history today; between man and the choices which impose themselves today, Sartre seemed to have lost the thread of his reasoning, to have turned backward to realism, to categorical obligations imposed on man from the outside, and worse, to notions of the politically opportune. Camus held firm, at the risk of exposing himself, defenseless, to the criticism of the dialecticians, and of seeming to pass brusquely from logic to emotive affirmation. It is certain that what induced him to remain firm was not an ideological system, but the sentiment, so vehemently expressed in *The Stranger* and in some pages of *The Myth of Sisyphus,* of the inviolable secret which is enclosed in every man's heart simply because he is "condemned to die." That is man's transcendence. That is man's transcendence in respect to history; that is the truth which no social imperative can erase. Desperate transcendence and truth, because they are challenged in the very heart of man, who knows that he is mortal and eternally guilty, with no recourse against destiny. Absurd such transcendence and truth—but absurd as they were, they were reborn every time that Sisyphus descended "with heavy, but equal, steps, toward the torment whose end he would never approach. . . ." This secret, like the "eternal jewel" of Macbeth can never be compromised or violated without sacrilege.

Albert Camus had known how to give form to this feeling and to remain true to it. Because of this, his presence added to everybody's world, making it more real and less insensate. And because of this, not of his fame, the young writer from Algeria has "grown" in my eyes, worthy not only of friendship but admiration. It was no longer a matter of literature, but of directly confronting the world. Literary space, that *trompe l'oeil* that had been invented in the nineteenth century to defend the individual artist's right to be indifferent, was broken. Camus (and, in his very different way, Sartre) by the simple act of raising the question of the value of existence, asserted the will to participate actively, in the first person, in the world; that is, to challenge directly the actual situation of contemporary man in the name of the exigence of a conscience whose rigor was not attenuated by pragmatic considerations. With this, one might say, he returned to the *raison d'être* of writing. Putting the world in question means putting one's self in question and abandoning the artist's traditional right to remain separate from his work—a pure creator. In the language of Camus, this signifies that if the world is absurd, the artist must live immersed in the absurd, must carry the burden of it, and must seek to prove it *for others*.

This was the real and the only valid meaning of *engagement*. Such a choice carried within itself the threat of the cancerous negation that Camus called nihilism. One had to go through the experience of nihilism and fight it. The simplest act of life is an act of affirmation; it is the acceptance of one's own and others' lives as the starting point of all thinking. But living by nihilism is living on bad faith, as a bourgeois lives on his income.

In 1946 Camus was invited to speak to the students of Columbia University in New York. I have kept notes of his talk, and am sure I can reconstruct it without betraying his meaning. The gist of the speech was as follows:

> We were born at the beginning of the First World War. As adolescents we had the crisis of 1929; at twenty, Hitler. Then came the Ethiopian War, the Civil War in Spain, and Munich. These were the foundations of our education. Next came the Second World War, the defeat, and Hitler in our homes and cities. Born and bred in such a world, what did we believe in? Nothing. Nothing except the obstinate negation in which we were forced to close ourselves from the very beginning. The world in which we were called to exist was an absurd world, and there was no other in which we could take refuge. The world of culture was beautiful, but it was not real. And when we found ourselves face to face with Hitler's terror, in what values could we take comfort, what values could we oppose to negation? In none. If the

problem had been the bankruptcy of a political ideology, or a system of government, it would have been simple enough. But what had happened came from the very root of man and society. There was no doubt about this, and it was confirmed day after day not so much by the behavior of the criminals but by that of the average man. The facts showed that men deserved what was happening to them. Their way of life had so little value; and the violence of the Hitlerian negation was in itself logical. But it was unbearable and we fought it.

Now that Hitler has gone, we know a certain number of things. The first is that the poison which impregnated Hitlerism has not been eliminated; it is present in each of us. Whoever today speaks of human existence in terms of power, efficiency, and "historical tasks" spreads it. He is an actual or potential assassin. For if the problem of man is reduced to any kind of "historical task," he is nothing but the raw material of history, and one can do anything one pleases with him. Another thing we have learned is that we cannot accept any optimistic conception of existence, any happy ending whatsoever. But if we believe that optimism is silly, we also know that pessimism about the action of man among his fellows is cowardly.

We oppose terror because it forces us to choose between murdering and being murdered; and it makes communication impossible. This is why we reject any ideology that claims control over all of human life.

It seems to me today that in this speech, which was a sort of autobiography, there were all the themes of Camus's later work, from *The Plague* to *The Just Assassins* to *The Rebel.* But in it there remained, discreetly in shadow, the other Camus, the one that I can call neither truer nor artistically superior, for he is simply "the other," jealously hidden in his secret being—the anguished, dark, misanthropic Camus whose yearning for human communication was perhaps even greater than that of the author of *The Plague;* the man who, in questioning the world, questioned himself, and by this testified to his own vocation. This is the Camus of the last pages of *The Stranger,* and especially the Camus of *The Fall* in which we hear his deepest being, the self-tormenting tormentor speak, resisting all forms of complacency and moral self-satisfaction. He wrote, "I was persecuted by a ridiculous apprehension: one cannot die without having confessed all one's own lies . . . otherwise, be there one hidden untruth in a life, death would render it definitive . . . this absolute assassination of the truth gave me vertigo. . . ." With these words, it seems to me, the dialogue of Albert Camus with his contemporaries, truncated as it is by death, is nonetheless complete.

Camus in America

by Serge Doubrovsky

Camus has had the luck, up to a certain point at least, of being a prophet in his own country. Yet it would scarcely be a paradox to say that he is a great American writer even more than a French one, inasmuch as the public makes the writer. Reservations or hostility either toward Camus's person or his work are virtually unknown on this side of the Atlantic. His works, that is, those which have been translated, are sold everywhere, cheaply, in paperback. Students throw themselves upon these texts with an insatiable hunger; courses, lectures, books, and articles on Camus always draw sincere and immediate attention. This is true not only on university campuses, but in all the groups and "milieus" that have cultural interests. This phenomenon is interesting enough, but in itself hardly extraordinary. Other writers also stir up the unanimous attention of contemporary opinion. What is unique in Camus's case is the depth of the public's attachment, its direct and heart-felt nature. Camus's death struck every thinking person here as a personal loss. I am not talking about the editorials and obituary notices that appeared in newspapers and magazines. I am thinking of people foreign to teaching or to literature who came to professors with tears in their eyes; to students of my acquaintance who vowed to fast several days at the announcement of his death. Poems in Camus's honor were born in every corner of the country, from pens both expert and clumsy. Whether in litany, elegy, or a few stammered words, sorrow sprang forth from the whole continent. Surely the death of no American writer, and much less any other foreign writer, would have excited such emotion in this country where literature is a secondary activity and often seems a poor relation among the arts. There were no tears at the time of Hemingway's supposedly fatal air crash several years ago, and Faulkner's death would arouse less emotion than a baseball player's retirement. Under these conditions, how can one explain the exceptional intensity of feeling solely about Camus?

"Camus in America." From *N.R.F.*, XCVIII (February 1, 1961), 292-296. Translated by Ellen Conroy Kennedy. Reprinted by permission of the author and *N.R.F.*

Pushed far enough, the answer might perhaps lead to an analysis and an evaluation of the whole of contemporary civilization as it exists in the United States. We shall limit ourselves to a few remarks. On the whole, it can be said that Camus is the great writer American literature has waited for and who never came. The generation of Faulkner, Dos Passos, and Hemingway already belongs to the past and to history. Its value is one of example and no longer of witness. It so happens that the succession is vacant. There are a hundred authors not wanting in talent, but there is no writer who attacks the problems of our time in depth. If happy peoples can be said to have no history, perhaps prosperous peoples have no literature.

While this may be so, prosperity is not happiness, and this hiatus, of which sociologists, psychiatrists, and priests make daily note, has found neither its spiritual elucidations nor its artistic expression. Through the allegorical turn of his mind, through his effort to confine himself to the universal, through his wish to give meaning solely at the level of the human condition, Camus offered in his novels an image of man bare and free enough of the particularities of nationality or history to be immediately accessible. Sartre, on the other hand, whose intellectual and personal approach is so deeply rooted in one moment of both pre- and postwar French consciousness—or "bad conscience"—intrigues, irritates, or fascinates Americans. In general, he remains fundamentally foreign to them. Camus, however, presents through literature what is for the Anglo-Saxon mind often the essential thing: an ethic. And this ethic finds fruitful soil here in America. I would not say that Americans are always sensitive to what is deepest in Camus's thought: the sense of a tangible, vital participation in life that one might call "the solar joy." What they like most is the *Old Man and the Sea* aspect of Camus, the concern he shares with Hemingway or Melville for man's struggle within the universe and against it. Camus continues and expounds a humanistic ethic that stresses effort more than success, and that unwittingly nourishes the ascetic spirit still alive in America in spite of the cult of success and well-being.

But even more, Camus's sense of the tragic goes to the heart of the American situation. In the polemic debate which separated them, Sartre reproached the author of *The Plague* for making the struggle against Heaven the central theme of human activity, for translating the "ideal" situation of occupied France's fight against Nazism into the Manichaean vision of a Humanity aligned together against absolute Evil. Sartre argued that this was a betrayal of the true conditions of man's struggle to make an ideal of humanity triumph. Now—and this is striking—the allegory of the plague retains all its force within the American context, where it seems to find a natural setting. In American society there are no class conflicts; racial conflicts never for an instant put the social structure in doubt; and nothing basic separates either political parties or spiritual groups. In the final analysis, because the collective organism is confronted neither with internal dissidence nor really harrowing problems, men of good will automatically find themselves united in the face of evil. There are racketeers and municipal corruption to fight. The condition of the Negroes must be bettered, and war waged on cancer or tuberculosis. In various guises it is always the same, universal fight. In one of the numerous "homages to Camus" that appeared spontaneously just about everywhere, an American poetess recently compared Camus to a doctor, and noted that it was not by accident that his spokesman, Rieux, was a physician—a telling remark. It is precisely the *medical* element in Camus that is most acutely felt here; the courage which rises above ultimate and inevitable failure, the day-to-day love for men as they are, and a certain confidence in man, in spite of faults which are never moral defects. Here, in short, is an ethics rigorously separated from politics, or, if you prefer, inseparable from the sort of politics that can be reduced to ethics. Camus's humanism is the spiritual face of American democracy.

It is true that if for Camus the human struggle can only end in provisional victories that will ceaselessly be questioned, American optimism tends rather to envisage a progress that is slow perhaps, but sure—a unilateral advance, in spite of retreats or pauses. At first glance one might see in this remark a conflict between two points of view. This would be to misunderstand the writer's role in America. The best American writers have attempted to give body and a voice precisely to those tragic elements that society officially wishes to ignore, but that survive in the unspoken consciousness of many. Hemingway and Faulkner spoke out for those who keep silent. So does Camus in our own day. Indeed, if there appears to be in America an oft-noted divorce between the country as a whole and its writers, it is not because the writers express thoughts contrary to those of their fellow countrymen, but rather that they express thoughts their countrymen choose to hide from themselves. Camus's case seems to confirm this hypothesis. For, at the very least, it is paradoxical that the most admired writer in America should be an agnostic, and even an atheist—this in a country where religion is indispensable on every public occasion and hardly to be distinguished from good manners. For in spite of the pious propaganda one meets in every circumstance, flaunted even on billboards and in advertising campaigns, America, as Americans are doubtless the last to realize, is one of the least religious countries in the world. And that is what makes for its great strength: a people entirely oriented toward this earth, fiercely resolved to make it produce everything it can for man. I would venture to say that it is not in *spite* of his atheistic humanism, but *because* of it, that Camus is so popular here. Here at last is someone who has expressed in black and white the secular ethics which is at the heart of this American civilization, where piety is most often merely a pious fraud. An American author who proclaimed these unorthodox truths would run a heavy risk of being ostracized. But since it is a foreigner and a Frenchman who undertakes to say what no one dares to say aloud or even perhaps to himself, all is well—and the faraway Camus meets only with acclaim.

Albert Camus: Militant

by Justin O'Brien

Perhaps the rapid, sweeping frame of Albert Camus was a compensation granted him by fate, which knew in advance, of course, that he was to have but forty-six years of life. If his career was to be complete and his renown universal, everything had to move swiftly, and the world had to accept him at once. His tragic death in an automobile accident on 4 January 1960 at the height of his creative life fits the growing legend of the man who once said: "I have too much youth in me to be able to speak of death." And yet, throughout his work he constantly returned to the contemplation of death; he was a death-haunted man.

The agents of fate who speeded Camus' world-wide reputation were legion: friends and publishers, translators from Norway and Finland to Yugoslavia and Portugal, from Poland to Japan. Most likely, he couldn't even have pronounced most of their names properly. Now that Camus is dead and his second posthumous work is to be published in America in my translation, I am urged to look upon myself as one of those myriad agents—a minor one because I didn't begin to translate his work until four of his books were available in English. But having frequented Albert Camus in all sorts of circumstances—on a lecture platform during his first visit to this country; in a speeding jeep crossing Paris, with André Gide in flowing cape on the front seat turning round to talk to us perched behind him; at a lunch table in Paris where the late American novelist Richard Wright was his other guest; in his office as an editor of the Gallimard publishing house; on a Parisian stage where he was rehearsing a cast of actors in *Caligula*—I early succumbed to the warmth, simplicity, and straightforward charm of the man who has been snatched from us. In his person, as in his writings, he established at once a fraternal relationship with those he was addressing and no one could remain impervious to his boyish smile.

That smile is uppermost in my memory, which now sees Camus most

"Albert Camus: Militant." From the *Columbia University Forum*, IV, No. 1 (Winter, 1961), 12-15.

frequently as a young visitor to our shores, quite simple and unaffected, leaning on the mantlepiece at Columbia's Maison Française, or in my apartment in Greenwich Village with a cigarette in his hand, answering questions thrown at him by a group of eager-eyed students sitting at his feet. Like an astute politician, he was ever particularly interested in youth, for he knew that the future lay in them. Besides—despite the weight of his experience, so different from any we had known—he seemed so young himself.

But my first personal contact with Albert Camus, even before seeing him in such intimate surroundings, took place in March 1946, very shortly before Knopf published the first Camus book here. I say "personal contact" because as an American officer in Paris in October 1944, I had first heard of the young novelist-dramatist-philosopher of whom all Paris was talking. His books were already out of print and unavailable but, knowing that the Gallimard firm always kept a certain stock in the cellar, I managed to come home with copies. Then, in early 1946, almost simultaneous announcements spoke of *The Stranger* to appear here and of Camus's first visit to America.

No American Francophile could remember any lecture in French that had ever drawn an audience of more than three hundred in New York. Yet, on the evening of 28 March 1946, we were to be at least four times that many in the huge auditorium at Columbia University known as McMillin Theater. To be sure, it was the first such manifestation, as the French say, since the war, and the three lecturers were named Vercors, Thimerais, Albert Camus.

The Silence of the Sea, published here by Pantheon in French and in English, and variously attributed to all the great French writers from whom we had felt so dreadfully cut off for four years, had established overnight the reputation of the pseudonym "Vercors." "Thimerais" remained unknown, for the *Editions de Minuit,* which had clandestinely published and circulated in 1943 his moving essay entitled *La Pensée patiente* (Patient Thought), had not yet reached us.

But many already knew that Albert Camus, at the age of thirty, had brought out a novel (*The Stranger*) that was greatly admired in France, an essay with a very strange title, and two plays. A few Americans in uniform had come back with copies of the newspaper *Combat,* of which Camus was said to be one of the founders.

This was about all that New Yorkers knew about the three young Frenchmen who were to speak on the 28th of March. But everyone was eager to hear French spoken again and to see in flesh and blood some survivors of the black years of the Occupation. M. Claude Lévi-Strauss, Cultural Counsellor of the French Embassy at the time, had the idea of holding the meeting under the patronage of an inter-university committee, and, inasmuch as I had just shed my uniform to resume duties as an associate professor of French at Columbia, he named me chairman of the committee.

Consequently, Vercors, Thimerais (whose real name, Léon Motchane, is better known among physicists and mathematicians than among literary people), and I picked up Albert Camus in midtown to arrange for the symposium. It was already announced as "The Crisis of Mankind" and the title must certainly have been Camus's. The day before the big show at Columbia, the four of us went up to Camus's room in one of those mothy hotels on upper Broadway. I shall never forget the utter simplicity and the smile, reminiscent of a Paris street-urchin, that distinguished the youngest among us, nor the admiring glance cast at him by an attractive girl in the elevator. The moment we were in his room and the athletic young man had stretched out on the bed with a few notes in front of him, he easily dominated the group.

And the following evening, however eloquently the two others spoke, Camus easily dominated the debate. Making no distinctions between victors and vanquished in the war, he rapidly sketched a horridly debased conception of man that was, he said, the legacy of World War II. Had not all of mankind, forgetting ancient ideals, descended to the very vilest means in its intramural strife? But with his conviction, and with his unassuming, youthful manner, the moment he launched into his unflattering subject—which permitted examples drawn from Algiers, Auschwitz, the streets of Paris and Madrid—it became apparent that he was in fact defending human dignity and asking justice for all. When he told us that, as human beings of the twentieth century, we were all of us responsible for the war, and even for the horrors we had just been fighting (the concentration camps, extermination by gas), all of us in the huge hall were convinced, I think, of our common culpability. Then Camus—who was never one to castigate without embodying an affirmative suggestion in his sermon—told us how we could contribute, even in the humblest way, to re-establishing the honesty and dignity of men.

Just then, one of our students passed up to the stage a note saying that thieves had stolen the receipts, intended for war-orphans in France. After Camus's moving remarks, I could do nothing but announce that the "Crisis of Mankind" was at the door and that our charitable endeavor would be of no benefit to French orphans. Fortunately, a man of good will rose in the middle of the audience and proposed that on the way out everyone pay his entrance-fee a second time. At once the two girls from whom the little black box had been stolen rushed out to the lobby and set up their box-office again.

No one was surprised to learn the next day that the second "take," the only one left, amounted to far more than the first one. After all, Camus had spoken meanwhile and everyone had left under the spell of his persuasive words. One of the other speakers, back in Paris, told the story to the *Figaro,* which published a half-column about it—all to the glory of America, the land of gangsters and of generous hearts.

And it is quite appropriate that Albert Camus should have first addressed his American public, or what was to become his American public, on such a subject. He was at the time still editor-in-chief of *Combat,* which had introduced a new purity and vigor into French journalism. In one of his early editorials he had opposed humanity to mediocrity as if it were quite natural to define mankind by what is not mediocre. And in all of his editorials he had militantly defended the dignity of man and man's aptitude for greatness. "The Camus of *Combat,*" writes Etiemble, "showed that a journalist can distinguish himself by character while distinguishing the language, making of an editorial or of the humblest article a work of art."

One of the best photographs of Camus shows him standing at the imposing stone in the printing plant of a newspaper. With a pencil in his right hand and the ever-present cigarette in his left, he is correcting one of his editorials while an attentive printer stands beside him ready to run off another proof. Camus looks confident and happy, although working under pressure. Did he not say in the last year of his life that there were two places where he had been supremely happy? One was on stage either acting or directing a company of actors and the other was a newspaper composing-room. In both places he belonged to a team working in harmonious effort toward the realization of a specific aim. And in both situations he was likely to be the moving spirit.

Unfortunately, Camus the journalist and polemicist is still inadequately known in America. And yet, throughout his too-short and most active life, he never abandoned the journalism that had been his introduction to writing. In Algiers in 1938, at the age of twenty-five, he had joined the staff of *Alger Républicain,* and the following year his forthright reportage on the misery of the Kabyle tribes of Algeria had caused a sensation and incurred the wrath of the government. He was even then working on his play *Caligula* and already planning his first novel, *The Stranger*. Unable to find work in Algiers because of the official distrust of him, he had gone to Paris, early in the Occupation years, to work for *Paris-Soir,* one of the biggest dailies. Now beyond doubt a professional journalist, he may even then have dreamt of one day having his own newspaper marked with his personal stamp. The opportunity came after he joined the powerful resistance movement known as "Combat" in 1942 and helped found the clandestine newspaper of the same name, of which he became editor-in-chief. Despite his postwar position as an editor in the Gallimard publishing house, despite his growing fame from the publication of *The Stranger* and *The Myth of Sisyphus* and the staging of his plays, *The Misunderstanding* and *Caligula,* he continued to edit *Combat* until 1947. There it was that he could exert his most direct influence. As one of his young associates, Roger Grenier, wrote of that period: "The whole administrative staff of the newspaper, the whole team of printers, all those who approached him, even if they had not read his books and were far removed from the world of books, realized fully who Camus was and were comforted and enriched by contact with him."

For several years after 1947, Camus held no regular position in journalism—partly because of uncertain health and partly because his income was then assured by his position with Gallimard and by the royalties from his growing shelf of books and plays. Yet he continued, through occasional articles and speeches, to take a stand in those causes that were dear to him. Then in the autumn of 1955, when the weekly *Express,* for which he had frequently written, became a daily with the impressive collaboration of such as François Mauriac, Pierre Mendès-France, and François Mitterand, he returned to regular journalism, contributing to *L'Express* at least two articles a week. It was then that his statements on the North African problem reached the widest possible public. After *L'Express* again became a weekly, Camus tended to avoid journalistic commitments that would tie him down to frequent deadlines. Still, his name continued to appear irregularly among the by-lines of numerous Parisian weeklies. Until his death in January 1960, Camus was never completely divorced from the career he had begun in Algiers as a youth.

By setting an example of lucidity and courage in facing and answering the questions that torment us, Albert Camus did leave behind a model of superior journalism. Whether read in the newspapers for which he wrote them or in the three volumes in which he collected them under the modest title of *Actuelles* (1950, 1953, and 1958), his articles gave the post-war generation the moral guidance it seemed to need. The very independence of mind that put him on the governmental black list in 1939 allowed him to attack simultaneously Russian labor camps and American support of Franco. In facing squarely the anguishing problem of Algeria from 1938 to 1958 (one whole volume of *Actuelles* is properly devoted to this), he saw steadily, as only an Algerian Frenchman could, both the point of view of the Arabs and that of the more than a million French in Algeria. And his stirring series of articles on the Hungarian revolt of 1956, the most forthright to appear in France, allowed him to repeat and to document his memorable statement that "None of the evils that totalitarianism claims to remedy is worse than totalitarianism itself." The longest essay in the entire collection is the now famous "Reflections on the Guillotine," in which he vividly and convincingly marshals all the arguments for abolition of the death penalty. But even those pages, with their balanced appeals to reason, to sentiment, and to the senses, are no more moving than the brief evocation of his co-worker in the Resistance, the young poet René Leynaud, executed by the Germans for his patriotic activity.

"The era of chairbound artists is over," Camus once wrote. And, although he did not invent the now-popular term *engagé,* he personified for our time the committed writer. He achieved in his personality as in his work a delicate equilibrium between commitment and aloofness, between the state of solidarity and the state of solitude. As he said in "The Artist and his Time":

> Even if, militants in our lives, we speak in our work of deserts and of selfish love, the mere fact that our lives are militant causes a special tone of voice to people with men that desert and that love. I shall certainly not choose the moment when we are beginning to leave nihilism behind to stupidly deny the values of creation in favor of the values of humanity, or vice versa. In my mind neither one is ever separated from the other and I measure the greatness of an artist (Molière, Tolstoy, Melville) by the balance he managed to maintain between the two. Today, under the pressure of events, we are obliged to transport that tension into our lives likewise. This is why so many artists, bending under the burden, take refuge in the ivory tower or, conversely, in the social church. But as for me, I see in both choices a like act of resignation. We must simultaneously serve suffering and beauty.

Obviously Camus's polemical and journalistic articles helped him maintain that personal equilibrium, without which his novels and plays would not be the consummate works of art they are. And yet, as he implies, the same tone of voice is in everything he wrote.

Indeed, the journalistic writings show once again, as does the first novel, that, from the start of his career, Albert Camus wrote with the assurance that belongs to maturity. And the Camus of *Actuelles* (for, despite having translated these pieces, I can see them and their title only in French) will always make me think of that evening in March 1946 when the young Pascal, or La Bruyère, or Voltaire stood up on the platform and told us off in our smugness and righteousness. It matters little by which of these names we call Camus, because he so obviously belongs among the moralists, with whom the French tradition abounds.

A Sober Conscience

by Wilfrid Sheed

Call a man the "conscience of his generation" often enough, and chances are he will soon become priggish, preachy, and mechanically compassionate; he will begin to spread his concern too thin, over all the world's problems, and to make the same hollow sounds of dismay over every new outrage—Suez, Hungary, juvenile crime. He will remain a good enough man, but without value.

The first thing to be said about Albert Camus is that he seems to have survived successfully this oppressive title and all the rather moist adulation that goes with it. The reader will find in this collection of his political essays *(Resistance, Rebellion, and Death,* Knopf, 1961) no single stale or faked emotion, no sign of the "personage" at work. He felt freshly about everything that came his way, and was prepared to hurl himself at it without regard to his reputation as a young sage: as a moralist, he kept no press clippings.

For a Frenchman, Algeria is probably the test. There is an enormous body of pious, uncritically pro-F.L.N. cant on the subject to which virtually every French intellectual subscribes. But listen to Camus on this:

> To be both useful and equitable, we must condemn with equal force and in no uncertain terms the terrorism applied by the F.L.N. to French civilians and indeed, to an even greater degree to Arab civilians. . . . The truth, alas, is that part of French opinion vaguely holds that the Arabs have in a way earned the right to slaughter and mutilate, while another part is willing to justify in a way all excesses. To justify himself, each relies on the other's crime. But that is a casuistry of blood, and it strikes me that an intellectual cannot become involved in it, unless he takes up arms himself. . . . We could have used moralists less joyfully resigned to their country's misfortune.

The merest common sense, at this distance: but in France, where the question is more pressing, and where fanaticisms are in constant, zany reaction to each other, common sense can require the highest intelligence. For a liberal intellectual like Camus, the massive influence of the Sartre school had also to be dealt with, and it is no small parenthetic tribute to his memory that he was able to coexist with Sartre without losing a jot of independence, and without setting himself up as a sort of counter-mandarin either.

Of course, Camus had a special stake in Algeria. "When the fate of men and women *of one's own blood* is bound, directly or indirectly, to the articles one writes in the comfort of the study, one has a right to hesitate and to weigh the pros and cons." Notoriously, the intellectual rebel thinks twice when his own ox is being gored. But Camus need not have apologized; he was never of that stamp. His compassion for, say, the Hungarians, comes through just as authentic and just as personal as his compassion for his Algerian kinsmen. "I am not," he writes, "one of those who long for the Hungarian people to take up arms again in an uprising doomed to be crushed under the eyes of an international society that will spare neither applause nor virtuous tears before returning to their slippers like football enthusiasts on Saturday evening after a big game. There are already too many dead in the stadium and we can be generous only with our own blood."

The same note is struck: he will not recommend others to shed blood until he has shed some of his own in the same cause. Interestingly, this is not because he rejects violence as such. His feeling seems to be that violence so alters one's total experience that those *outside* it cannot give rational advice to those *inside* it; they would simply be talking about different things.

Several writers of our time have conveyed this same feeling about the mysteries of violence, George Orwell most notably among English-speakers. Like Thomas Aquinas, who "saw" something just before his death that made all his writings seem like straw, these men seem to have "seen something" which makes a good deal, anyway, seem like straw. Symptomatically, Orwell says that during the Thirties he suddenly gave up trying to write beautifully, cultivating thereafter a style of puritan simplicity. Camus also has a bare style. What they had seen was terrorism, and it made even literature seem comparatively trivial.

It is this sense of having seen something that gives Camus's writing whatever haunting quality it has. Although he uses in his political essays a narrow method, scorning adornment, variation of tone, even for the most part wit, one reads on, with the feeling that this man *knows* something. He does know, of course, about the French occupation; but his understanding goes further than that. He also knows about Hungary, by some kind of extension, and about the condemned cell and the frightened child. He knows about the twentieth century.

This is why Camus is able to maintain, without straining, such a consistent level of moral intensity. He really cares about each case of suffering that comes to his attention, because it strikes some chord of remembrance. Perhap the best section of the book concerns a poet-friend who was killed in the resistance. "A first group of six left the truck and started toward the trees. The machine guns immediately crackled behind them and mowed them down. A second group followed, then a third . . . Leynaud's friends simply wonder whether he was in the first group or one of the later groups." Not a word of rhetoric, or a hint of false sentiment; with memories like that a man needn't concern himself with taking attitudes, or placating Sartre, or shoring up his reputation as a conscience. He has more pressing things on his mind.

If there were nothing in Camus but outrage, however, even honest outrage, I suppose we would prefer him in pretty small doses. But there is another great attraction: the constant play of intelligence in his work. As a French polemicist, he perhaps had no choice (Camus makes a distinction between wise and foolish intelligence: he may have been thinking about French polemicists.) But he conceived it also as a matter of duty.

In the chapter entitled "Defense of Intelligence," he cites the anti-intellectualism of the Nazis as one of their indispensable characteristics—a traditional French gibe at the Boche, perhaps, but more than that coming from so serious a man as Camus. He personally had felt the brute burden of their "philosophies of instinct," and had found his own refuge in intelligence. Everything refers back to terrorism with Camus; it obsessed his imagination and gave it fire. "We are speaking of the kind [of intelligence] that is backed by courage, the kind that for four years paid whatever was necessary to have the right to respect." He saw this as the skeleton key to all dictatorships, the instincts tyrannizing over the intelligence; certainly, he had earned the right so to see it.

I have talked about Camus's seriousness and relative lack of wit. It is never precisely humorlessness, only economy. His touch is actually quite light, and he is never turgid or self-important. But he will seldom stray from his path for an aside or the shadow of a jest: there seems to be no time for that. Neither his health, which was always treacherous, nor his views of events, allowed him time to burn. He had seen his first warnings about Algeria (published in 1939) ignored, and subsequently watched his birthplace descend into nightmare. He had seen a lot more. But none of it reduced him to hysteria, only to brevity.

Whether this makes for the best kind of writing was a question that troubled him when he bothered to think about it. He holds a long and comparatively indecisive soliloquy concerning the future of art and artists. Should they ally themselves with causes? But yes. Should they remain detached? Truly. And are these two together possible? Manifestly not. Camus knows when he has failed to answer a question. But for once, one feels that the discussion has been remote, anyway, that Camus had already answered it for himself and that he was prepared to leave other artists to their own devices.

He was much more interested in life than in art. And while recognizing intellectually the importance of the latter, his own deepest concern did not extend far beyond his own art. For the first time in the book (and this discussion comes towards the end) there is a sensible diminution of intensity. Perhaps, he suggests, there will be no place for artists in the future. He cares about this, of course—Camus seems incapable of not caring about anything—but compared with what has gone before, he leaves the question with almost a shrug. An Englishman in the same position might not even have bothered to bring it up. Camus gives it rather conventional attention.

It may seem an irritation—it would surely have seemed one to him—that discussions of Camus always circle around the man rather than his books. But I find in recapitulating this last book that Camus does somehow remain, while many of his ideas blur and fade. Most of them were ideas of the moment, written in unextinguishably hot blood, but for yesterday's newspapers. They are admirable, they are original (if seldom strikingly so), but they fade. What lingers is a feeling that they were the right things to think at that particular time, and would be again in similar circumstances; and that the man who thought them was a good man.

But this is not quite true of everything in the book. Every now and then, Camus says something that sticks like a burr and keeps an enduring interest. For instance, the following from a speech given in a Dominican monastery, a speech neither conciliating nor truculent:

> The other day at the Sorbonne, speaking to a Marxist lecturer, a Catholic priest said that he too was anticlerical. Well, I don't like priests who are anticlerical any more than philosophers that are ashamed of themselves. Hence I shall not, as far as I am concerned, try to pass myself off as a Christian in your presence. . . . For a long time during those frightful years I waited for a great voice to speak up in Rome. I an unbeliever? Precisely. For I knew that the spirit would be lost if it did not utter a cry of condemnation when faced with force. . . . It has been explained to me since that the condemnation was indeed voiced. But that it was in the style of the encyclicals, which is not at all clear. The condemnation was voiced and it was not understood! Who could fail to feel where the true condemnation lies in this case. . . . What the world expects of Christians is that Christians should speak out, loud and clear, and that they should voice their condemnation in such a way that never a doubt, never the slightest doubt, could rise in the heart of the simplest man. . . . But it may be, and this is even more probable, that Christianity will insist on maintaining a compromise or else on giving its condemnations the obscure form of the encyclical. Possibly it will insist on losing once and for all the virtue of revolt that belonged to it long ago. In that case Christians will live and Christianity will die . . .

and so on, in the same vein and better in its entirety.

The man who went out of his way to say that to a group of Dominicans not only was a conscience; he had one.

And even when he wasn't using it precisely to our taste, it made him the kind of chivalrous opponent that every movement ought to pray for (although possibly few do), one, that is, who had the courtesy to expect virtue in others instead of just taking it for granted in himself.

Sartre versus Camus: A Political Quarrel

by Nicola Chiaromonte

The news in Paris is the public break between Albert Camus and Jean-Paul Sartre on the issue of Communism. I hope American readers will not think the fact that these two famous Parisian intellectuals could be aroused by such an issue to the point of ending a ten-year-old friendship is another sign of European belatedness. This polemic and this break are in fact a sign that in France ideas still count, and, more particularly, that French intellectuals cannot easily reconcile themselves to the divorce between principles and political life which has been the mark of the postwar years all over Europe. Moreover, the arguments exchanged between Camus and Sartre touch upon questions of general intellectual import. Finally, the Communist issue will be a live and significant one in Europe as long as the Communist parties retain their strength. The fact that they are still strong is not the fault of the intellectuals. And while the Communist issue is alive, it is worth the trouble to study its phenomenology.

At the origin of the Sartre-Camus clash, which occupies a good part of the August issue of *Les Temps Modernes,* there is *The Rebel.* With this book, Albert Camus attempted to do something that Jean-Paul Sartre has never found the time to do, namely, to give an account of the reasons which led him to take the position he took with regard to the political ideologies of our time, and more particularly Communism. Camus had taken part in the resistance as a writer and a journalist. He had been the editor of a daily paper after the liberation; during this period he played a public role, and took political stands. Having withdrawn from public life in order to devote himself to his writing, he felt that he was under the obligation of thinking through the ideas that he had been expressing in

"Sartre versus Camus: A Political Quarrel." From *Partisan Review,* XIX, No. 6 (November/December, 1952), 680-687. Copyright 1952 by *Partisan Review.* Reprinted by permission of the author and *Partisan Review*

articles and speeches. In other words, he felt intellectually responsible for his political commitments, and attempted to live up to this responsibility. For this, if for nothing else, he deserves credit.

In the author's own words, *The Rebel* is intended as "a study of the *ideological* aspect of revolutions." This has to be stressed because, as we shall see, the attack launched upon the book by *Les Temps Modernes* is all based on the assumption that Camus had meant his work to be primarily a political manifesto, if not a new *Das Kapital*. Briefly summarized, the main thesis of *The Rebel* runs as follows: (1) Nihilism, already implicit in the Jacobin myth of terroristic violence, has been brought to its extreme consequences by contemporary Communism. But nihilism is not exclusively a political phenomenon. It is rooted in the history of modern consciousness, and its origins can be traced back to such strange "revolts" against reality as Sade's, Lautréamont's, and Rimbaud's. Philosophically, the Hegelian notion of reality as "history," and of human action as a dialectical series of "historical tasks" knowing of no other law than their realization, is one of the main sources of ideological nihilism. From Hegel, in fact, Marxist prophecy is derived, with the vision of a "happy end" of history for the sake of which, in Goethe's words, "everything that exists deserves to be annihilated." This is the aspect of Marx emphasized by Communist fanaticism at the expense of Marx's critical thought, simply because apocalyptic prophecy, being as it is beyond the pale of proof, is the surest foundation of a ruthless orthodoxy. (2) At this point, the revolutionary myth finds itself in absolute contradiction with man's impulse to revolt against oppression, leading to systematic enslavement rather than liberation. (3) By denying that human life can have a meaning aside from the "historical task" to which it must be made subservient, the "nihilist" must inevitably bring about and justify systematic murder. The contradiction between the revolutionist who accepts such a logic and the man who revolts against injustice in the name of the absolute value of human life is radical. And the very absurdity of this contradiction should convince the man who insists on acting for the sake of real humanity that he cannot escape the classical question of the "limit." To begin with, the limit of the idea of "revolt" is, according to Camus, the point where the idea becomes murderous. Contemporary ideologies, the revolutionary as well as the reactionary ones, are essentially murderous. Hence they must be refused once and for all, at the cost of one's being forced into what the ideologists call "inaction," but which, in fact (except for the self-satisfied and the Philistine), is a refusal of automatic action and an insistence on choice, real commitments, and the freedom to act according to authentic convictions on the basis of definite situations, rather than follow ideological deductions and organizational discipline.

This is a rather crude simplification of Camus's thesis. It should, however, be sufficient to indicate that, no matter how debatable the arguments and the conclusions, the question raised by Camus is a serious one, and deserves to be discussed seriously at least by those people today who, while not pretending to have at their disposal any new systematic certainty, are aware of the sterility of the old political dogmas. Let us notice in passing that until recently Jean-Paul Sartre was not unwilling to recognize that he belonged in the company of these people. As a matter of fact, he went so far as to write that the biggest party in France was that of those who abstained from voting, which proved how deep among the people was the disgust with the old parties, their methods, and their ideologies; a new Left, he added, should try to reach those masses.

An attentive reader of *The Rebel* will not fail to notice that, in his own peculiar language, and in terms of general ideas rather than of specific moral problems, Camus formulates against the modern world the same indictment as Tolstoy. For Camus, as for Tolstoy, modern society does not recognize any other norm than violence and the accomplished fact, hence it can legitimately be said that it is founded on murder. Which is tantamount to saying that human life in it has become a senseless affair. Tolstoy, however, believed that, besides retaining an "eternal" value, Christianity was still alive in the depths of our society among the humble; hence he thought that a radical Christian morality: non-violence, could offer a way out. Camus is not religious, and much more skeptical than Tolstoy as to the moral resources of the modern world. He does not advocate non-violence. He simply points out the reappearance, through nihilistic reduction to absurdity, of the need for a new sense of limit and of "nature."

No matter how uncertain one might consider Camus's conclusions, his attack on the modern ideological craze appears both strong and eloquent. Of course, if one believes in progress, one might still maintain that Nazism and Stalinism were the result of contingencies, factual errors, and residual wickedness. But progressive optimism is precisely the notion that Camus vigorously questions. His arguments cannot be easily dismissed by a philosophy like existentialism, which stresses so resolutely the discontinuity between human consciousness and any "process" whatsoever, and which in any case makes it very difficult to go back to the notion that man's ethical task is to "change the world" through historical action. This not only because the idea of "changing the world" is a radically optimistic one in that it presupposes precisely that fundamental harmony between man and the world which existentialism denies, but because only if man is "historical" through and through (as Hegel and Marx assumed) is the definition of a "historical task" possible at all. Now, the main existentialist claim was the rediscovery of an essential structure of human consciousness beyond historical contingencies. From this, going back to Hegel and Marx seems a rather difficult enterprise, one, in any case, that requires a lot of explaining.

Yet, lo and behold, in the first attack against *The Rebel,* launched in the June issue of *Les Temps Modernes* by one of Sartre's faithful disciples,

Francis Jeanson, this critic found no better line of attack than to accuse Camus of "anti-historicism." His arguments can be summarized as follows: (1) by rejecting the cult of History which seems to him characteristic of the nihilistic revolutions of our time, Camus places himself "outside of history," in the position of the Hegelian "beautiful Soul," which wants to remain pure of all contact with reality, and is satisfied with the reiteration of an abstract Idea void of all dialectical energy; (2) by criticizing Marxism and Stalinism, Camus accomplishes an "objectively" reactionary task, as proved by the favorable reviews of his book in the bourgeois press; (3) intellectual disquisitions are a fine thing, but the task (the "choice") of the moment makes it imperative to struggle in favor of the emancipation of the Indo-Chinese and the Tunisians, as well as in defense of peace; this cannot be done effectively if one attacks the Communist Party, which, at this particular moment, is the only force capable of mobilizing the masses behind such a struggle.

This was bad enough. Much worse, and much sadder, is the fact that in his answer to Camus's "Letter to the Editor of *Les Temps Modernes*," Sartre himself did little more than restate his disciple's arguments.

In his "Letter," Albert Camus had addressed the following remarks among others, to Sartre:

> To legitimate the position he takes toward my book, your critic should demonstrate, against the whole collection of *Les Temps Modernes,* that history has a necessary meaning and a final outcome; that the frightful and disorderly aspect that it offers us today is sheer appearance; and that, on the contrary, in spite of its ups and downs, progress toward that moment of final reconciliation which will be the jump into ultimate freedom, is inevitable. . . . Only prophetic Marxism (or a philosophy of eternity) could justify the pure and simple rejection of my thesis. But how can such views be upheld in your magazine without contradiction? Because, after all, if there is no human end that can be made into a norm of value, how can history have a definable meaning? On the other hand, if history has meaning why shouldn't man make of it his end? If he did that, however, how could he remain in the state of frightful and unceasing freedom of which you speak? . . . The truth is that your contributor would like us to revolt against everything but the Communist Party and the Communist State. He is, in fact, in favor of revolt, which is as it should be, in the condition (of absolute freedom) described by his philosophy. However, he is tempted by the kind of revolt which takes the most despotic historical form, and how could it be otherwise, since for the time being his philosophy does not give either form or name to this wild independence? If he wants to revolt, he must do it in the name of the same nature which existentialism denies. Hence, he must do it theoretically in the name of history. But since one cannot revolt in the name of an abstraction, his history must be endowed with a global meaning. As soon as this is accepted, history becomes a sort of God, and, while he revolts, man must abdicate before those who pretend

> to be the priests and the Church of such a God. Existential freedom and adventure is by the same token denied. As long as you have not clarified or eliminated this contradiction, defined your notion of history, assimilated Marxism, or rejected it, how can we be deprived of the right to contend that, no matter what you do, you remain within the boundaries of nihilism?

This is a stringent argument. Sartre did not answer it, except by insisting that "our freedom today is nothing but the free choice to struggle in order to become free . . . ," and that if Camus really wanted "to prevent a popular movement from degenerating into tyranny," he should not "start by condemning it without appeal." "In order to deserve the right to influence men who struggle," Sartre admonished, "one must start by participating in their battle. One must start by accepting a lot of things, if one wants to attempt to change a few," which is, among other things, a theory of conformism, or at least of reformism, not of revolution and drastic change. Because if one "must start by accepting a lot of things" in order to change "a few," then why not begin by giving up wholesale notions such as "capitalism," "communism," the "masses," et cetera? If he had cared to answer further, Camus could easily have retorted that it was precisely the awareness that "one must start by accepting a lot of things" if one wants to obtain real changes that had persuaded him to give up ideological radicalism. While Sartre, for the sake of changing "a few things," is ready to swallow a totalitarian ideology plus a totalitarian organization.

One thing is certain: Sartre is more intelligent than that, and knows much better. How can he then, in polemic with a man like Camus, imagine that he can get away with taking over the most ordinary kind of journalistic arguments?

The answer, I believe, must be found in the phenomenology of the amateur Communist, a type widespread in Europe today, especially among the intellectuals.

The first thing to say about the amateur Communist is that he is by no means a "fellow traveler." He does not receive either orders or suggestions from the Party; he does not belong to any "front organization," and, except for an occasional signature, he does not give any particular help to the Communist cause. What he is interested in is the defeat of the bourgeoisie and the victory of the proletariat. A truly independent Communist, and, within the framework of the Communist *ideal,* a liberal, that is what he is. His points of contact with official Communism are two: (1) he considers it obvious that the Soviet Union is a socialist, that is, a fundamentally just state; (2) for him, it is self-evident that the Communist Party, being the party of the "masses," is also at bottom the party of social justice and peace. Hence, he supports both these institutions in principle, but by no means on all counts. The totalitarian mentality is utterly foreign to him. As for the difficulties and ambiguities of his position, he is perfectly aware of them. But, precisely, "one must accept a lot of things, if one wants to change a few."

One would surmise that, being neither a Communist nor an anti-Communist, neither a totalitarian nor a liberal, and insisting as he does on the difficulty, if not the illegitimacy, of a resolute political stand, the amateur Communist should be a rather Hamletic character. At this point, however, we witness a remarkable phenomenon: the fact of participating (at a variable distance) in the massive intellectual universe of Communism (*i.e.,* of being able to use Communist arguments without subjecting himself to the rigid rules by which the militant Communist must abide) gives the amateur Communist a singular kind of assurance. Far from feeling uncertain, he feels very certain, and behaves as if his position were not only politically sound, but also guaranteed by the laws of logic, ethics, and philosophy in general, not to speak of history. Which amounts to saying that he enjoys both the prestige of the Communist uniform, which he shuns, and the advantages of the civilian clothes, which he ostensibly wears. He considers himself "objectively" a Communist, insofar as he embraces the proletarian cause, but "subjectively" a free man, since he does not obey any order from above. The last, and most refined, touch of such a character is the conviction he often expresses that, in case of a Communist victory, he will be among the first to be "liquidated." His heretical orthodoxy will thus receive even the crown of the martyrs. In what substantial way these refinements can further the cause of the oppressed is, on the other hand, a question that should not be asked. The important thing here is that the unhappy consciousness of this believer without faith should continue to feed on contradictions, since contradictions are to him *the* sign that he has a firm grip on real life.

A man of Sartre's talent cannot be forced into a "type." But the fact is that, since 1945, every time they took a stand on contemporary politics, he and his friends have been behaving more and more like amateur Communists. Worse still, they have been more and more satisfied with taking over the usual arguments of the Communist catechism, and this with an arrogant refusal to justify their position in terms of the philosophical tenets with which they fare so well. They have been behaving, that is, as if, once they had declared themselves in favor of the Proletariat, the consistency of their ideas was a matter of automatic adjustment of which no account was due to "others." By so behaving, these philosophers have obviously fallen victim to the most intolerably dogmatic aspect of Communist mentality: the idea that being a resolute partisan can make short work of all questions.

The crudeness of the arguments used by Sartre against Camus cannot be explained if one does not assume that, having established an intellectual connection with the Marxist-Leninist-Stalinist mentality, he is intellectually dominated by it. Personally, of course, he remains independent. That is precisely why he, an intellectual, can be a victim of the delusion that intellectual assent has no intellectual consequences. But, having reached the conclusion that "participation" in the Communist system is the most effective way to pacify his political conscience, it follows that the philosopher of "anguished freedom" participates in the moral smugness which the system guarantees to its proselytes. From moral smugness to intellectual arrogance the step is short indeed. Once one has adopted a certain logical system, it is of course absurd not to avail oneself of the arguments that, from such a point of view, are the most effective.

It remains that Jean-Paul Sartre has not answered Albert Camus.

The latest news has it that the communist weekly *Lettres Françaises* has offered the excommunicated Sartre a political alliance. It is unlikely that the editor of *Les Temps Modernes* will accept such an offer. He prizes independence too much. He will not give any direct help and comfort to the Communist Party. He will simply continue to spread the intellectual confusion by which the Communist Party benefits.

Albert Camus's Algeria

by Roger Quilliot

You will not find it hard to believe me if I tell you that I suffer because of Algeria as others may suffer because of their lungs.

Essays, short stories, novels: all of Camus's works are related to Algeria and are rooted there: *The Plague, The Stranger, L'Envers et l'endroit* (Betwixt and Between), as well as *Noces* (Nuptials), *L'Eté* (Summer), and *Exile and the Kingdom*. There is one exception which, as such, is illuminating: Camus situated *The Fall,* a short story expanded to book length, in the grey mists of Amsterdam. Clamence, lost in the canals of the Dutch inferno, secretes his bad faith—that of a "judge-penitent" who, in the act of saying his *mea culpa,* strikes another's breast. In contrast, Algeria, or rather the Mediterranean of which it is only a boundary, may represent unconsciousness or lucidity, but never hypocrisy. When Camus again wished to express the jealous desire for life, he created Martha, a Slav, who, living in cold Czechoslovakia which is untouched by any sea, dreams of waves dancing in sunlight. Martha is one of the living dead, as are the Just, exiled in frozen Russia, cut off from happiness by a thirst for justice, and cut off from their own people by their unrelenting obsession. The latter have renounced youth and love; they kill so that Russia may be beautiful. Martha, who has renounced nothing, kills so that she may one day come to know life and beauty on the shores of the Mediterranean. As opposed to the lands of ice and death, Algeria is the incarnation of love of life, natural beauty, and the splendor of the world. Beautiful like the sea, Algeria is sterile like the sea; alive like the sun, like the sun, it is murderous.

From *L'Envers et l'endroit* to *Exile and the Kingdom,* Camus discovered in Algeria the pendulum swinging from yes to no, from life to death, from abundance to sterility. These, poverty, Belcourt, and his mother's small flat taught him. But a few kilometers away, the beach offered him its

"Albert Camus's Algeria." From the *Revue Socialiste,* October, 1958, pp. 121-131. Translated by Emmet Parker. Reprinted by permission of the author and the *Revue Socialiste.*

treasures. Not far from Algiers the Roman ruins at Tipasa, buried under exuberant and richly colored vegetation, sang of the victory of life over death, of ever-renascent nature over the ephemeral constructions of man. But further toward the south, Djemila, eroded by the wind, spoke of the permanence of death and the annihilation of stone under the sun. For the sun is life-giving, but the sun kills. It rides high in the sky, it dazzles Meursault's eyes, and it triggers the murderous shot—the sun is the real murderer. It strikes down oppressively on the day of the trial, similar in its cruel and blinding relentlessness to the prosecutor's accusations; its brutal flash is like the blade of the guillotine. The desert at the edge of the wheatfields, the red of the hibiscus and the dull sand, the odor of flowers and the smell of human misery, the starving Kabylia and the modern buildings of Algiers—Algeria is full of contradictions, a land of men and an inhuman land.

People there also carry within them their contradictions: indolence and brazenness of bodies stretched out on the beaches, the naïve cult of the body and latent mysticism, aloofness and familiarity, amiability and violence, the concomitant taste for exhibition and mystery. In "The Minotaur" and in "Summer in Algiers," Camus describes with humor or with gravity his fellow countrymen who, like himself, are so ready to burn up their lives for fear of losing them. Algerians are capable of patient resignation, but they also have a capacity for revolt which sometimes reaches a pitch of insane fury. Caligula, who is Roman and who personifies an evil which spread over the banks of the Weser and the Moskva, is kin to the men of Algeria who, passive for many years, become suddenly armed for their misfortune by the frenetic desire to live, combined with the sudden despair of dying. From that moment the Plague draws closer; it hovers nearby, watching Oran, the city that turns its back to the sea.

Undoubtedly, the Plague of which Camus speaks symbolically came to us from the East. It swept over Europe, and it seemed to Camus that Africa would be spared, protected by the equilibrium inherent in classical thought, the Mediterranean moderation which he found exemplified in the balance between the Ancient Greek gods of light and darkness, between Apollo and Dionysus, between Socrates and Callicles. He had confidence in the fierce individualism and earthiness which had once motivated the Spanish anarchists in their struggle against the "right" of the Falangist state and the "right" of the Stalinists. Yet Camus knew better than anyone that Cadiz still lived in a state of siege; neither the sea nor the sun serves as protection against the implacable laws of the Plague. They only render the triumph of evil more overwhelming, more tragic, as in Oran encircled by barbed wire. Beauty outlawed, men living amid fear and hate, observation towers and barbed wire, the compounds for the pest-ridden victims—no doubt that at the moment he wrote his novel, Camus rejected them for Algeria, his homeland. He knew it was capable of bloody uprisings, massacres, the basest passions, and the worst acts of violence. But he could not imagine that it might give way to a reign of systematic terror and cold violence, to the spirit of the Inquisition. The conclusion of *The Rebel* makes this clear. Moderation!

From Casablanca to Beirut, from Damascus to Seville, the Mediterranean world is shaken by convulsions; Socrates drinks hemlock everywhere along its shores. And in the face intoxicated by pain and blood which his fellow countrymen turned toward him Camus no longer recognized Algeria, but only the absurd and the temptation of annihilation. The gentle lines of the Chenoua, the caressing bite of the sea, the tea roses of Tipasa, smooth as cream—these are the deadly nuptials which Algeria celebrates today. And those who were astonished by Camus's silence were very shallow indeed.

• • •

It had been some time since he had seen the first rats die in the stairways, the rats of colonialism, an old sickness that was dragging on in Algeria. Camus did not consider the presence in Algeria of people of French origin as illegitimate, or even contestable. His father's family had fled the German occupation in 1870, seeking a new Alsace on Algerian soil. But no justice was being rendered the mass of Arabs, most often condemned to a life of misery for which even the difficulties of Camus's own childhood provided little basis for comparison. As did the Leftists at that time, Camus dreamed of substituting for these two Algerias that were juxtaposed rather than intermingled, an Algeria without fault, without discrimination, borrowing from official language, peopled by Frenchmen—each entirely equal to all others. For practical reasons, he thought it well to turn to a rat-exterminating enterprise in vogue at that time: the Algerian Communist Party. But he discovered in less than a year that the struggle against the Plague in Algeria furnished a social pretext to a branch office more intent upon rationally exploiting suffering for the profit of the home office than upon progressively abolishing it. Since a certain preference for the living human being inclined him toward the living Arab of today rather than toward the Arabs of the century to come, he decided that the Communist method was not the most desirable one.

Some time later the Popular Front brought him new hope.

> In 1936, the Blum-Violette Project made the first step, after seventeen years of stagnation, toward a policy of assimilation. It proposed nothing revolutionary. It took up once again the proposal to grant civil rights and electoral status to 60,000 Mohammedans. The relatively modest project raised an immense hope among the Arab population. . . . The powerful "*colons*" grouped in financial committees and in the Association of Algerian

Mayors set in movement such a counteroffensive that the project was not even presented before Parliament.

Three years of inertia: Algeria sank back into oblivion. In the midst of the Nazi vociferations, who was to take notice of colonial problems? Who even among the European settlers or the rich Mohammedans was to concern himself over the misery of the Arab mountaineers or the Kabyle peasants? In 1939, a famine devastated Kabylia. To this famine, Albert Camus, one of the reporters for the Socialistic *Alger Républicain,* devoted a lengthy news report, hoping to move, if not the administration, at least the mass of his fellow countrymen. I think that I was the first to draw attention to that series of articles, remarkable already for their style, their restrained feeling, and their humane sentiment. As he follows the "itinerary of a famine," it is in human beings that Camus takes an interest. He continually cites actual incidents which he had witnessed with his own eyes, using statistics only to support and give generality to the facts.

He noted the failings and the needs; he was careful not to make of this level-headed indictment of generalized negligence a polemic weapon against any particular administrator. Camus wished to be of service to the Kabyles rather than to damn those responsible for their difficulties. As he repeated again and again, what he proposed were reparations for the former, not expiation on the part of the latter. In the realm of justice, he had no desire to appeal to the tribunals that punish; he appealed rather to the courts of arbitration which order that amends be made.

His findings remain sadly up-to-date: "Kabylia is an overpopulated area; it consumes more than it produces." Consequently there is famine, and one can almost hear La Bruyère's or Bossuet's words of indignation over the lot of the seventeenth-century peasant when Camus writes:

> I think I can state that at least fifty percent of the population sustains itself on herbs and roots while waiting for assistance from administrative charity in the form of distributions of grain. . . . At dawn in Tizi-Ouzou I saw children in rags fight with Kabyle dogs over the contents of a garbage can. To my questions people answered, "It's like that every morning."

Nonetheless the imperturbable administration continued to enforce the customary regulations.

• • •

"What remedy has been found for such suffering? I can answer without hesitation, 'Only one: charity.'" Politically oriented charity, moreover, the administration of which was left to the discretion of the *caïds,* local Mohammedan chieftains. Furthermore, practically nothing had been done about the unemployment that affected one-half of the population. Nothing had been done about the "insulting wages" that made of working conditions in the Kabylie "a regime of slavery." The settlers objected that the output of the Kabyle worker was inadequate. Here Camus takes a firm stand "against that abject line of reasoning which deprives a man of strength because he does not have enough to eat, and then wants to pay him less because he lacks strength." They also invoked the Kabyle's mentality and his minimum needs:

> I know of nothing more despicable than these arguments. It is despicable to say that these people adapt themselves to any condition. . . . In the attachment of a man to his life there is something stronger than all the suffering in the world. It is despicable to say that these people do not have the same needs as we have. If they had no needs such as these before, we would have created them a long time ago. It is strange to see how the very nature of a people can be used to justify the debasement in which one keeps them, and how the proverbial reticence of the Kabyle peasant can legitimize the hunger which gnaws his stomach. No, it is not in this way that things must be viewed. . . . The truth is that we rub elbows daily with a people who live three centuries behind the times, and we are the only ones who are insensitive to this incredible anachronism.

• • •

The rats continued to die nevertheless, invading the gutters and the mouths of sewers. In 1945, the Arabs rebelled at Sétif—a bloody popular uprising, followed by pitiless repression. At that time Camus was directing *Combat.* He left at once for a three-week trip with the intention of informing the indifferent mother country. As the years of World War II were coming to a close, who else was concerned with the "incident" at Sétif? While Hiroshima was being wiped off the map, how unimportant these individual massacres seemed. At the source of the drama Camus found the ever-present suffering of the people: "Algeria in 1945 is plunged in a political and economic crisis which has always been endemic there but which has never been so acute." Because of the lack of rain the harvest was extremely poor; for lack of reserve provisions famine ravaged the entire country. The little wheat in Algeria was being sold on the black market or unequally allocated. Theoretically the Arabs' ration was five-sixths that of the European settlers; in reality it was one-third or one-half. Hunger and injustice were painfully awakening the political consciousness of a people who had remained passive until that time.

Most certainly France had chosen the way of assimilation, and the ordinance of March 7, 1944, continued, on the whole, along the lines of the Blum-Violette Project—but ten years behind schedule. Now, Camus notes,

France's defeat and her loss of prestige have intervened as also the landing of 1942 which put the Arabs in contact with other nations and awakened their capacity for comparison. Finally there is the Pan-Arab Federation which is a constant temptation for the North-African populations.

He affirmed with bitterness that the policy of assimilation did not correspond to the given situation. In 1945, he wrote:

I have just read in a morning paper that eighty per cent of the Arabs want French citizenship. But I can sum up the present state of Algerian politics by saying that they indeed *wanted* it, but that they no longer want it . . . Arab opinion, if I am to believe the results of my investigation, is indifferent to the policy of assimilation.

The integrationists might have done well to consider this statement.

Ferhat Abbas and the Socialist Aziz Kessouz symbolized this evolution. They had once demanded assimilation; they now insisted upon "the recognition of an Algerian nation tied to France by bonds of federalism." Not for a moment does it occur to Camus to reproach Ferhat Abbas, "that product of French culture," with his earlier statements on the non-existence of the Algerian nation. Instead he seeks to understand the Arab leader's evolution, and an analysis of Ferhat Abbas's "Manifesto" proves eloquently that the French had missed an opportunity sometime earlier. General Catroux, in 1943, had accepted this text as a basis for discussion. The French administration, however, had taken the uprising at Sétif as a pretext for the imprisonment of the "Friends of the Manifesto." "Pure and simple stupidity," Camus replied. If Ferhat Abbas were mistaken in considering assimilation as an unattainable reality, "it would have sufficed to make that reality attainable in order to deprive the friends of the Manifesto of any tenable argument."

Then years passed by, in which a new status for Algeria was conceived and allowed to abort in trumped-up elections—ten years, in the course of which Camus had to bear witness for his Mohammedan friends who were imprisoned and dragged before the courts; ten years of hope and disappointment, during which the insane war in Indo-China, the contradictions of French policy in Morrocco and in Tunisia succeeded in awakening despair among the Arab masses and hope among the most intransigent Nationalists. The former could expect nothing more from the will of the French nation; the latter based their hopes on the incoherence of its decisions. It was then that rebellion broke out. A savage rebellion, as excessive in its objectives as in its means. Camus could understand a terrorism like that of *The Just Assassins* which recoils from murdering children and strikes only at the guilty, which offers life for life, as Kaliayev or Sophia Peroskaya once did. But he could not understand a blind terrorism which struck preferably at the innocent or the enlightened; nor a reactionary terrorism which attacked schools and all symbols of modern life; nor the mutilations that resulted from barbaric instincts, superstition, and religious fanaticism. The form of rebellion which Camus advocated must find its limits within its own structure. Standing firmly against oppression, the rebel affirms his right to live, but his rebellion begins to decay at the moment when, in its turn, it gives way to organized oppression and terror. Typically, Camus takes this occasion to recall the rebel to a respect for life. Though he may deplore the fact that these "forgotten men," the Arabs, have taken arms against "the dream of a power which thinks itself everlasting and forgets that history always marches forward," he can still excuse them. But when they in their turn come to dream of eradicating the existence of the French in Algeria, to deny the presence of a million Frenchmen, in Camus's eyes they exceed the limits of justifiable rebellion and bring down suffering upon everyone.

The elections were drawing near. French policy could be made flexible. Therefore Camus, in *L'Express,* launched toward both sides the appeal of Socrates to the Athenians. Like Montaigne refusing to choose between Guelphs and Ghibelines, like Romain Rolland combatting both French and German lies, Camus wanted "to place himself in the no man's land between two armies and preach, in the midst of bullets, that war is a deception and that bloodshed, if it sometimes carries history forward, carries it forward to further cruelty and suffering." Since Parliament was procrastinating, he would himself undertake to explain to both sides that life is of prime value and that power and justice lose all meaning in the middle of a cemetery. He was aware of the chasm which separated the Metropolitan Frenchman and the Algerian settler. Therefore he reminded the former that they had also benefited from colonization and that they had closed their ears to the cries of suffering of the Arabs. Rather than cause the settlers to band together from "a bitter sense of solitude," and so force them to unite in "dreams of criminal repression or of spectacular secession," Camus suggested that it would be better to arouse and sustain in them a liberal state of mind which would prepare them for reasonable compromise. Of the French settlers he asked that they loyally recognize the defeat of the policy of assimilation, "first of all because it has never been implemented, and secondly because the Arab people have retained their individuality which is not compatible with ours." A national Arab individuality exists and the dream of reconquest leads straight to abandonment. Finally he asked the militant Nationalists to renounce their intransigent position as well as the temptation of Pan-Arabism. To all he issued an appeal for the protection of civilians so that the hellish cycle of hatred might be broken.

He took up this appeal for a civil truce in Algiers on January 22, 1956, but passions were already such that the *ultras* jeered at him and attempted to attack him. They could not forgive him for having approved a few days earlier the Socialist declaration according to which there could be no unilateral negotiation: "In order for negotiations to take place, each side involved must take into account the rights of the other and must concede something in the way of a settlement." They could not forgive him his proposal for a round-table discussion which would assemble representatives of all the divergent views on Algerian interests. The twenty-second of January prefigured the sixth of February, the day when Algiers mobilized in opposition to the President of the Council, cried him down, and threatened him so successfully that he yielded to the mob. That was the day, according to Camus, which set in motion the machinery of repression. This first concession to the spirit of violence brought about the banishment from Algeria of the last pocket of liberals. The "Algerian Community" Aziz Kessouz had proposed was to disappear. M. de Maisonseul, a friend of Camus, also guilty of wanting a truce, was himself imprisoned. Each day the helplessness of the civil authorities grew more apparent and pacification took on the tortured countenance of war.

The Arab Nationalists, on the other side, stiffened their resistance accordingly. Their demands became more and more unacceptable. It is true that part of the French press sustained them in the hope of an early and complete success, and condemned the French settlers without reservation. Camus recalled to a sense of decency the judge-penitents who, like Clamence in *The Fall,* willingly placed the burden of guilt on others and sought to expiate the sins of the entire nation by mortifying the flesh of a few of its sons.

> There are those who pass without transition from a speech on the principles of honor or of fraternity to a worship of the accomplished fact or of the cruelest faction. I continue to believe, however, in the case of Algeria as in all other cases, that such aberrations on the part of the right as well as on the part of the left point up clearly the nihilism of our time.

Faithful to himself, Camus refused to condone fanaticism. In his eyes the revolt of the Arabs posed the problem of their oppression which demanded reparations; it did not resolve it any more than fear on the part of the French justified blind repression. Terrorism and torture reinforced and complemented one another to the supreme satisfaction of totalitarians of whatever breed they might be. Both attitudes—the events proved it—were as ineffective as they were immoral. To render passions calm and sober: such was the object of Camus's statement. "But," he added, "its effects have been nil up to now; this book is also the story of a failure." It is only too true that the most sensible words, once passions are unleashed, are dispersed in the winds. Hence, only silence remained for Camus who needs must render justice to both sides—

incapable of choosing between two forms of violence, two totalitarian movements.

When weariness seemed to have overcome both camps, and the most confident were worried, he chose to speak out once more.

> An Algeria made up of a federated people and bound to France seems to me to be preferable, in terms of plain justice, to an Algeria bound to the Islamic Empire which would accomplish nothing, insofar as the Arab people are concerned, except to increase their poverty and suffering, and which would tear the Frenchmen of Algeria from their native land.

In a final note, he gave an outline of what this new Algeria should be. First he defined basic principles: condemnation of colonialism, of the repeated lie of assimilation, of the unjust allocation of tax revenues, of scornful attitudes; he also condemned the claim to total independence and asserted the right of indigenous French settlers to remain in Algeria. A federal structure, which Camus borrowed from the Lauriol Plan, would have to be worked out. The Algerian Federation would only exist on an individual basis because of overlapping of different ethnic groups in the same areas. Therefore, in the early stage, the French Parliament would include a Metropolitan section (approximately five hundred deputies of which fifteen would represent the French settlers) and a Mohammedan section of about one hundred members. The latter would legislate separately on problems pertaining to the Arab population, the former on problems pertaining to the settlers, and Parliament, in a united session, would legislate on common problems. The administration would be responsible to each of the sections or to the combined legislative body, depending upon the problems involved.

In the second stage, when the French Commonwealth would have been set up, the Algerian Regional Assembly would express the local autonomy of Algeria and be integrated through the channels of the Federal Senate and the Federal Government into the whole Commonwealth —this requiring a constitutional revision.

If I have insisted on these close ties with Algeria it is because nothing of what Camus wrote should be unknown to us; because in these articles he treated with rare good faith and a rare strength of conviction a country which was close to his heart and which, even while he was in voluntary exile, remained his native land in which he was passionately interested. He knew what he was talking about, and he said it with as much sustained fervor as moderation and objectivity. He entered into the arguments of both sides and he strove to render justice to each. The reading of *Actuelles III* can only be profitable to those who are haunted by the Algerian tragedy. All of those, finally, who admire Camus will see him as he actually was: passionately devoted to justice but careful of preserving human lives; a rebel, but restrained in his revolt; lucid, and disdainful of the procedures of base polemics; and finally, close to men and the world in which they live, love, and suffer—alone like all those who are dissatisfied with over-simplifications, who are nevertheless closely involved in the action unfolding: "I knew also that it would have been pleasant to abandon oneself to an evening so surprising and so grandiose, but that the suffering whose flames burned red before us imposed a kind of ban on the beauty of the world."

Albert Camus and the Christian Faith

by Thomas L. Hanna

I

Those who have read only the literary works of Albert Camus have surely been struck by the essential role which the Christian faith plays in these works. In both his novels and his plays there emerges at some point an element of Christianity, either in the form of an idea or in a person or both. In fact, it readily becomes apparent that in all his literary pieces Camus is centrally concerned with religious-moral themes and that these constitute much of the force and attractiveness of his works. In one of Camus's earliest works, the four lyric essays entitled *Noces* (Nuptials), we notice that the central ideas about which this lyricism is woven are those of sin, death, duty, immortality, and hope. These essays, completed during Camus's twenty-fourth year, gave witness to the arrival of a religious thinker who was soon to take a unique position in the battle of ideologies which now dominates contemporary thought and letters. In recent years Camus has established himself as one of the most prophetic and lucid philosophers of our times. He is one of those rare events which are characteristically given us only by French civilization: a superbly articulate philosopher and writer. Moreover, Albert Camus is today's most articulate non-Christian thinker.

To characterize Camus as a religious-moral philosopher means to say that his preoccupation is with questions of the nature and meaning of men, their hopes, their possibilities, and their destiny. And within this area Camus has established a positive humanism, a religious philosophy which, to many, is the first move toward what has been termed a "new humanism."

What is mandatory is that, if there is to be such a thing as a new humanism, it cannot be developed in isolation from the great religious alternatives which the Western world possesses. This is to say that such a philosophy must be honest and articulate in the reasons it offers for

"Albert Camus and the Christian Faith." From *The Journal of Religion,* October, 1956, pp. 224-233. Reprinted by permission of the author and The University of Chicago Press.

rejecting the claims of Marxism and the Christian faith. Camus has not been remiss in this, inasmuch as a large portion of his philosophical work has entailed a criticism of the Marxist and Christian positions, and this is one reason for the importance of his thought. In this criticism Marxism has been the central and most urgent concern of Camus, and in *The Rebel* the sections dealing with Marxist theory and prophecy constitute one of the most trenchant critiques of Communist thought and action ever written from the viewpoint of moral philosophy. But, if large sections of Camus's philosophical works are devoted solely to Marxism, this is not the case with the Christian faith. Camus has nowhere, up to the present, dealt at length with Christian theology. But yet all his major works are filled with direct or indirect references to Christianity, and these constant references create the atmosphere in which Camus's positive thought moves. This lack of an extended critique of Christianity is explained by the fact that, although Camus is an anti-Communist, he is not an anti-Christian—he is simply a non-Christian. As such, he has never cut himself off from conversation with Christian thinkers but stands in a relation of tension to Christianity, directing his criticism to the moral effects of this faith without condemning its ultimate sources, even though he does not accept them. And, certainly, this is as it should be, for any Western philosopher who begins with the assumption that the Christian faith is an illusion and hence entirely discredited is suspect of irresponsibility or willful ignorance. Although Marxism is, for Camus, the most urgent problem to which he addresses himself, it is the Christian faith which is the most fundamental issue and the one with which he must most clearly come to terms. And, as shall be seen, in coming to terms with the Christian faith, Camus feels that to a large extent one has come to terms with Marxism and with the underlying reasons for the ills of the twentieth century. What shall be done, then, is to sum up the many remarks which Camus has made concerning Christianity and present a general statement of both his understanding and his criticism of the Christian faith.

II

Camus's estimate of the Christian faith is summed up most simply in his remark that "in its essence, Christianity (and this is its paradoxical greatness) is a doctrine of injustice. It is founded on the sacrifice of the innocent and the acceptance of this sacrifice" (*The Rebel*). This is to say that, to Camus's mind, Jesus of Nazareth was an innocent man unjustly killed; from no point of view can he rule out the fact of the injustice in this event. Hence, when Christians, viewing this event, accept it as a sacrifice—that is, when they accept it as right and necessary—they have denied the one undeniable truth in this event which is that it is horrible and unjust that an innocent man should be killed. This is what is paradoxical in Christianity. And the greatness in this paradox is that Christians have, in this metamorphosis of injustice, found an attitude which transcends and minimizes the abiding reality of human suffering.

It is here that are found the fundamental motives of the Christian faith as well as Camus's own thought, that is, in the problem of evil and death. For Camus the first data of religion and morality are the evil and death that are part of the abiding condition of men. Whether or not there be goodness or God is not a primary evidence of human existence —suffering and death are. The question is what this primary evidence teaches us and what we do about it. Only after the reality of human evil is given does the question of God and ultimately man's submission to or revolt against God arise. These theological questions have neither meaning nor reality without this primary reference.

So that this fundamental aspect of Camus's thought might be clear, we may take a dramatic illustration from his novel *The Plague*. During the height of the plague which has stricken the North African city of Oran, the central figures of the story are about the bedside of a child who is suffering from the last stages of bubonic plague. Dr. Rieux has just received a shipment of a new antiplague serum which he had administered to the child, and the group, which included the priest, Father Paneloux, stayed by the child waiting to see what effect the serum would have. The men silently witness the child's sufferings as the plague remorselessly saps away his life; they are as overwhelmed by their own helplessness as they are by the agony of the dying child. The child's movements grow weaker, until finally they are stilled: he is dead. Dr. Rieux leaves the room hurriedly with a strange look on his face, and Father Paneloux attempts to stop him at the door. Rieux turns on the priest fiercely, saying, "Ah, that child, anyhow, was innocent, and you know it as well as I do!" Rieux leaves the building, and Paneloux follows him outside, where he finds Rieux sitting on a bench.

"Why was there that anger in your voice just now? What we'd been seeing was as unbearable to me as it was to you."

Rieux turned toward Paneloux.

"I know. I'm sorry. But weariness is a kind of madness. And there are times when the only feeling I have is one of mad revolt."

"I understand," Paneloux said in a low voice. "That sort of thing is revolting because it passes our human understanding. But perhaps we should love what we cannot understand."

Rieux straightened up slowly. He gazed at Paneloux, summoning to his gaze all the strength and fervor he could muster against his weariness. Then he shook his head.

"No, Father, I've a very different idea of love. And until my dying day I shall refuse to love a scheme of things in which children are put to torture."

In this scene Camus has shown us two men who have seen and recognized the same human evil but have given two clearly different responses to it. One man has accepted this evil as finally good even though it is beyond his understanding how God will, in the end, transform it in accordance with his purposes. The other man can only revolt against what he has seen and ceaselessly "refuse to love a scheme of things in which children are put to torture."

Here, then, in the sufferings of a child, is a test case. It is out of such stuff as this that religions are spun, and it is an event such as this that Camus points to as evil. Camus's response to this problem is simple; that is, if this is a world in which innocents must be tortured, and if there be a God who rules, guides, or sanctifies this world, then God is unjust. The given evidence of evil is there, and, if the idea of God is introduced, then there is no other conclusion. If men are to speak of God, a personal and sovereign God, then there is introduced into human experience an infinite gulf between the sufferings of men and the designs of God—a tension which demands submission or revolt. If God rules, then God is responsible: this is a first consequence of the idea of a personal God which first appeared in the Old Testament. And with the appearance of a personal God there also appears religious guilt, crime, and revolt on the part of man. The prototype of this is Cain, and we, Camus says, are the children of Cain by way of this inheritance. It is from this understanding that Camus goes on to explain the significance of Christ:

> From this point of view, the New Testament may be considered as an effort to reply in advance to all the Cains of the world in softening the visage of God and in invoking an intercessor between him and man. The Christ came to solve two principal problems, evil and death, which are essentially the problems of rebels. His solution consisted first of all in taking on their condition. The God-man suffers also—with patience. Evil and death are no longer absolutely imputable to him inasmuch as he suffers and dies. The night on Golgotha has so great an importance in the history of men only because the divinity, ostensibly abandoning its traditional privileges, lived through to the end the anguish of death and of despair. Thus is explained the *lama sabactani* and the awful doubt of the Christ in agony. The agony would be light if it were sustained by eternal hope. That God might be man it is necessary that he give up hope. (*The Rebel*)

In Christ man is reconciled to God because God has shared man's condition, and with this knowledge man can accept his condition without revolt. Only the willing sacrifice of an innocent God could justify the long and universal suffering of men. Thus, Christ closed the gulf between heaven and earth.

The originality of Christianity, Camus holds, is that it brought together within itself two notions which up to that time had never been linked:

that of mediation and that of history. The idea of mediation was Greek and that of historicity was Judaic, and it was the synthesis of the latter with the former that made possible the spread of Christianity throughout the Mediterranean world. It is the characteristic of historical attitudes that the natural world is not considered as an object of contemplation but of transformation. The first Christians impatiently awaited the end of the world and, in lieu of this, later assisted in the mastery and transformation of the world; human action and thought was centered in history, for there is a plan, a goal, a destiny, to be fulfilled within this history. In contrast, the characteristic of the Hellenic notion of mediation was to obey and admire nature, and it is this aspect of Christianity which flowered most fully in the Albigenses and in St. Francis. Camus insists that this was the true strength of Christianity, and it was this that held its historical tendencies within bounds, at least for a time. When one feels that the natural world about him is God's world and is expressive of God's nature, then this world obtains a certain value and holiness which tends to eradicate any impatient contempt for nature and any desire to subjugate it to the realization of historical goals. This latter desire is what Camus has termed "the German ideology."

Thus, in response to the primary human evidence of evil and death, Christianity posits a sovereign God whose will to lead the world from its given condition to a chosen condition is in part counterbalanced by his loving relation for the world as it is. The paradoxical greatness of this faith is that it poses the "should" against the "is" of this world but yet cannot bring itself to despise the "is." From the viewpoint of morality, this is the certain effect of the central doctrines of the Christian faith. As long as these conflicting attitudes are held together, Christianity can attain to a love of the good that is of this world without seeking to change it and yet be able at the same time to accept the evil that arises in the world as somehow justified within the higher purposes of the guiding hand of God. Understood in this manner, Camus does not feel that Christianity is a religion of resignation. In reply to an interviewer who spoke of it in this manner, he said:

> But I would think twice before saying as you do that the Christian faith is a resignation. Can one put down this word for a St. Augustine or a Pascal? Honesty requires that we judge a doctrine by its summits, not by its subproducts. And in the final analysis, little though I know about these matters, I have the impression that faith is not so much a peace as a tragic hope. (*Actuelles*)

Camus understands, then, that in its best moments the Christian faith is active in its cultivation of beauty and goodness and sustained by a tragic hope in its acceptance of evil and death. And this is the Christian position which Father Paneloux puts forth in his two sermons in the attempt to bring meaning into the plight of a city beaten by the plague. It is true that, following the death of the child, Paneloux's second sermon was more moderate and less certain than the first; but the difference between the two sermons consisted in saying that, if the plague be not the punishment of the sins of the people, it is at least part of the designs of God, so mysterious they may be, and must, in faith, be accepted and finally loved. As a Christian, Paneloux is driven to the wall by the horror of the plague, and he realizes that in such extreme circumstances it is a question of all or nothing for the Christian. Either he maintains his faith that God is the ultimate ruling force in the universe, bringing good out of all the evil which he allows to afflict men, or else he takes his place with Dr. Rieux, Tarrou, and all the rebels of the earth in maintaining that this evil and this death are unbearable and that either there is no God and men must ceaselessly struggle with their single powers against the plague of life or else, if there be a God, he is a murderous, unjust, and incomprehensible being who is the supreme enemy of men. Given human evil and death, either God is innocent and men are guilty or else God is guilty and men are innocent. The death of a child poses the alternative of all or nothing for the Christian faith.

III

When Camus turns to a consideration of events in the modern world, it is with this understanding of Christianity in mind, and it is only against the background of two millenniums of Christian tradition that he feels we are able to interpret recent political history in the Western world. Stated simply, it is Camus's belief that the balance between the Greek notion of mediation and the Judaic notion of historicity was first undermined in the Middle Ages and that subsequently the deep-rooted historical consciousness of Western Christian civilization has taken full sway and is accountable for the peculiar direction toward totalitarianism which contemporary history has taken. It is from the time of the Inquisition and the eradication of the Cathari heresy that Camus dates the disappearance of the balancing power of the Hellenic elements of Christianity. From this time onward the Judaic elements became increasingly the dominant force in Western life.

The significance of this dissolution of the unique synthesis in Christian theology is that the myth and symbols by which Christians had described the divine drama which was unfurling itself through time were now brought into a historical focus.

> The beautiful equilibrium of humanity and nature, man's consent to the world which underlay the rise and splendor of all ancient thought, was broken to the profit of history first of all by Christianity. The entrance into this historicity of the nordic peoples—who do not have a tradition of friend-

> ship with the world—precipitated this movement. From the moment that the divinity of Christ was denied or when, at the hands of German ideology, he symbolizes nothing more than the man-God [rather than the God-man] the notion of mediation disappeared; a Judaic world was resuscitated. The implacable God of armies reigns once more, all beauty is defamed as a source of useless pleasure, nature itself is enslaved. From this point of view, Marx is the Jeremiah of the historical God and the St. Augustine of the revolution. (*The Rebel*)

What Camus is saying is that, with the advent of the modern period and of critical reason, Jesus was discovered to be not God but man, and with this discovery Western civilization had come full circle back to the realities of evil and death from which it had arisen, leaving human suffering unjustified and unexplained beneath the veiled face of a sovereign God. "To the exact degree in which the divinity of Christ had been denied, pain became once more the lot of men. Jesus, frustrated, is but another innocent whom the representatives of the God of Abraham had executed in a spectacular manner" (*The Rebel*). But, if the loss of Christ brought men once more in face of evil, it did not leave men in the same state of mind as before, because men knew now that history was their vindication, and it was in their hands to realize the promise that history holds. The whole cosmic drama of God's plan came to be translated into terms which men could understand and of which history seemed capable. The modern world adopted from Christianity the hope for a Kingdom which men could realize and the promise of a Kingdom which reason or history would guarantee.

With this new vision, the stage for contemporary history was set. And the age of reason was not long in discovering that, if the values men seek lie at the end of a historical process which men will achieve, then God is useless in the history of men. This is the idea which was emerging in the revolt of social and metaphysical thought of the nineteenth century. And nothing is more obvious, Camus maintains, than that socialism and atheism go hand in hand: "All socialism is Utopian, and first of all scientific. The Utopia replaces God with the future. It then identifies the future with morality; the only value is that which serves this future" (*The Rebel*). It is for this reason that Camus insists that to understand the history of Christianity is to understand Marxism. The Marxist prophecy is nothing more than the perennial Christian-Judaic vision of God's plan moving history toward an apocalypse; but the vision is now totally within history. The religious pretension of Marxism is obvious in its refusal of men as they are in the name of men as they shall be. Marxism, like Christianity, places its ultimate values outside history, and history itself is the sacrificial effort to achieve these values. Marxism shares Christianity's impatience with the "is" of this world in the light of a "should" which is beyond history. The apocalypse of history in the classless society is no more justified than the coming Kingdom of Heaven. In both of these faiths the injustices and evils of this life are transformed into temporary goods in the light of the apocalypse. It is the promise and the certainty of the ultimate justification of the cause which make it possible for men to give themselves willingly as a sacrifice for this cause. When the ultimate values of human existence lie beyond and at the end of history, then men can die meaningfully only on an installment plan —the justification of their sacrifice will come only at the end of time.

In this regard Camus has pointed out that Christians have a certain justification for entertaining the hope of history's end, inasmuch as for them history has a beginning. For the Marxist, however, history had no beginning: what is always has been. And, if there be no beginning, how can Marxists reasonably insist that an end of history is conceivable? What guaranty is there that, when the society of classes gives way to a society without classes, a new antagonism will not arise to challenge the classless society? Having divorced itself from the Christian myth of creation, Marxism can never conceive of history as anything but an eternal becoming, whose values and justification are eternally in the future, and the injustices and the sacrifices that were wrought for the sake of this future will ever remain injustice and meaningless sacrifice. It is in the midst of such hopeless and murderous aspirations that contemporary history moves, and it is in the face of this that Camus raises the cry for a life in which values are found within history and within human action itself and not above or beyond history. He argues that, so long as we live with values which are posited absolutely and transhistorically, we shall not avoid murder. For it is only when one is absolutely certain of his values that the nonexistence of other men is justified. But, if the values of men are posited within the relativities of human history, then no man can with certainty sacrifice the lives of others for this uncertain value. The effort to validate these uncertain values of human existence was the purpose of Camus's most distinguished philosophical work, *The Rebel*. Against the aspiration for totality, conquest, and perfection in human history, Camus places a history in which men have limits, and knowledge has uncertainties, and values have relativity. To attempt to transform men into the image of an absolute value is not to fulfill them but to murder and deform them. For men are not infinitely plastic; they are not things which can be endlessly molded and changed. They have limits, and to go beyond these limits is only to add to the total of suffering in human history. It is this limit which all men find within themselves and which is shared in common by all men that is the only source of value which men possess. It is the only real value in human existence. And it is when this limit, this value, is transgressed that men revolt. Revolt, alone, is revelatory of human values and, as such, constitutes an essential dimension of human experience. It is on the basis of such an understanding of human value that Camus is able to say to a religion of historicity, "Does the end justify the means? This is possibly so. But what will justify the end? To this question, which historical thought leaves hanging, revolt replies: the means" (*The Rebel*).

IV

It is a curious thing about the thought of Albert Camus that he has not estranged himself from Christian readers. This may possibly be because Christian thinkers have not as yet realized the full import of what he has said about the Christian faith. Whatever the reason may be, it is interesting that, when Christians pick up the works of such a man as Sartre, it is largely with a mind to refute; but, when Christians pick up the works of Camus, it is with a mind to learn. It is encouraging and admirable that there continues to be a healthy dialogue between Camus and Christian thinkers. However, in the several formal exchanges which he has had with various representatives of the Christian faith, Camus has not been so gently dealt with as he himself has dealt. Like David Hume, he has come to learn that for one who stands outside the church it often requires a great amount of Christian charity in order to deal with Christians. Perhaps what stands in the way of more cordial relations is Camus's implacable honesty. There is no better evidence of this than the address which he gave in a Dominican convent to a group of Catholic clergy, in the course of which he said:

> What the world awaits from Christians is that they speak loud and clear, and that they express their condemnations in such a manner that never a doubt, never a single doubt, may rise in the heart of the simplest man. It is that they leave off with abstraction and that they face up to the blood-stained visage which history has taken today. . . . When a Spanish bishop blesses political executions, he is no longer a bishop, nor a Christian, and not even a man, he is a dog, like all those who from the height of an ideology command this execution without doing the work themselves. (*Actuelles*)

These are exceedingly clear words, and it is even clearer that Camus speaks them not with an animus toward Christians but from the positive point of view of a human value which has been denied. What alone concerns Camus in his thought about Christianity is its response to evil and death. "I share with you the same horror of evil. But I do not share your hope, and I continue to struggle against this universe where children suffer and die" (*Actuelles*).

It is especially in regard to the notion that he is a pessimist that Camus seeks to define himself in contrast to both Christianity and Marxism, and it is here, in terms of simple contrast, that the genius and the classic clarity of Camus's thought are fully evident:

> Christians and Communists will tell me that their optimism is of a more extended scope, that it is superior to all others, and that God or history, according to the case, are the satisfactory terminations of their dialectic. I have the same argument to present. If Christianity is pessimistic in regard to man, it is optimistic in regard to human destiny. Well then, I will say that although pessimistic in regard to human destiny, I am optimistic in regard to man. (*Actuelles*)

And certainly this is the amazing optimism of Camus, which so peculiarly confounds the normal manner in which modern men think—although not the manner in which they doubt. For this is the about-face which Albert Camus has effected in his philosophy and in his literary pieces, and it is this unexpected and yet so compelling reversal which is the contribution of his genius to our times. At first glance, it is a strange and artificial world in which Camus moves, until suddenly the thundering realization comes that this is our world of which he speaks; it is the history which daily moves about us, except that now it has attained a definitive clarity. Camus immerses us as he himself is immersed in the tragedy and tense hopes of the mid-twentieth century; he is, as he says, "a child of his times." This world and the history lying behind it, which Camus has delineated in his philosophical works, is the world that is in turn found in all his literary works. Meursault, the little functionary of *The Stranger,* is no abnormal man; he is you or any man moving through life, choosing with uncertainty, living with ultimately no pattern of life to which to mold himself, when suddenly he is put into the position of being judged by legal standards of absolute value. And, once absolute values are put against the life of relativity which Meursault has lived, it is obvious that Meursault is guilty and that he has led a criminal life. When, in *The Plague,* an entire city is quarantined within guarded walls at the merciless hands of the plague, the suffering and death which ensue cannot be explained and justified in terms of God's higher purposes; they must be recognized for what they are, horrible and revolting, and men have no other choice than to hate the plague and do all within their power to defeat it. The plays, *The Misunderstanding* and *Caligula,* show us what happens in a world whose values exist beyond history and how murder and absurdity are the logical consequences of such a world. And in the later plays, *State of Siege* and *The Just Assassins,* Camus shows us how, in a world delivered entirely unto history, men suddenly discover abiding values within the revolt into which such a world has driven them. It is the moral philosophy which underlies these novels and plays that gives them their force and desperation, and it is only in terms of this larger philosophical position that the literary works of Camus can be fully understood. For Camus is first of all a philosopher with serious moral and religious concerns, and all his literary productions serve as functions of these concerns.

We come to understand the thought of Albert Camus only after we have probed the full significance of his optimism about man and his pessimism about human destiny. For this throws us back to the abiding evidence of evil in human existence. For the Christian the ultimate character of the universe is good, and in this he finds his hope and the ability to transcend and accept, to a degree, the evil in the world. But what, at this point, has become clear about the thought of Camus is that for him the ultimate character of the universe is evil and that consequently men are always uncertain and always threatened; whatever goodness there be in life, it is in men, and this goodness is created only in the struggle of men to preserve and enlarge this area of goodness which they alone know and which they alone can guarantee. Value and truth lie within men, and it is only by virtue of the contrast which a threatening world presents to men that they become conscious of the salvation which lies within them. However strange this attitude toward the world may seem at first glance, further reflection will show that it is not after all either strange or even novel. Those who have come to know the thought of Sören Kierkegaard will here recognize remarkable similarities in what might be assumed to be quite disparate philosophies. More interesting still is the fact that Camus's attitude at this point is solidary with that of Christian orthodoxy in its depiction of man's life as a "trial." In face of the threatening character of the world, Camus calls men to revolt. And the call to revolt is nothing more or less than a call to create; to transform the inhumanity of the world into the image of man, to humanize what is inhuman—in short, to civilize. This is the "new humanism" put forth by Albert Camus—a humanism whose final and only goal is the uncertain and mortal lives of men, creatures who are not infinitely pliable and suffering but are limited and infinitely precious and must at all costs be defended against those who would judge their lives and history by that which is foreign to their lives and history. But, after all, we ask, what is man? Man, replies Camus, "is that force which always ends by holding off gods and tyrants" (*Letters to a German Friend* in *Resistance, Rebellion and Death*).

Albert Camus: The Dark Night before the Coming of Grace?

by Bernard C. Murchland, C.S.C.

When the Nobel Prize for literature for 1957 was awarded to Albert Camus, a singularly dedicated man of our century was honored. Both as an artist and a man the outstanding characteristic of M. Camus is his total and tortured involvement in the world of his time. He is concerned with the intellectual, political, and moral climate in which we live. He questions traditional values, the future of mankind, and explores at great length the conditions necessary for human living today. "What meaning can be salvaged from the world?" is the restless question that runs through Camus's plays, novels, essays, and journalistic writings. "We are at the extremities now," he writes of modern man's plight. "At the end of this tunnel of darkness, however, there is inevitably a light, which we already divine and for which we have only to fight to ensure its coming. All of us, among the ruins, are preparing a renaissance beyond the limits of nihilism."

The positive quality this passage signals is essential to an understanding of Camus's work. There is a temptation for those only vaguely familiar with his writing to associate him with a rankly negative school of existentialism, to class him (with Sartre and others) among the philosophers of the absurd and nihilism. This is particularly true, I believe, of the American public. An article in one national review awhile ago very unfairly referred to him as "a man of childless thought."

Camus himself, on several occasions, has endeavored to correct this accusation. In an interview with the French press he said:

> When I ask what is deepest in me, I find that it is the desire for happiness. I have a great interest in people. I have no contempt whatsoever for the

"The Dark Night before the Coming of Grace?" (Originally titled "Albert Camus: Rebel.") From *The Catholic World,* CLXXXVIII, No. 1126 (January, 1959), 308-314.

> human race. I believe that one can feel proud to be a contemporary with so many men of our times whom I respect and admire. . . . At the heart of my work there is an invincible sun. It seems that all this does not constitute a particularly sad outlook.

It was between 1936 and 1937 that Camus's first essays appeared, unheralded and largely unnoticed, in two volumes: *L'Envers et l'endroit* (Betwixt and Between) and *Noces* (Nuptials). There is in these essays a kind of proud and somber Hellenism. Camus celebrates the espousals of man with the flowers, the sea, and "all the light of the world." He expresses a sensual romantic happiness that is strangely tempered with a note of tragedy, an awareness of the discord between man and the world. While the young author sang a pagan song of deliverance, abandoned himself to the "happy lassitude of my nuptials with the world," felt the "poetic luxuriance" of things and perceived the "duty of happiness," there was already a hint of anguish and absurdity in his work.

"The Minotaur" describes the city of Oran with glowing euphoria:

> The sea rumbles a bit down below. Yet already the sun, the faint breeze, the whiteness of the asphodels, the sharp blue of the sky, everything makes one fancy summer—the golden youth, then covering the beach, the long hours on the sand and the sudden softness of evening. Each year on these shores there is a new harvest of girls in flower. . . . At eleven A. M. coming down from the plateau, all that young flesh, lightly clothed in motley materials, breaks on the sand like a multicolored wave.

Then Camus's thought gravitates toward the other pole of his universe, toward "the conscious certitude of a death without hope."

Suddenly, the dominant climate of enchantment dissolves completely into a bitter and pained obsession with the absurd. It is important to understand that this obsession was to a great extent dictated by a personal experience. Between 1937 and 1942 Camus spent much time in a sanatorium. The shock of physical sickness had a brutal effect upon his sensibility. The note of death detected in his youthful essays swells to a loud protest against the treachery of life. A life that had only wanted to sing was now forced to contend with absurdity. What meaning could such a life have? This personal crisis found expression in the short play *Caligula* which was written in 1938 and published in 1943—a fierce and unique picture not only of one man's tragedy but of the tragedy of the modern world.

In *The Stranger* (1942) and *The Myth of Sisyphus* (1942), (as well as another play called *Cross Purpose,* published in 1944), Camus attempts to conciliate his obsession with the absurd and his mystique of sensual happiness. (He had gone to Paris in 1940 where the slaughter of World War II and his active role in the resistance were experiences that deepened considerably his earlier experience of illness.) These works explain each other and are concerned primarily with the crisis of the individual, with man as a lonely exile struggling for happiness and meaningfulness beneath the immense and senseless burden of existence.

The Myth of Sisyphus, the first of Camus's two important philosophical essays, reveals a new depth in Camus's own thinking. The question raised in the beginning of this book is: how can a life that has no meaning best be lived? Camus considers the possibility of suicide and writes that "it is the only truly philosophical problem." In the context of this discussion he examines what he calls the "absurd walls" within which the drama of our human condition is played out. The sentiment of the absurd is "a light without radiance," which can strike anywhere at any moment. The banality of daily life is quite as effective in bringing about its emergence as the disaster of global warfare. The rhythm of abstract, depersonalized, uncreative activities crumbles into absurd chaos before the question: what does it all mean?

Infirmity, ignorance, irrationality, nostalgia, the impossibility of distinguishing the true from the false, our radical inability to know ourselves or others, the implacable mystery of the world—these are some of the elements of the absurd as Camus envisioned it at this time. It was the sum total of all the antinomies and contradictions man is heir to, compounded by the conditions of World War II and Camus's personal experiences. Reason can do very little to introduce motives of hope, unity, and harmony. Religion is even more impotent. The logic of absurdity concludes to the necessity for suicide. But at this point Camus revealed his positive genius. To take one's life would be, in the final analysis, an act of cowardice, of bad faith. We simplify the problem by avoiding it. We must live if we wish to maintain what we believe to be true. "To live is to make the absurd live," says Camus, "To make it live is, above all, to face it squarely. Unlike Eurydice, when we avert our gaze, the absurd dies. Thus, revolt is one of the few philosophical positions." It is in this perspective that Camus introduces his courageous metaphor of Sisyphus. Like the mythical hero, man must accept the limitations of his condition. He must accept absurdity with lucidity and conquer it through sincerity and loyalty.

Sometime between 1942-44 Camus reached a new level of development. In his four *Letters to a German Friend,* he proclaims: "I continue to believe that this world has no superior meaning. But I know that something in it has meaning: it is man, because man is the sole being to insist upon having a meaning." Camus's vision now expands to include the suffering and unhappiness of all mankind.

This sense of universality goes considerably beyond the struggle of the individual Sisyphian character in *The Plague* (1947) and *The Rebel* (1951)—another fiction-philosophical combination at a new level of significance. In these two powerful works (perhaps Camus's best) the values of justice, loyalty, and courage appear much more positively on the frontiers of the absurd, values that are as indisputably authentic as they are adamantly anti-Christian. Camus has never wavered in his atheism. Christianity has always appeared to him as another of the pointless ideologies in the name of which men are subjugated and massacred. He has excluded it from his vision as a matter of principle.

The Plague permits of several interpretations. It is first of all the record of a physical epidemic, of a city beseiged by some uncontrollable disease which strikes down the innocent and outflanks all efforts made to curb it. In another sense, it is a chronicle of World War II, the war of the occupation and imprisonment of some two million Europeans. The tragedy of Europe is transplanted to Oran and reduced to artistically manageable proportions. At still another level, *The Plague* reaches a note of impressive depth in its concern with the presence of evil in the world. There is, finally, a moral dimension—something new in Camus —introduced in the person of Tarrou. With him, the theme of moral evil, the evil that men inflict upon each other, reaches its greatest intensity. Through Tarrou, Camus's own ideas of commitment, dedication to the plight of others, and courageous stand against violence and injustice are made clear.

The Myth of Sisyphus was concerned with the problem of suicide. In *The Plague* Camus substitutes this problem for that of a strange form of martyrdom, a kind of religion of happiness through atheistic sanctity. (The problem of absurdity is reduced to Tarrou's question: "Can one be a saint without God? That is the only concrete problem I know of today.") But there is in this new emphasis an undeniable deepening of Camus's thought. He has gone beyond the exterior manifestations of absurdity to recognize the reality of spiritual death in the world. The root of absurdity is within us. When Tarrou dies in the presence of Dr. Rieux (who narrates the story), we witness an outstanding example of disinterested love—one of the high points of modern literature. Here Camus realizes that there is no harm in being happy. It is only being happy alone that cannot be justified. This sense of solidarity, based upon sacrifice and personal responsibility for the world, is the price of happiness.

It is paradoxical that a work so authentically impregnated with charity should be at the same time the most anti-Christian of all Camus's books. For it obviously is a work which aims to prove most clearly that man can construct, without the help of God or of rationalistic thought, a creative humanism of high nobility. Wherever two or three people are gathered together, there is hope, Camus seems to say. However irremediable and definitive man's imprisonment, he can now rejoice in a sense of dignity and an innate feeling of sympathy that suffices to make him great.

The Rebel, Camus's second philosophical essay, furthers the line of thought adumbrated in *The Plague*. Revolt, in Camus's mind, is a creative effort that makes absurdity meaningful, or rather enables us to transcend absurdity, by protesting against it; it postulates a "human nature" that must be respected, a terrestrial brotherhood that must be defended; and it creates a moral value rooted in the idea of moderation and the respect for limits.

As a matter of fact, the idea of revolt is at the very heart of Camus's thinking. It is the key at once to his notion of happiness and the meaning of life as well as the purpose of social action and artistic creation.

In many ways, Camus is restating the basic principles of liberal humanism. In a deeper sense, he is exploring and justifying the immense potential man has for becoming himself. The Christian might profitably take up where Camus leaves off to examine the implications of this vision in respect to his own situation in this world. It would be too much to say that his position can be adopted without modification as a basis for Christian humanism. But it has merits that command our interest. Camus is not unique in his preoccupation with the absurd. What makes him unique, and what stirs sentiments of admiration in those who read him, is the courage and logic with which he refuses to compromise the dignity of man.

Camus's latest stage of evolution has defined his positive dynamism much more sharply. Here his art becomes more serene, disinterested and assumes something comparable to a redemptive dimension. In *The Plague* he was interested primarily in serving men, not saving them. But in *The Fall* (1956) and his recent collection of stories, *Exile and the Kingdom,* he stresses the new values of penance and expiation. The themes of transcendence, the creative value of suffering and human solidarity are added to the Camusian vision. The French writer exhorts us, with the fervor of the moralist he cannot help being, to count ourselves among those who do battle against the accumulated guilt and ignorance of the world.

It has been suggested that Camus is tending toward a religious conversion and the Catholic Church has been mentioned in this context. Certainly the development of his work must, if it continues, ultimately culminate in some spiritual position. The narrator's name in *The Fall* is a strong clue to the voice crying in the wilderness. It is quite possible that the novel expresses a realization of sin and unworthiness—the dark night before the coming of grace. There are also further symbolisms: the reader is told by Camus to identify the canals of Amsterdam with the concentric circles of hell; the title of the book is essentially religious; the concern with man's guilt links it to the Mauriac-Greene tradition and it seems to be an authentic cry for salvation.

But it would not do to force this conclusion. We must bear in mind Camus's immense gifts of irony. In *The Fall* he could conceivably be satirizing the whole notion of guilt and protesting its being used as a weapon for enslaving men and deadening their creative powers for self-transcendence. One cannot be sure. But in *Exile and the Kingdom* he returns to the same redemptive themes and in this case it is more difficult to admit of the irony interpretation.

It seems that this new dimension of Camus's work is something far greater than irony or satire. Roger Martin du Gard has said of him: "Each new work carries him one step further on a solitary way, laid out in advance." It is impossible at this time for the critic to say just where.

This evolving, incomplete character of Camus's work is one of the most disconcerting things about it, and accentuates the danger of confusing the part for the whole. Many of Camus's individual statements and even books must be interpreted in view of his development. We must be careful to distinguish the enduring deep themes of his art from the experimental framework of much of its expression. Indeed, it is necessary to share to some extent in the author's own uneasiness and search for equilibrium in order to weigh precisely the meaning of what he is saying at any given moment. It is primarily within Camus's own peculiar perspective that he should be judged.

Camus does not rate substantially as a metaphysician. His work represents the effort of a creative soul confronting his times and striving to bring as much of our actual situation as possible into the light of expression and understanding. He has attempted to translate his own experience into a statement of some universal relevance and patch together, in his way, the pieces of a broken world. And it is for his achievement in this that we must admire him. It would be the sheerest of nonsense for the Christian to consider his position invalid because it does not make room for the traditional categories of grace and redemption. Camus, I believe, is exploring these in accordance with his own talents. He has seen man caught in what is quite possibly the most absurd situation of history. Yet he has not lost his admiration for him. In a very concrete way, he has set himself the task of creating a climate of values, a refuge from meaninglessness, a kind of salvation. He has experienced the highly prized Christian joy of helping his brothers and defending justice. He has realized, as he wrote in *The Rebel* that "real generosity toward the future lies in giving all to the present." One thinks of the stress such men as Bloy and Péguy laid upon the necessity for a temporal revolution as a guarantee of eternal salvation.

Rilke wrote in his *Book of Pilgrimage:* "I know that all paths lead to the arsenal of things where there is no life. Yet there is a great miracle in the world: I feel that all life is lived." That paradox quite adequately summarizes Camus's own pilgrimage through absurdity to a high sense of purpose. We may, I think, confidently expect yet more admirable work from an artist who, after all, has only begun to exercise his genius.

Camus the Pagan

by Henri Peyre

No writer from the Old or the New World has been mourned in English-speaking countries with the same intensity of grief as was Albert Camus in the first weeks of 1960. A pall of gloom seemed to have spread over literature. The spiritual guide of many a confused and searching soul had most absurdly been ravished. No other writer, neither William Faulkner, in truth coolly admired in his native country, nor T. S. Eliot who has not donned his mantle of sage and prophet since the *Four Quartets* and whose dramatic attempts have scored a steady decline since *Murder in the Cathedral,* not even André Malraux, too peremptory and aloof in his cryptic lyrical assertions on silent voices—expressed in sonorous periods—could, in the sixth decade of our century, rival the prestige of Camus, the lay saint. Spontaneous tributes to him sprang up in colleges and readers' clubs, resounded on the radio. That pagan writer, who had treated the chaplain in *The Stranger*, the Jesuit preacher in *The Plague,* the renegade priest in *Exile and the Kingdom* with undisguised hostility, found himself posthumously serving as a theme for many sermons. The bitterest of his fables, *The Fall,* was even interpreted by charitable souls, unwilling to dispense such an intelligent negator of their doctrines from the unsavory felicity of their paradise, as the prelude to Camus's eventual adhesion to the Christian faith. He who had once been invited discreetly not to remain "a Pascal without Christ" was hailed, through his sarcastic and garrulous lawyer turned into a judge-penitent, as a St. John the Baptist.

"It is frequently out of a pagan soul that the best Christian soul is made," wrote Charles Péguy in his *Clio, Dialogue of History and of the Pagan Soul.* It may be, though nothing supports such a conjecture, that Camus at sixty would have embraced Catholicism. Certainly, he disliked anti-clericalism and, in one of his last pronouncements on the subject, in September 1956, while denying that any signs of a turn to the Church should or could be read in *The Fall,* he added: "I do not believe in God,

"Camus the Pagan." From *Yale French Studies,* No. 25 (special Camus issue) (Spring, 1960), pp. 20-25. Copyright 1960 by *Yale French Studies.* Reprinted by permission of the author and *Yale French Studies.*

that is true, but I am not thereby an atheist." Camus was then growingly anxious to set himself apart from the Existentialists of the militantly atheistic band—suspiciously anxious to do so, indeed, in the eyes of this writer, for one remains convinced that, for all practical purposes, Camus should be regarded as an Existentialist in all but a very few respects such as the priority of existence over essence. He would not have protested so much against such an alignment but for his fear of being turned into a follower of more relentlessly logical philosophers and of sectarian politicians.

But partisan attempts to annex the dead or to distort cryptic allusions in their writings would be to treat unworthily a man such as Camus, who was honesty and nobleness incarnate in his intellectual development. The works of Camus, as they stand interrupted by fate, utter a pagan message which is to be set beside that of the great pagans of antiquity and that of some of the modern pagans to whom Christianity owes an immense debt of gratitude—for they have asked the right questions and constrained Christians to evolve ever more satisfactory answers to them. "Neo-paganism is the great spiritual phenomenon of our age"—thus wrote, in *The Drama of Atheistic Humanism* (1944), the eminent Jesuit thinker, Father Henri de Lubac, who deplores it, but courageously concedes that many noble souls, indeed many "blinded Christian souls" are attracted to the renovated paganism of today.

Instinct and doctrine blend in Camus's pagan assertions. His early series of essays, *Noces* (Nuptials), sings a paean to the wedding-feast of sky, sea, and the Algerian earth, supplemented by several equally rapturous prose canticles in honor of his "invincible summer" burning through the hours of distress and squalor in his youth. Their motto is a vehement denial of any longing for another life. Four pages before the volume closes, he propounds the conclusion: "The world is beautiful and, outside it, there is no salvation." The opening lines of the book are a disclaimer of all myths and intellectual structures erected to frustrate or to justify man's naïve desire for earthly happiness. "There is but one love in this world. To embrace a woman's body is also to retain, close to one, that strange joy which descends from the sky to the sea . . . I love this life with abandon and I want to speak of it freely; it fills me with pride at my human fate." *Hic et nunc:* here and now Camus, the young Pagan, like his three immediate predecessors in French literature, the Gide of *Fruits of the Earth,* Montherlant, and Giono, wants to savor the delights of life. The notion of hell appears, but as a pleasant joke, conceived by the imagination of most virtuous persons. Immortality, and any ultimate rewards promised to those who elect the Pascalian wager, are spurned. "I do not choose to believe," states the worshipper of the wind at Djemila, in *Noces,* "that death opens onto another life. To me it is a closed door." Those delusions are but an attempt to unburden man of the weight of his own life. And Camus prefers to carry his burden himself.

Noces was first published in Algiers, the very same year as *Caligula* was composed, in 1938. A little later, while France was living her first year of oppression under the German yoke, a renowned scholar, Jérôme Carcopino, brought out a collection of essays, *Aspects mystiques de la Rome païenne,* in which he analyzed the strange, almost mystical, consent to the mystery of death inscribed on many a tombstone in Camus's own country. "Non fui, fui non sum; non desidero." "I was not, I was, I am no more; I have no regret," thus, in Latin or more often in Greek, it was inscribed on the epitaphs of their relatives the North Africans of the early centuries after Christ, perhaps imbued with the half-mystical doctrines of thrice greatest Hermes. But it would be rash to assert that Camus's paganism is necessarily that of a North African or even of a Mediterranean. North Africa, after all, has produced its good share of Fathers of the Christian Church, from Tertullian to St. Augustine. Alexandria, the deserts of Egypt, and the coast of Syria, where the sky and the earth differ but little from Algeria, have contributed a large number of cenobites, saints, mystical philosophers and poets, agnostics and delirious exponents of Revelation, to Greek speculation, to Christianity, and to Islam. Latin lands have produced more mystics than northern climes.

Camus's true spiritual motherland was classical Greece. In 1948, long after the ordeals of disease and of the prolonged state of siege of World War II had cast a pall of gloom over his early rapturous Epicureanism, Camus asserted the collective guilt of our, and his, age, responsible for having exiled Helen. We are the apostates of the cult of Greece. "We lack the pride of man which is fidelity to his limits, clearsighted love of his fate." On May 10, 1951, in the *Nouvelles Littéraires,* Camus reasserted his preference for Hellenic values over Christian ones: "I feel closer to the values of the ancient world than I do to the Christian ones. Unfortunately, I cannot go to Delphi to become initiated." Few systems of ethics have ever been nobler than those of the Epicureans and of the Stoics; but, like Jansenism and Presbyterianism at their most demanding, they refused to come to terms with the weaknesses of mortals, avid for self-pity and anxious to display their frailty and their shame on the public square. The name of Pascal has been invoked in connection with that of Camus, perhaps too lightly. A writer in the Christian monthly *Esprit,* Simone Fraisse, rightly argued, in March 1959, that much deeper affinities linked Camus to Lucretius. To the Latin poet, Epicurus was already a man in revolt, spurning the concept of Providence, haughtily consenting to his role of Sisyphus: he did not deign to indict the gods, for they had no share in the evil of the world. They passively watched it. Camus read his own mood as a rebel, intoxicated with the absurd, in the "prodigious image of divine sanctuaries swollen with the accusing corpses of the plague" which closes Lucretius's sixth and last book. But he added to Lucretius's resigned pessimism the modern concept of men's solidarity. After writing in *Noces* that "there is no shame in being happy," he had a character in *The Plague,* Rambert, remark, when faced with the omnipresence of evil: "There is shame in being happy all alone."

Much wishful thinking has been lavished over *The Fall.* After *The Plague,* which Camus had characterized in *Le Monde* in 1947, in an interview given to Claudine Chonez, as "more anti-Christian than his other books," readers of misguided good-will, lured by the title, thought they could descry anticipatory signs of a Christian attitude in *The Fall.* Meursault was in a sense an innocent sentenced for a crime which he had committed but not willed, and could be viewed, as Camus owned ("paradoxically," he underlined) as "the only Christ that we deserve." To searchers for allusions, Meursault's last wish for a large crowd to witness his execution, "so that all be consummated" might even recall the "consummatum est" whispered by the crucified Christ in the nineteenth chapter of St. John. But the hero of *The Fall* is an embittered, sarcastic nihilist, a garrulous talker merging his own guilt in the guilt which he instills in all those whom he forces to listen to him. If anything, that baffling tale should be read as a satire of the self-indictment practised by Christians and atheistic Existentialists alike, by Dostoevsky's "buffoons" as Camus called them in his "Exil d'Hélène," and by the advocates of universal and unlimited responsibility. After Tarrou and Rieux, the mouthpieces of a lofty ethics which did without God so that nothing be ravished from man's prerogatives, those idealists dreaming of being saints without God and pure of all expectation of any reward, Clamence strikes us as a totally desperate and sneering cynic. The book, unlike *The Plague,* truly has "no exit." Clamence's hell is, as in Sartre's play, the judgment of men, the glaring presence of the others.

Camus is profoundly opposed to all Christianity stands for: first the notions of incarnation, of grace, of redemption, of repentance, and of collective guilt for some sin committed, unbeknown to us. In that sense, as Camus himself remarked in the interview given to the *Nouvelles Littéraires* on May 10, 1951, and as J. P. Sartre had shrewdly explained as early as February 1943 ("Explication de *L'Etranger*" in *Les Cahiers du Sud*),[1] Camus stands at the opposite pole from Kafka, "the novelist of impossible transcendence": for Kafka, enigmatic signs appear to point to an inhuman and undecipherable order; for Camus, there is no transcendence whatever. The very notion of sin, he avers, is meaningless to him. "There are words that I have never quite understood, such as sin" (*Noces*).

But Camus's most original revolt is against hope, "cette petite Espérance," with which Péguy was convinced that the French people had concluded a secret pact. Camus indicts hope as a form of resignation, robbing man of energies which he needs, in order to enrich a God who "hardly needs them," "Christ, eternal robber of energies," vituperated the adolescent Rimbaud in an early poem. Tarrou dies, never having known

[1] Translated and reprinted in this volume, pages 108.

hope. In *Noces,* Camus had strikingly declared that hope in "otherness," which serves as an excuse for man to bear placidly with the evils of this our life, undermines the courage needed by men to cope with all too real ills here and now.

> From Pandora's box, in which swarmed the evils of mankind, the Greeks let out hope after the rest, as the most dreadful of all. I cannot imagine a more moving symbol. For hope, in spite of what many believe, is equivalent to resignation. And to live is not to be resigned.

Pinning their hopes on another life, too many Christians complacently regard this one as a vale of tears, in which happiness is out of place, since we are all guilty. Even when he adapted *Requiem for a Nun* and voiced his admiration for Faulkner, Camus rejected the belief in "fundamental culpability" which the Mississippi novelist has never shaken off. In several of his books and in the essays collected in *Actuelles,* Camus referred to the massacre of the Innocents, perpetrated by Herod and necessary to Christian mythology. He saw Christianity itself as resting "upon the sacrifice of the innocent and the acceptation of that sacrifice" and preferred revolt, which alone can establish justice. He rose against the damnation of unchristened children, long accepted by the Church, and the evil uses of the phrase "nemo bonus," "There is none good but one, that is, God" attributed by Matthew (xix, 17) and Luke (xviii, 19) to Christ.

Camus's attitude toward Christianity was most clearly stated in a dialogue he held with the Dominicans of La Tour Maubourg, on the Paris Left Bank, in 1946, subsequently published in *Actuelles I,*[2] and in a debate in which he confronted Mauriac, on January 11, 1945, also published in the same volume. Waxing impatient at the glib charge of pessimism (or of nihilism), flung at him and at other Existentialists by Christians complacently draped in their allegedly consoling faith in another life, Camus sternly retorted that though "a pessimist where man's destiny was concerned, he was an optimist where man was concerned." He added:

> I believe I entertain a just idea of the greatness of Christianity; but there are a number of us in this persecuted world who feel that, if Christ died for certain men, he did not die for us. And at the same time we refuse to despair of man. If we do not cherish the unreasonable ambition to save him, we wish at least to serve him. We consent to be deprived of God and of hope, but not to do so easily without man.

Christian thinkers, even in a country like France where Catholic writers are often eyed with suspicion by Rome, have not hesitated to proclaim their debt to agnostics or to pagans, like Camus, who attempted to derive

[2] Translated in *Resistance, Rebellion, and Death* (Alfred A. Knopf, Inc., 1961).

the logical consequences from the Nietzschean death of God. Jean Lacroix, in *Le Sens de l'Athéisme moderne* (The Meaning of Modern Atheism) (1958), duly published with the church's *nihil obstat,* wrote of "man's prodigious attempt of recuperation of his total humanity" which is that of modern atheists. He personally recognized his immense gratitude to his atheistic friends, "for they have taught him not to cheat." In the same number of the *Cahiers du Sud,* "Permanence de la Grèce," in which had appeared Camus's essay on Greece, "Helen's Exile," a Greek scholar, the Dominican Father Festugière, broad-mindedly admitted that subscribing or not subscribing to an established religion is an irrelevant detail. There are ultimately only two kinds of men:

> Those for whom religious problems exist and those for whom they do not . . . Some people may have religious faith, may practise that faith outwardly without experiencing the anguish of religious problems. They may attend mass, take communion at Easter, fulfill the varied obligations of Christian law through a feeling of tradition, or through the simple desire to fulfill what is due in respect to the divine, or even to liberate themselves from some disquietude, once for all, through observing the rites instituted by men for that purpose, so that, having observed them, they may no longer have to think about them. Conversely, one may adhere to no creed whatever, perform no religious practices, yet be tortured throughout one's life by the problem of God, of what He is, of the relations between God and man.

Eighteen centuries ago a great North African theologian, the master of an impetuous prose, Tertullian, had declared: "oportet haereses esse": there must be heretics and agnostics if traditional faith is not to sink into complacency and inertia. Camus's world is one of universal condemnation to death, as Pascal's world was. But to the stranger, to the unfortunate men of good will in Oran harassed by the plague, to his companions in the Resistance, to the unbelievers of today who spurn the use of those small screens which Camus declared he had seen in Italian museums, through which the scaffold was concealed from men sentenced to death, to the bitter characters sketched in *The Fall* and in *Exile and the Kingdom,* the issue seems to require an anti-Pascalian answer: what are the positive values which persist in this world of mortals sentenced to death? Such paganism or disbelief in Christian values is a novel phenomenon of the twentieth century. Camus noted it in a curious footnote to his article, "Portrait d'un élu," in *Cahiers du Sud,* April 1943: "Contemporary unbelief does not rest on science as it did toward the close of the last century. It denies both science and religion. It is no longer the skepticism of reason in the presence of miracle. It is a passionate unbelief."

The Ethics of Albert Camus

by Serge Doubrovsky

For Sartre, Mauriac, and many others who may or may not have written, the deep shock felt, at Camus's death, combined with personal sorrow, is the feeling of a work suddenly stopped in full momentum, mutilated. As Malraux said long before, through Moreno in *Man's Hope,* "The capital thing about death is that it renders irremediable all that which has preceded it. . . ." For the writer, however, all the effort of writing is directed, before death, at escaping death. The author dead, the work continues; it lives. It can not progress, but it can be enriched. It could not be modified, but through its relation to new minds it can be renewed. . . .

During Camus's lifetime already, in order to neutralize his message, attempts were made to ossify his work, to disarm it by means of one or two often repeated epithets. At first, the word was "existentialism." Camus protested in vain on many occasions against the appellation and the affiliation, going so far as to attack by name the philosophy that was attributed to him: to no avail. One can still consult several manuals, especially the Anglo-Saxon ones; there lies Camus under the heading "existentialism." But this is not really troublesome; and existentialism is a scarecrow only for imbeciles. Although it is, in fact, an error in classification, it wrongs no one. More serious, is the stereotyped image: Camus, the moralist par excellence of the immoral twentieth century; the austere, just, righteous preacher. We need only consult the obituary notices. Some congratulate him for it, others detest him for it. His will to be ethical, his moralism is praised or denounced: it is none the less an established fact. Some people do not hesitate to speak of "Jansenism" and Camus, like Racine's Phèdre, becomes a Christian without grace. Or again, Camus is not a believer and that is just the point: a professor of ethics, he knows only a professor's ethic, two or three abstract notions which he exalts. There again, in spite of his protestations, Camus had been witness to his metamorpho-

"The Ethics of Albert Camus." From *Preuves* No. 116 (October, 1960), 39-49. Translated by Sondra Mueller and Jean-Marc Vary. Reprinted by permission of the author and *Preuves*.

sis: "Like everyone, I tried as best I could, to correct my nature by means of an ethic; that is, alas, what cost me most" (*L'Envers et l'endroit*).

Morality? What morality? That is what we should like to examine here. When re-reading Camus, we are struck by the repetition of a certain number of terms that seem to come out of a course on ethics: justice, happiness, revolt, etc. These words reoccur repeatedly, like a call to order, in the editorials of *Combat* and in the polemical exchanges with his contradictors. In his personal and philosophical essays they are constant themes of meditation, focal points of his thought. All Camus may seem to be contained in his choice of a particular glossary. Yet, and this is remarkable, these key words are never rigorously examined and really given a definition. It might be objected that the words "absurd" in *The Myth of Sisyphus,* "revolt" in *The Rebel,* are analyzed at length, and often in an authoritative way. But the analysis is, so to speak, horizontal rather than vertical, proceeding by extension rather than by inclusion. Revolt leads back to the original emergence of value, the emergence of value to the consciousness of evil, the consciousness of evil to the inverse affirmation of happiness and justice. But what of happiness, justice? The contents of these concepts, their immediate and far-reaching implications, the dialectic of inclusion or exclusion that relate them are all latent. Though Camus feels these concepts, he does not explore them in depth, in the sense that Sartre, for example, links his phenomenological descriptions of shame, fear, and anguish to a complete and rigorous view of man. In our opinion, the value of Camus's processes of thought derives from the very fact that they are lived rather than reasoned. "I am not a philosopher and I know how to speak only of what I have experienced" (*Actuelles II*). This does not mean, of course, that a philosopher must of necessity speak about what he has not experienced. But in so far as he integrates experience within a system, he transforms it. Dialectics gradually take the place of intuition.

Phenomenology is set in motion, truths must fall in and be arranged. In contrast, Camus has no system, no general framework, no philosophy. He grasps firmly only a few discontinuous truths which grip him: "I held on to truth as much as it held me" (*The Stranger*). We may as well get used to it. We can argue for and against, put in balance . . . integrity and entirety, existence and philosophy, and raise all the problems of a philosophy of existence. This is what Jaspers did, and others besides. At any rate—and this is to the point—it is impossible to extract a "morality" from Camus's various intuitions and an "ethic" from his meditations on ethics. Camus's thought has been reproached both for its lack of practical application and for its excessive morality. But we may well question the notion of an ethic devoid of practical applications, an ethic, if ethic there be, defined as an ensemble of rules and precepts. What Camus's monotonous and powerful appeal to "justice" or to "happiness" reveals is in fact, an existentialist tension, rather than any rules for living. Above all, Camus is a poet, or to be more exact he has the sensitivity, the vision of a poet. But can a man innocently be a poet in our century? Insofar as Camus clothes his intuitions with reasoning, he distorts them.

"A man's work is nothing other than the long voyage to rediscover by the detours of art the two or three simple and great images which first gained access to his heart" (*L'Envers et l'endroit,* preface). All Camus's thought resides in a few elementary childhood experiences, in the way they "opened" him to the world. The famous "Mediterranean wisdom" with which he was so often taunted, is not, as was wrongly claimed, a luxury born of a bourgeois culture. As a child, and a child of illiterates, Camus, at the time of his fundamental experiences had not attained the realm of culture. He attempts rather, consciously and sometimes awkwardly, to recapture the *precultural* springs of existence. The fundamental existential experience that haunts Camus and which he tried to express through the lyrical descriptions in his first essays—works to which one must always return because they never ceased to be true for him—through the myths of the "Algerian race" and the "towns without pasts" (is there a writer who does not create his own myths?), in the last chapters of *The Rebel* in brief, is the world lived as heat and light, is the sun.

Sartre, in the analyses at the end of *Being and Nothingness,* has sufficiently emphasized the importance of the tangible in presenting immediate symbols for the interrelation of our consciousness and the world; in his "psychoanalysis"—to use Bachelard's word—of snow, of the viscous, etc. It is not surprising that no theoretical analysis of the solar can be found in Sartre since, after all, the sun seems absent from his personal universe. Or, to state matters more exactly, it plays a negative role: "I shan't do anything worthwhile, except perhaps, at nightfall. That's because of the sun. . ." (*Nausea*). The redeeming virtues of night are defined in relation to the negated sun; it is because they are *anti-solar* that they give Roquentin a temporary respite from nausea. There is, of course, the disappearance of light ("Nausea remained down below, in the *yellow light*"), but what especially counts is the disappearance of heat: "I am happy: the cold is so pure, so pure tonight." Night leads back to cold, cold to purity. We follow the slope, the orientation of Roquentin's existentialist reverie: "Am I not myself a wave of chilled air? To have neither blood, nor lymph, nor flesh . . . To be only a part of the cold." The sun is no longer "Noon the just" of Valéry's "Graveyard by the Sea," "Noon up there, motionless Noon," the plentitude of being against which the revolt of life must be affirmed: it is the *vital* force itself. Camus considers the sun in the same way as does Sartre, but only to oppose Sartre as he opposed Valéry. Camus's sun, unlike Valéry's, is not the manifestation of a spherical form of being, closed in on itself. . . . It is always the sun shining on the ruins of Tipasa, the sand beach of *The Stranger,* or the sea. It is light felt not as a distant purity, but as a fecundating bath. It is the unifying force of the cosmos: "From the earth to the sun a heady alcohol rises over the whole expanse of the earth, making heaven sway" (*Noces*). Gliding over all things, penetrating all things, overwhelming in its presence, the sun is the very symbol of that vital participation through which the realms of nature and of man are united: "Outside the *sun, kisses* and wild *perfumes,* all seems futile to us" (*Noces*).

The theme of the "sun," therefore, defines the fundamental category in Camus's ontology: participation. It is perhaps worth recalling here young Camus's vivid interest in Plotinus. His experience is the very opposite of Sartre's nausea. Sartrean "nausea" has its source in the double awareness of subject and object, of the absolute separation of consciousness and nature—in man's impotent negation of being as he tries symbolically to "reject" a world from which he is effectively rejected. With Sartre, we live a godless Cartesianism, whereas in Camus we detect a Bergsonism but without teleology. Though life in Camus's work no longer moves in an ascending and reassuring direction, it still has impetus; though it has lost its finality, it has preserved, so to speak, all its vitality. The body is the place where man and nature meet in a happy "marriage."

In the solar world of Camus, the muscular indolence and eurythmy of bodies reigns without contest. Animality is fully accepted. Camus is far from thinking in terms of self-enjoyment or of a hedonistic retreat within. ("To take pleasure in oneself is impossible." *L'Envers et l'endroit,* preface). The body is the privileged place of joy, because it is the locus of harmony, and union is in fact unison. Physical love places human beings against the background of Being, and participation in the act of love is the symbol of a deeper participation. Meursault feels his love for Marie while swimming: "The water was cold and I felt all the better for it. We swam a long way out, Marie and I, side by side, and it was pleasant to feel how our movements matched, hers and mine, and how we were both in the same mood, enjoying every movement." Nor is it by chance that Meursault's love for his mother, instead of being a latent and permanent sentiment, as required by psychological myths which are only disguised forms of morality, always wells up from sudden perception: "Through the rows of cypress trees . . . that tawny brown and green earth . . . I understood Mother." The spontaneous identification of earth and mother defines Meursault's "cybelian" [Cybele: goddess of the earth] mode of existence, plunging to the telluric sources of his being where in the words of the poet Claude Vigée, all love is "a happy incest."

It is easy to see how an ontology such as this can affect ethics. Vital participation is both act and value. We can mask fact for others and for ourselves, but a value will emerge precisely at the time of the unmasking. In this light it should be noted that at the end of *The Stranger,* Meursault's famous "awakening" and his accession to the ethical life do not arise out of the rejection of his past "animality," or of his physical mode of existence: of his adherence and adhesion to the moment, to the earth, given him in a succession of sensations; of his fidelity to the present and to presence in spite of all the attempts of society to create a continuous time and a logical world. On the contrary, the imminence of death makes explicit those values which heretofore had been implicit only. Meursault's life, suddenly limited and arrested, is not struck retrospectively with absurdity, as happens for Sartre's Pablo, in *The Wall:*

> Death had disenchanted everything. . . . If someone had come to tell me that I could go home peacefully . . . it would have left me cold: a few hours or a few years of waiting, it's all the same, when one has lost the illusion of being eternal. I was anxious about nothing; in a sense, I was calm.

In contrast, Meursault says,

> That meant, of course, I was to die. Also, whether I died now or twenty years hence, this business of dying had to be got through, inevitably. Still, what troubled me in my reasoning was the terrible jump my heart gave at the thought of twenty years of life yet to come.

Threatened with annihilation, life gathers and concentrates its force, becomes conscious of itself and proclaims that it is the only value: "And I, too, felt ready to start life all over again." Far from rendering life absurd, death is the element which gives it its full meaning. Life retrieves and reabsorbs death, and in its very defeat triumphs, since death which denies life succeeds only in reaffirming life. In Cybele, Apollo and Hades were reconciled:

> In a few moments, I shall throw myself down among the absinth plants letting their fragrance invade my body and, all prejudices to the contrary, I shall know that I am fulfilling the truth which is the truth of the sun and will also be that of my death.

(*Noces*). This, of course, suppresses neither the reality nor the horror of death. For death is not manifest only at the end of a life, but at its very heart, and then it is called suffering. With Meursault, the problem, in a sense, was posed too simply, too neatly. His beautiful animality is to be destroyed, but it is not impaired. He is going to die a lusty young man, but he will not suffer in the flesh.

With *The Plague,* we move from death suffered in full health to death suffered in illness. Pus mingles freely with the absinth plants of *Noces* (Nuptials), which reappear at the end of *The Stranger*: "The cool night air, veined with smells of earth and salt, fanned my cheeks. The marvelous peace of the sleepbound summer flooded through me like a tide." Flesh does not perish only, it disintegrates. It does not disintegrate after death only, but in life. Life and death are not only opposed one to the other, they inter-penetrate. The problem becomes more painful and more complex, but it remains fundamentally unchanged. This is made clear in the significant episode toward the end of *The Plague,* the end of the long combat with Evil and the long conversation between Rieux and Tarrou, who from all this draws the lesson: "Do you know," he said, "what we ought to do for friendship's sake?" "Whatever you wish," said Rieux. "Take a dip in the sea; even for a future saint, it's a worthwhile pleasure." The friendship between the two men, like the love of Meursault and Marie, regains its essential truth in the contact with water, as the two men swim "in the same cadence": "For some minutes, they advanced with the same cadence and vigor, alone, far from the world, liberated at last from the city and the plague." The narrator had already spoken, at the beginning of the passage, of "the outer world which can always save everything . . ." Rather than the stoic pronouncements he sometimes coined, this is the intuition which lies at the center of Camus's ethic.

If our analysis is accurate, it ought to help us get rid of two misunderstandings which weigh disastrously on the work and the person of Camus. First, the famous "heroism," to which we are told his message can be reduced. This error contains a share of truth, like all errors. The Tarrou side of Camus, in truth the temptation of heroism, is apparent in Camus's tendency to refuse emotion, in the kind of inflexibility with which he comes to grips with fate and which is often reflected in stiffness in his style, in his constant search for the concise phrase. "What interests me," says Tarrou with simplicity, "is to know how one becomes a saint." Evidently, Camus, too, is interested. But in his moments of weakness, when the demands he makes upon himself grow weak, Rieux, who, after all, is the narrator of the book and who survives whereas Tarrou dies, answers his friend, his alter ego: "I have no taste, I believe, for heroism and sainthood. What interests me is to be a man." "Yes, we are seeking the same thing, but I am *less ambitious.*" One can easily understand why heroism is a facile solution, a least effort: as the characters of Malraux's *Man's Fate* show, heroism is essentially a turning in on oneself by a confrontation with death. . . . Camus moves in the opposite direction when at the end of *The Rebel,* he says that "in order to be a man" one must "refuse to be God"; when he breaks away from the ultimate ambition of heroism, it is because he is not thinking in terms of a closed, circular ethic; it is because all his thought tends to define an ethic of "openness" to the world and to others, an ethic of participation.

There is a certain form of participation which is called enjoyment. Apropos of Camus, Gide has often been mentioned, and Camus has been taken to task for affinity with the apostle of hedonism, at a time when "commitment" was considered indispensable. Hedonism, too, is one of the temptations Camus faced (who does not have his own?) but it is incompatible with the fundamental direction of his thought, with his "existential project." "Self-enjoyment is impossible; I know it, in spite of the great talents I could have applied to it" (*L'Envers et l'endroit,* preface). Camus finds this hedonism impossible, not in the name of an abstract morality, but because it is the nature of the body, of the "body proper" as the philosophers would say, to turn toward the world and be in harmony with the world. Resemblances with Gide in vocabulary or thought—sensation, present moment, light, sun, landscapes, etc.—are only superficial. . . .

There is no Gidian hedonism in Camus. Camus's faithfulness to ever-repeated fundamental experiences is quite opposed to Gide's variety of experiences. The fundamental paucity and poverty of Camus's imagery of nature contrast sharply with Gide's varied landscapes, with Gide's many sentimental wanderings through reality as flitting "from flower to flower, from one thing to another" (La Fontaine). Camus's imagery is always drawn from the ruins of Tipasa, sun on rock, or the Mediterranean, the sea. When removed from his element, visting Prague or the Scandinavian countries, Camus becomes lost, bewildered. Whereas Gide experiences everything in the plural, Camus experiences things in the singular. His solar experience is one of destitution and denudation. His is a "proletarian" relationship to the world, the relationship of someone who has nothing and whose contact with objects is not expressed in terms of having. Camus's domain is *being,* and this returns us to our preceding analyses of the vital force. The only possession is a rejoicing which is a participation.

Since heroism and hedonism are rejected, more from an ontological point of view than an ethical one, or to put it otherwise, once the concept of possession in the form of domination of self or of the world is disqualified, there obviously remains a basic problem to be solved in Camus's thought: that of the relationships between being and doing. This is the very heart of the quarrel between Camus and existentialism, a quarrel that caused so much ink to flow over the last ten years. One can easily follow the evolution of Sartre from *Nausea* to *Red Gloves:* all ontological solutions are closed to thought. Where consciousness is the illness of being, where the "for-itself" exists only as a continuous opposition to the "in-itself," and where the aim of the human being underlying all others is to synthesize the two contradictory entities—in other words, where, as Malraux had already stressed in *Man's Fate,* man's dream is to be God, any position which seeks a solution in being is necessarily doomed to failure. "Bad faith," which all Sartre's work is there to uncover and track down in all its machinations, is nothing but man's desperate effort to give the consistency of being to his existence, *to make himself exist* through symbolic possession of the world, through other people's view of him, etc. From then on, man is a "useless passion." The concept of authentic action is opposed to the state of real transcendence of the "absurd." "A priori, life is senseless . . . but it is up to you to give it a meaning" (*Existentialism is a Humanism*). The important word here is *give*. "Bad faith" can introduce itself in our way of "giving a meaning," in such a manner as to have this meaning remain intentional, symbolic. Meaning can be given to one's life through deeds alone, or more precisely through actions, that is to say, a manner of behaving which is not an end in itself (this would be falling into heroism, an attitude denounced in *The Flies*), but which aims at an objective transformation of the world. Since history is the actual medium in which man comes into contact with the world, the existentialist philosophy of action will be a philosophy of historic action, entirely oriented toward *the future*. Sartre: "Existentialism will never take man as an end, for a man is always in a state of formation" (*Existentialism is a Humanism*). De Beauvoir: "It is in the light of the future, which is the meaning and very substance of the act, that a choice will become possible" (*For an Ethic of Ambiguity*). Simone de Beauvoir herself draws the consequences of this attitude in the following statement: "Men of today will be sacrificed to those of tomorrow because the present appears as the 'facticity' that one must transcend toward freedom." In this respect, the whole purpose, the whole effort of Camus's philosophy is directed at shutting this door so dangerously left open on the sacrifice of the living to the men of the future and at reinstating the inalienable value of the present in opposition to the future.

"This argument accepts life as being the only necessary good . . ." (*The Rebel*). The moral philosophies of Sartre and Camus are what one could call "unidimensional philosophies," the one basing itself completely on the idea of liberty, the other on that of life. It is not accidental that throughout this essay we have pursued the parallel, or rather that we have been pursued by this parallel between Sartre and Camus. A perpetual confrontation such as this—which faces us in our every thought and action—does no more than express the absolute need of our time to redefine itself completely. Malraux had already said, "The age of the fundamental is beginning again," and in spite of the complexity of the problems, the fundamental choices are simple. A philosophy of liberty directed exclusively toward action is a philosophy of abandon, of the radical separation of man and world, a philosophy in which the world becomes acceptable only when transformed by man. This explains the value given to the manufactured object in Sartre's work, the detailed analysis of the artifact and of all relations connected with the use of things, whereas, in contrast, Roquentin's "nausea" is triggered by the feel of a pebble on the beach. The dangers of such an existentialist attitude can easily be grasped: by denying itself communion through actual presence, it does away with the present in favor of the world transformed, "acted upon," i.e. the future. By cutting off humanity from being, by enclosing man in the humane and denying being to the human, it tends to upset the balance of existence leaving it in a false equilibrium, so to speak.

Philosophers like Merleau-Ponty have attempted to help man out of this dead end and to re-establish him on his ontological foundations. That is exactly what Camus does in the realm of ethics. To expect salvation to emerge from action is to postpone the justification of the action indefinitely, to perpetually refer to the problematical end of history. In her systematic effort to define an existentialist philosophy, Simone de Beauvoir was aware of the dangerous mirage inherent in the concept of distant goals: "The end justifies the means only if it remains present to us, if it is completely revealed during the enterprise itself" (*For an Ethic of Ambiguity*). However, because of the lack of a point of reference, of a permanent criterion, in short, of an absolute value, or, more exactly, because liberty is the only absolute value he possesses, the existentialist philosopher finds himself placed in a position forever oscillating between the end and the means: "One cannot judge the means without the end which gives it meaning, any more than one can detach the end from the means which define it." But from where then will the definition, the meaning, come? Under its humanized surface the world is absolute chaos. Man, we have been told, cannot be taken as an end since he is perpetually in the making. The refusal to take man himself as an end is all the more understandable since Sartre's theoretical analyses of our relationships to others as well as his literary investigation reveal that "hell is other people" and that for man "his number one enemy is man"; and this without our being able to blame any political system, since Sartre considers that it is an unchangeable ontological situation, a characteristic of man's condition and therefore impervious to any possible modification.

Freedom then remains as the supreme goal. But since freedom is a fact or if one wishes, facticity, as well as transcendency (we cannot not be free, we are *condemned* so to be), and therefore differs from a value that has yet to be, we can conceive of goals *for* freedom but not of freedom as a goal. For we cannot confuse liberty and liberation without being insincere. The chained slave is free as both the theoretician in *Being and Nothingness* and Orestes in *The Flies* know[1]; if he wants to be freed, it is because he wishes to find himself moving once again within the circuit of humanity; it is because he wishes to *live*.

Here we discern another value that liberty can no longer define. It is no longer possible to shut man up inside his own ipseity, to say with Simone de Beauvoir that man's problem consists in "pursuing the expansion of his existence and in recovering this very effort as an absolute." In a different manner, we have come back to the fruitless circularity of heroism. Human activity must open itself to the world, must sur-

[1] "*Jupiter*: If you dare pretend that you are free, then the freedom of the prisoner loaded down with chains in the corner of his cell will have to be vaunted as well as that of the crucified slave.—*Orestes*: Why not?"

render itself to the world and rediscover its natural source and dwelling, must live the experience of the sun. Simone de Beavoir herself says this admirably well when she writes;

> To wish man free is to wish for being, it is to wish for the revelation of being in the joy of existence. . . . It is when our movement toward freedom takes on the consistency of pleasure, of happiness, that it assumes its real and palpable form in the world. . . . If we do not love life in our own selves and through our fellow man, it is useless to try to justify life.

This is exactly what Camus says throughout his work. But one can wonder how such an existential outlook is compatible with the existentialist attitude. How can the revelation of being be made through joy if the basic experience of being is expressed through "nausea"? How can one desire being and at the same time set up consciousness as the very negation of being? An orientation toward happiness, an unconditional love of life are indeed the concrete basis of all ethics, but then we need to change ontologies. What happened in fact was that the ethics of ambiguity surreptitiously passed from Sartre to Camus. And if in the last analysis we wish to give a concrete basis to moral philosophy, we must go back to the words of Camus: liberty opens upon life and the philosophy of existence upon the philosophy of being.

We now have before us one of these arresting Camus truths. The "yes" triumphs over the "no." "I came to realize that at the core of my revolt lay a consent. . . . How does one sanctify the union of love with revolt?" (*Noces*). But simultaneously an inverse reaction takes place: revolt exists side by side with consent: both find expression in an equilibrium of opposites. Therefore we have not reached one of those philosophical "principles" that would allow us tragically to "deduce" a philosophy, an axiom from which we could draw laws and precepts as in the good old days of rationalism. Hardly has the "yes" been posited before the "no" rises in opposition. "Man is the only creature that refuses to be what he is" (*The Rebel*). Horror and injustice exist within our own selves, in others, and in the world. Thus in a simultaneous "yes" and "no" Camus defines a dialectic of confrontation, of opposition, of anguish without transcendence. Camus's well-known "concept of limitations" simply means that an affirmation of life must be made which does not end in a complete negation of the world. Camus knew full well that to emphasize the "vital" was not without danger. Nietzsche had encountered the same problem only to fall into the "superman" trap and into the error of biological expansionism; we are well aware of what followed when these ideas were taken up by others. Life can be deadly; the sun kills, as Meursault finds out when he shoots the Arab without reason: "My eyes were blinded by a curtain of salty tears. I felt only the sun beating down relentlessly upon my forehead. . . ." The pure and simple submission to vital forces without the counterweight of moral revolt ends in the destruction of these forces; vitalism escapes nihilism only on the condition that life accept a sacrifice: it must cease to limit itself to the individual; it must transcend itself by moving into the realm of the universal: "Within the limits of the 'absurd' experience, suffering is individual. Starting with the movement of revolt, we are aware of suffering as a collective experience, as everyman's adventure. I revolt, therefore we are" (*The Rebel*). This defines the evolution of Camus's thought from *The Stranger* to *The Plague*.

A moral philosophy of action is thus superimposed upon—one might even say spans—a philosophy of being. This is the sensitive core, the touchstone of any doctrine today. Action in Camus's eyes must remain faithful to its twofold origin, the "no" sitting in judgment, and the "yes" ready to "change life but not the world." Divided at its source, action can only be charged with anguish. Since it no longer attempts to reach the absolute, which is found only on the level of being, it can only be imperfect. "Poverty prevented me from believing that all is well in history and in the world; the sun taught me that history is not everything." Camus has often been criticized for rejecting history because he did not accept it exclusively. The fact that he set it in a broader ontological context does not mean that he substituted the concept of history for something else. But at a time when history, in the case of many, has become the only dimension of the human drama, Camus refers us to something which underlies history and without which history could not exist.

In the course of the debate caused by *The Rebel,* Sartre criticized Camus for placing human values in "the battle of man against heaven" and by so doing forgetting the concrete and historical reasons for action. It is quite true that in a way *The Plague* presents a perfect situation in which all human beings can unite to fight the inhuman. But, after all, the book is also an allegory and must so be understood. It does not negate history, but extracts an ultimate meaning from it. If man habitually can and should (most of all, perhaps) fight man, it is insofar as man becomes a scourge and assumes the role of the plague. The oppressed says to the oppressor: "Get out of my sun." Action as conceived by Camus can never be satisfied with being a praxis; it is never a form of salvation in itself; it is never circular at any time. Though necessary, it is always deceptive, in fact somewhat mystifying if it is not rooted in the world of the present, in life itself. As Simone de Beauvoir so aptly said, "If the satisfaction of an old man drinking a glass of wine has no value, then production, wealth, are only empty myths." Man is not "the future of man"—to use the words of the poet Francis Ponge, so dear to the existentialists—he is man's present.

Immediate practical consequences stem from Camus's moral philosophy which some have described as being so ethereal: "I shall have pleaded my case . . . so that *from this very moment* the agonizing pain of man be lessened" (*Actuelles*). No appeal to the realm of ends, of the future, can justify any attack on the present, on life which is an inalienable value. Camus squarely sets up an ethic of being in opposition to the ethics of action, and at this point he breaks with existentialism and Marxism. Camus never denied that in certain exceptional cases, the use of violence might be a weapon, but he always refused to accept that it might become a policy. A simple nuance perhaps, but for millions of human beings, one which is capital in importance. In this sense certainly, Camus was the conscience of our time, repeating in vain perhaps what Ionesco was to illustrate in his play *The Killer*: that we could not build the "shining city" in defiance of nature without immediately bringing the Killer into existence.

One might object that it is very easy to be a "conscience" and this obviously raises the whole problem of the "clean" and "dirty" hands having an equal chance of bringing some consolation. But, we ask, how does the evolution from *The Stranger* to *The Plague,* from the subjective to the "we are" attitude find its application on the practical level? Camus proposes an ontology; nevertheless a concrete ethic, in other words, a policy, still has to be defined, for it would be pointless to establish an "Algerian" ethic which would not begin by dealing with Algeria, for example. And how will the "yes" and "no" offset each other in this particular instance? "What we need is to define a modest policy, a policy just as free from any trace of Messianism as from the nostalgia of a Garden of Eden" (*Actuelles*). Will Camus's ethic of moderation then end up only in a policy of moderation? When Camus writes, "There is only one thing left for us to try, and that is honesty without illusion, a wise loyalty . . . ," this wisdom may seem limited and disappointing, but we must admit that there exists no ethical or political position that does not have its pitfalls. The pitfalls inherent in the concepts of absolutism in action or history are too obvious these days to require any comment. What Camus called the nihilism of efficiency at any cost has more than shown its inhuman consequences. But the opposite danger of abstention and inactivity is also present. It is a real danger and no formula exists which allows us to evade it. Both the middle of the road and the royal road can be fatal. The first, however, offers our civilization more chances of survival than the second, whose end we know only too well.

We shall not discuss those personal commitments or refusals to be committed which concern Camus alone. We merely note that, when necessary, Camus paid with his own person, and that his reticence very often coincided with a near withdrawal. But he never claimed that he was playing an exemplary role nor did he ever set himself up as a model. Passionately in search of an ethic, he never claimed he was a moralist. As his preface to *L'Envers et l'endroit* (Betwixt and Between) clearly shows, he was aware that he was fallible. The exponents of virtue who dream of being judges are dealt with in *The Fall*. To those who demand coherent, satisfying, and clearly stated policies—to systematic minds, to the organizers and administrators—we can only answer that Camus, like the most beautiful girl in the world, can give only what he possesses.

In contrast to the fundamental experience described in most contemporary philosophies, he had a certain happy experience of being which appeared basic to him: he passed it on to us. Around him and in history he sees the consequences of uprooting: he tells us about them. Camus, who is a thinker though not a philosopher, instinctively perceives certain truths. They had escaped minds dialectically better prepared than his own, but minds that did not know how to extract consequences from these truths or who did not wish to extract them. He recalls these consequences inexorably, monotonously. He rediscovers the values of life and happiness lost in the tumult and terrors of our age. He places happiness, that is to say, the reconciliation of man and nature, above ethics and simultaneously rectifies the indifference inherent in nature, his own nature, through an ethic: solitude exploding in the movement of the heart toward his fellow-man. "Rieux straightened up and said in a firm voice . . . that there was no shame in preferring happiness.—Yes, said Rambert, but there may be shame in being happy all alone" (*The Plague*).

This is the existentialist tension in Camus's thought that no theoretical formulation, no dialectic process can resolve. Camus gives us only two ends of the chain which we must hold at any cost. In its authenticity, Camus's "moderation" is quite the antithesis of comfortable, mediocre moderation. It is a painful and perpetual effort. The true contact with being and with others is not given. It can only be conquered over the commonplace, over habit. The tenacious will to come to grips with the present is not easy to maintain when one knows just how easy it is to count on the future or the past for one's own justification. "Moderation" is the only way through which to live and adhere completely to life. Basically, the discontinuous intuitions powerfully restated by Camus, once elucidated, reveal less what we should do than *what we should not do*. One cannot be a hero, a pleasure seeker, or a judge, and this is the sense of Camus's opposition to Malraux, Gide, or Sartre.

Camus's work does not set up an ethic, but in a way it does propose "prolegomena to any future ethic." As Claude Bourdet said in the conclusion of an article "Camus and the problem of Clean Hands," "If the time should come when in spite of present ups and downs France turns toward socialism . . . then the warnings of Camus against the degradation of revolution may be useful to those who will then be facing certain dangers . . . " If we lose a certain relationship to being, existence founders. These are the "traps" detected, the warning cries, desperate at times, that Camus raises in our time, clarion calls of the poet echoing through a city of philosophers and rhetoricians. Lacking that logical coherence which so often is only superficial and illusory, the warnings, the cries, the call possess an internal cohesion born of an unshakable certainty. If it goes deeply enough, analysis uncovers not a mine of ideas but an outpouring, a vital spring. There we must take our arguments to be refreshed. It seems that for Camus this is what constitutes all ethics. It must be *existential* in the full sense of the word, or it does not exist, or it becomes an anti-philosophy dedicated to man's destruction. No formula, no effort of discursive thought can absolve us from recreating experience ourselves within ourselves. Human beings though interdependent stand alone Today, this is a truth not easily acceptable. Camus is neither the man in the street nor the "organization man." He is the man in the sun, on the lone naked rock, who knows that once the plague has come he must re-enter the city. It is he who said, "My human passions have never been 'against,'" and who during the struggle and beyond it, never forgot the reasons to love. This sun, this knowledge mean little to empire builders or creators of systems. Nevertheless, should the era neglect them, it will rush to its doom, and man's fate will be sealed the day he forgets how to love—in spite of evil and suffering this creation without a creator.

Albert Camus: A British View

by S. Beynon John

The English translation of Camus's *The Rebel* provoked a number of extravagant estimates of this talented French author and succeeded in distracting attention from what is, surely, his chief claim upon our interest: his power as an imaginative writer. So far as his philosophical forays are concerned, Camus is likely to remain something of an exotic in England. He typifies that marriage of intense intellectual abstraction and moral passion which excites across the Channel, whereas, in England, it more frequently exhausts. This English reaction is not simply the product of a bluff Philistinism, as some French critics affect to believe. It has its roots in our empirical tradition, our suspicion of those incandescent aphorisms, at once stylish and abstract, that dazzle the society of Parisian literary cafés where writers of imaginative fiction make their sudden raids into the territory of social and political theory. We turn, I fancy, with more ready sympathy to the play of the creative imagination in the medium of fiction, and here, Camus has most impressively configured for us a strange, haunting and significant world of his own.

As one might expect, the clues to any understanding of Camus lie, in the first instance, in the intellectual climate of his youth and young manhood and in his personal experiences during this period. Camus's own reaction to life was nourished and confirmed by the nihilism prevalent in much of French thought and literary sensibility between the last two wars. The elements which formed this climate of feeling were not novel. They had existed in the previous century, often provoking the usual reactions to nihilism, but in the twentieth century they reached a new degree of intensity which suggested to some of the sensitive and intelligent a new *kind* of experience. Repeated destructive wars, the accelerated growth of mass society, the generalized despair of mass unemployment, the unparalleled advances of technology, the doctrines and techniques of the totalitarian state—all represented what Peter Drucker describes as

Albert Camus: A British View." (Originally titled "Albert Camus.") From *Modern Languages,* XXXVI, No. 1 (December, 1954), 13-18.

the "return of the demons." In a word, these forces tend to awaken in individual man the sense of his victimhood in the world. New scientific theories, too, seemed to challenge still further men's assumptions about the nature of experience. Among these we must count the delayed implications of Freud, and discoveries about the nature of the physical universe, especially those of Einstein. Two general conclusions were often drawn from the play of these factors. Firstly, they appeared to break up traditional values and beliefs about the nature of man and his place in the universe. Next, in the degree to which they menaced individuality or made it the prey of unconscious impulses (as with Freud), these forces seemed to impair the density of individual existence and to provoke the idea that man was adrift in an absurd universe. Such a climate of thought and feeling inspires, at least in part, the spirit of radical negation, *la hantise du néant* (the obsession with nothingness) that is to be found in the work of writers as various as Paul Valéry, André Malraux, and Albert Camus, and the temptation—evident in Malraux and Camus—to mistake intensity of sensation (a means of being confirmed in one's own existence) for the rhythm and warmth of life. It is as if, among the ruins of belief, subjective experience alone has validity, though it is often filled with an almost vertiginous sense of the suffering and estrangement of man.

The circumstances of Camus's own life in Algeria were such as to make this prevailing sensibility especially congenial. Born in 1913, in Mondovi, of a poor working-class family, he was reared by his widowed mother and knew a degree of privation. He entered the University of Algiers, maintaining himself by a variety of occupations, manual and clerical, but, after completing the *licence* and a piece of post-graduate research on the relations between the thought of Saint Augustine and Plotinus, tuberculosis forced him to give up his hopes of a career in the University. During this period he underwent a number of important intellectual and literary influences, notably those of André Malraux and Dostoevsky, whose work he met and, in a sense, lived in stage versions produced by an experimental theatre group to which he belonged. The nihilism and the spirit of revolt evident in these writers were all the more influential in that they matched his personal vicissitudes. The other seminal experience of these early years was Camus's encounter with nature along the North African littoral. We find it expressed in two short collections of semi-autobiographical essays which provide a map, as it were, to his sensibility and his metaphysical preoccupations at this time. The more important of these, *Noces* (Nuptials) (1938), extends in range and power the travel sketches which had formed a part of his first collection, *L'Envers et l'endroit* (Betwixt and Between) (1937), raising them to the level of a sumptuous hymn to the world of physical beauty and the life of the senses. The four essays contained in *Noces* were composed between 1936 and 1937 and represent the notations of a metaphysical pagan in the face of changing landscapes. Each essay has its own distinctive resonance and mood but all are united in the persistent confrontation of the permanence of nature with what is sensual and mortal. Pervading all the muscular paganism and the insistence upon a "common resonance between man and the earth" is the horror and rejection of death. Man is revealed here as a web of sense, highly sensitive to the assault of sea, cloud and flower; obsessed with death, and caught up in a passionate revolt against the natural order of things in which he figures as a victim. In these essays, it is the décor that dominates, especially as Camus feels himself, at moments, to be just another element in the life of nature.

> Like a pebble made shiny by the tides, I was polished by the wind, worn down to the very soul. I was a bit of that force upon which I floated, then much of it, then all of it finally, merging the pulsings of my blood with the great sonorous beatings of that natural heart ever-present, everywhere. (*Noces*)

This identification of himself with nature leads Camus to treat wind, sun and sea almost like allegorical presences. Does not the very first page of *Noces* refer to the "gods that speak in the sun"? Here man is envisaged as the "locus of a polytheism," to borrow a phrase used by Aldous Huxley in describing the ideas of D. H. Lawrence, a writer with whom the early Camus has certain affinities. In this sense, *Noces* is directed away from the human world to a larger, non-human collectivity. The tendency of this polytheism is to personalize nature at the expense of man; it reflects the general and the non-human at the expense of the particular and the human.

What elements may be disengaged from these formative years? A pagan receptivity to nature complicated by a tragic apprehension of man's estrangement in the world; a rich sensuality married to the anguished anticipation of death; and, finally, a sense of man's victimhood coupled with the revolt against that order of the universe which permits it. From this point onwards, Camus's career offers a distinct shape.

First comes the period roughly contemporary with the Second World War (from 1938 until the middle of 1944), when his early tragic intimations are deepened and his sense of man's estrangement in the world raised to the power of obsession. During this phase, a marked congruity exists between Camus's philosophical themes and the situations and tonality of his imaginative fiction. Both reflect man's estrangement and the absurdity of human existence. The profound pessimism of Camus's work at this period may be thought of as the legacy of French military and moral collapse. At least, that collapse appears to sanction his earlier intuitions, since it is evidence of a world in which the arbitrary reigns supreme and men are crushed beneath the heedless pressure of history. On the other hand, the fact that Camus is engaged in the very positive activity of the French Resistance argues a commitment to life, an affirmation of the worth of living, which are at variance with the tone and themes of his literary production. It is the tension between these two attitudes that supplies the key to understanding *The Myth of Sisyphus* (1942), which both registers the force of the temptations of nihilism and attempts to find a way out of the nihilist impasse without flying into the arms of religion. *The Myth of Sisyphus* expresses, in terms of formal ideas, themes Camus had previously realized imaginatively in the first draft of *Caligula* (that of 1938, left substantially unchanged in the stage version of 1945), and in his novel, *The Stranger* (early 1942); themes he will restate in dramatic idiom with *The Misunderstanding,* written in 1943 and first produced in 1944. The philosophical essay defines Camus's concept of the absurd as the encounter between man's innate need of order and purpose and the blank indifference of nature. A study that begins with suicide insists upon the recognition of the fundamental absurdity of life, urges the living out of this absurdity in a constant tension of revolt and, finally, arrives at an acceptance of life symbolized by the labor of Sisyphus. These ideas have their center of gravity in the experience of nullity and the absurd and it is this experience that animates Camus's imaginative writing.

The novel and the two plays of this period configure the sense of estrangement and create a tragically *elliptical* world through which the characters move as though in a trance. In *The Stranger,* as Sartre has brilliantly suggested, Camus deliberately suppressed all casual connections in the syntax and atomized the sense of temporal duration, by the constant use of the perfect tense, so as to stress the degree to which Meursault's world is arbitrary and absurd. The central dichotomy of the novel lies in the juxtaposition of two conflicting versions of the same set of events: Meursault's dry, laconic account of his Mother's burial, his liaison with Marie, and his eventual murder of a strange Arab, and, on the other side, the more sinister versions of these same events as seen through the eyes of the prosecution and its witnesses at Meursault's trial. This narrative technique adroitly conveys the sense of men's mutual incomprehension in the world. A number of grotesques (Salamano, with his mangy dog, and the eccentric lady absorbed in ticking off the radio programs are the most prominent) confirm the impression of absurdity. Meursault is not the villain of the piece. Villainy implies efficacy and responsibility, while he is just another *thing* in nature, obedient to the pulsations of the midday sun. *The Stranger,* far from being a transcription of the real world, is an allegory, a veritable myth of the absurd as incarnated in Meursault. Here, as in *Noces,* it is the inhuman and undifferentiated *collective* forces that dominate: sun and sea, presences of nature; the town of Algiers itself. The initiative, the particularity and the baffling complexity of men are absent.

Camus's mythopœic faculty also finds expression in *The Misunder-*

standing, where, by using for its plot a sensational news item discovered by Meursault on a scrap of newspaper hidden in his cell, he obviously intends to create a sort of contemporary myth about the nature of man's existence in the world. Camus combines the form of Grand Guignol and the substance of metaphysical anguish. This story—about a long-absent son who makes a fortune, returns home and is murdered by a mother and sister who fail to recognize him—is nothing but an extended metaphor on the human condition. This is the world without signs or sense, the absurd world in which man is never at home. Credibility, motivation—these criteria simply do not apply, since we are not in the human world but in that abstract zone of symbols where the puppets of the absurd twitch into counterfeit life.

Caligula confirms the impression of an abstract and over-intellectualized theatre. The same blank and inhuman world is crystallized about the career of this mad Roman emperor whose lunacy is transposed from the historical to the metaphysical level. His is that "encounter with nothingness" provoked by the death of his sister, Drusilla, with whom he has been enjoying an incestuous relationship. Death brings him up sharply against the central truth of existence: "Men die and they are not happy." Where Meursault and Martha register the fact of life's absurdity, Caligula attempts to outbid it. He demonstrates the bankruptcy of total revolt, the terrifying consequences of the lust for the absolute.

These three works reveal a deliberate transposition into fiction of the philosophy of the absurd. They are abstract and exemplary, the graphic expression of a myth. But, in his third period, from 1945 to 1951, Camus fails to realize imaginatively the transition from nihilism to a sort of "reverence for life" (to use Schweitzer's expression), which he successfully accomplishes at the level of the discursive intelligence, in his philosophical argument. Briefly, the ideas elaborated between these two dates, without marking a complete break with the desperate negativity of *The Myth of Sisyphus,* are distinguished by a more truly human accent and constitute, to a much greater degree than formerly, an affirmation of the value of human life. A significant shift in ideas takes place, beginning with the closing pages of *Letters to a German Friend,* passing through the many articles and lectures written between 1945 and 1948 in *Combat* and elsewhere, and culminating in the final words of *The Rebel.* Camus has moved away from the hectic metaphysical revolt and the moral scepticism evident in his early ideas so as to embrace, in the face of Nazi conquests, the moral conviction that "any mutilation of man is irretrievable." He has abandoned the notion of "total" revolt under the accumulated evidence he derives from his study of the anatomy of modern European revolutions. Man is fallible, political theories are relative, automatic progress is a mirage, and freedom is threatened in every generation. Man must resist the temptations of the absolute and return to the old Aristotelian concept of moderation. These conclusions are banal but their timing makes them especially relevant and they bear the imprint of a lived experience.

These themes are transposed into the imaginative fiction of Camus's third period. Whereas his early heroes had been the victims of a sort of fatality of the absurd, the major figures of *The Plague* (1947), *State of Siege* (1948), and *The Just Assassins* (1949) revolt against the arbitrary. Unlike Caligula, though, they keep their revolt within human limits and, through it, manifest the fraternity of suffering by which men are united. Nevertheless, the imaginative world crystallized about this more human doctrine rarely conveys any convincing sense of life. Characters still lack human density, variety, and the element of surprise. Indeed, both *The Plague* and *State of Siege* are impressive in their total effect, but the individuals in them are reduced in scale and power by the force of great collective entities: the plague itself, the animated mass of the town, and the distant but disturbing presence of the sea. Consequently, neither Dr. Rieux nor Tarrou nor Father Paneloux quite comes alive for us. We perceive what they represent, but they do not seem to possess a life beyond the exigencies of this allegory in which an isolated and plague-stricken town symbolizes the human condition. Grand, however, that admirable comic creation, is above such criticism. He, and, to a minor degree, certain of the grotesques in *The Plague,* like the asthmatic Spaniard or the man who spits on cats, suggest something of the spontaneity of life. This is entirely absent from *State of Siege* where the deliberate adoption of the conventions of allegory intensifies the sense of abstraction. The conflict between death and suffering, that is, the power of evil, and the power of human love, construed in its largest sense and verging on the Christian concept of charity, is here articulated through a number of types and personifications. The Plague is incarnated in a sort of barrack-square martinet; Cadiz is the world, and a Chorus represents mankind. The action oscillates between the Plague and a young student, Diégo, who, along with his fiancée, Victoria, symbolizes Camus's attachment to purely human values. Both are insipid and lifeless, whereas a certain force is evident in the collectivities, the Plague, the Chorus and the sea that symbolizes liberty, which is not dispersed by Diégo's final victory, achieved through self-abnegation. Only at the level of political satire, in scenes of angry farce, does the play come to life.

The Just Assassins, it is true, is not dominated by these impersonal forces, but it is geared to abstract ideas. The debate over means and ends, which divides this group of Russian terrorists, imposes a rigid pattern on the characters involved. Hence, Ivan, the "delicate murderer," and Stépan, the case-hardened revolutionary for whom the end justifies all, draw life, less from their own personalities, which are "flat" and unexplored, than from the necessities of the dialectical counterpoint in which they are engaged. The debate between conscience and violence is remarkably well sustained, but an impassioned monotony continues to be the mark of Camus's characterization.

In the light of this brief interpretation, it may be possible to discern what factors inhibit the sense of life in Camus's fiction. They are, I suggest: the appeal of negation, the polytheistic experience of nature, and the force of abstraction.

Even when his thought passes beyond nihilism (and his whole intellectual development is an attempt to transcend its paralysing attraction), Camus retains the negative cast of mind that the encounter with nihilism had engendered. The act of faith, though not necessarily in a Divine Providence, required for a real acceptance of life and the possibility of human happiness is rarely made convincingly in Camus's imaginative work. His thought is centered on death, though certainly not as a "consummation devoutly to be wish'd," and this single-minded concentration inevitably affects the rendering of life in his pages. It falsifies life by equating it too readily with intensity of physical sensation. Camus's atheism is clearly an integral part of his experience of negation and it helps to drain his work of individuality and variety. I mean by this that Camus's use of myth is a response to the vacuum created by the "death of God" and the disintegration of traditional religious belief. Myth is a substitute for faith and the metaphors of religion, and myth, by its very nature, is anonymous and collective: it swallows up the individual life.

This tendency is intensified by the character of Camus's response to nature. He experiences nature so vividly that it comes alive, manifests itself in living presences which nullify man, and creates a feeling for allegory that permeates novels and plays alike. Allegory, like myth, is directed away from the life of particular men toward the general and the abstract. In a word, Camus has no difficulty in experiencing the reality of what is diffused and collective, but this very power impairs his feeling for the density of individual human existence.

Finally, Camus's philosophical intention is too obvious in all his imaginative writing. Situation and character often seem forced and contrived, as if the ratiocinative intelligence is, so to speak, too strong for the imaginative alloy in which it is working. In spite of this, Camus's novels and plays have an undeniable relevance and fascination for the contemporary reader. The vision of the world which he communicates may seem distorted, but it is a recognizable and significant distortion which illuminates man's predicament in the modern world. It was Camus's gift to recall us to an awareness of our human condition.

The World of the Man Condemned to Death

by Rachel Bespaloff

There a man takes right away the place his way of facing death assigns him. The mind itself loses its dominion.

Julien Sorel: *The Red and the Black.*

Reduced to its simplest expression, Camus's thought is contained in a single question: What value abides in the eyes of the man condemned to death who refuses the consolation of the supernatural? Camus cannot take his mind off this question. All his characters bring an answer; one has only to listen to them.

The Stranger

In *The Stranger,* Camus has already perfected his instrument: that realism which I shall call "cryptic," to distinguish it from naturalistic realism. Moreover, he had at his disposal an already perfect form, Gide's *récit,* which he could freely adapt to his needs, thus having an extraordinary economy of means. Gide had shown him what use could be made of the *I* to express the most intimate experience with the maximum of detachment. Objectivity with Camus does not strive to create an illusion of reality, for it is precisely the real which is being questioned. It strives, rather, to give the sensation of the fragmentation, the incoherence of a world which has, so to speak, lost its nuts and bolts. It behooves the reader to furnish the answer to the question suggested by a description which is given without commentary. Camus wanted to show an alienated subjectivity by letting the character depict himself through acts which do not express him. The difficulty was the greater as the *récit,* by its very nature, supposes a narrator who arranges past events according to the meaning he confers upon them—whereas here, precisely, the meaning is lacking. The narrator has lost the key to his own secret: he has become

"The World of the Man Condemned to Death." From *Esprit,* January, 1950, pp. 1-26. Translated by Eric Schoenfeld. Reprinted by permission of *Esprit.*

a stranger to his own life. He holds only facts, and facts are nothing. Therefore, he cannot give his existence a meaning which would establish its unity. Having neither past nor future, he has only a present which is crumbling away and does not become memory. Time, until the final revolt, is nothing for him but a succession of distinct moments, which no Cartesian God pieces together, which no vital impulse spans, which no remembrance transfigures. Camus has rendered admirably this fall of the present into insignificance through a paradoxical use of the first person narrative. The main character gives an account of the facts as they occurred in his life up to the eve of his execution, without the perspective of the immediate past, without extension and without resonance. Nothing is explained, but everything is revealed by the tone and the structure of the work, by the contrast of the two climaxes: the almost involuntary murder, where "the red explosion" of the sun plays a more important role than the man, and which marks the culmination of fatality; the revolt which gives birth to freedom within the confines of a destiny narrowly bounded by death. The art of Camus's *récit* lies in the subtle use of the processes which take the place of analysis, in the way the discontinuity of existence is emphasized through the continuity of tone which places all events on a single plane of indifference.

And yet, the alienation is far from being complete. A stranger to himself and to others, Meursault has a homeland: sensation. Interiority has, so to speak, emigrated from the soul to the body, and only moments of happy sensation restore a friendly world to the exile. In this sense, Camus's hero is a sort of plebeian brother of Gide's *Immoralist* who gives to the exaltation of the body the value of a protest against the false seriousness of a morality which finds it can come to terms with injustice. Though he does not condemn social oppression, nor tries to fight it, he denounces it through his quiet refusal to conform to the defiant attitudes one expects of him. One realizes that this indifferent man is intractable in his absolute respect for truth. On this point, he exhibits a surprising and even heroic firmness, since, in the end, it will cost him his life.

Camus, like Malraux and Sartre, belongs to a generation which history forced to live in a climate of violent death. At no other time, perhaps, has the idea of death been linked so exclusively to that of a paroxysm of arbitrary cruelty. Even on the plane of tragic humanism—Corneille's and Shakespeare's plane—death did not take on this kind of aspect; purveyor of glory, it was the arbiter of greatness. Nothing of the sort today. The smoke of crematories has silenced the song which from Chateaubriand to Barrès, from Wagner to Thomas Mann, had not succeeded in exhausting its modulations. Henceforth, in the vicinity of death, tortures replace ecstasy and sadism voluptuousness. Moreover, the immense certainty that there is a cure which the Christian associated with death, and his infinite hope that death was the winged sentinel of a fatherland, have slowly been wearing out. Nothing remains but naked death, in a storm of cold violence. Never before had death come to man with the new face now modeled by its millions of slaves. Neither the cult of the dead, nor any belief in glory, nor any faith in eternal life accompany death into this hell. This is the image of death which is woven into every page of Camus's work.

It is to Camus's credit that he always keeps its image before his eyes and ours whenever he comes to grips with the problem of the will to power. From *Caligula* to *The Plague,* Camus covered the same ground as had Malraux from *The Conquerors* to *Man's Fate*. Like Malraux, he confronted this problem with the aid of Nietzsche. The drama for this Nietzschean generation was that it lived on Nietzsche's thought and had simultaneously to deal, in actual fact, with its caricatural realization on a practical plane. It exalted the will to power in the individual at the very moment it prepared to fight it outside in the form of imperialism. To assess the seriousness of this situation, one need only consider the contrasting attitudes of the Napoleonic and the Nietzschean generations in regard to the will to power. Balzac and Stendhal clearly discerned the limitations of the man who, in their eyes, incarnated sublime energy. Napoleonic dictatorship, it is a fact, had not then degraded the conscience of the individual, nor seriously impaired the independence of his mind. Imperialism had not then taken the form of that anonymous violence which appears wherever it has succeeded in absorbing the various nationalisms, mixing the classes and welding them into those new conglomerates, political parties, transforming cruelty into discipline. The Napoelonic generation was therefore able to glorify energy as the principle of a form of human greatness which humanity as a whole can attain only through the individual's will to rise beyond himself. True, Balzac, great tragic poet that he was, revealed the self-destructive character of the passion for possession, and Stendhal diagnosed fundamental evil with perspicacity, when he noted that party spirit kills off true passions so that "one then commits the worst acts of cruelty, without cruelty." None the less, their ideal of the great energetic personality necessarily entails a hierarchy of values based on the growth of the will to power. Stendhal's Julien Sorel (*The Red and the Black*) dreams of "distinctions for himself and freedom for all." Though he scorns what he attains—"Is love (war, success) then no more than this?"—the disappointment is partial and does not put into question the value of existence. When, after he has been condemned to death, Julien examines and judges himself, he can absolve himself. He has carried out without flinching the "duty" toward himself which his will to greatness had prompted: this certainly is his absolute. His ambition is dead and no longer in question; only true love survives in him. But the truth of happiness, arising out of his shattered ambition, does not discredit the demands of a heroic will. And so great is the force of this imperative, that in a last flash of revolt Julien will sacrifice to it his life, rather than have to owe it to a society he despises.

The position of the modern hero is quite different. His "Is it no more than this?" stops at *this* and becomes glued to it. His existence has been dislocated under the weight of "*this*": absurd contingency, absurd necessity. Compare Meursault's attitude to Julien's as both face death. Just as he had not premeditated his crime, Meursault neither judges it nor assumes it. In contrast, Julien enters wholly into the least of his decisions. "My crime was premeditated," he tells the jury. Meursault neither gambles nor loses; the disconnected time in which he loses his way cannot find consummation in the moment. His entire existence is nothing but a misunderstanding, and it is through a misunderstanding that he eventually gives and suffers death. "I have not *lived in isolation* on earth," says Julien, "I had the powerful notion of *duty* . . . I was not carried away." Meursault is carried away, as his generation was to be carried away into war, by the combined effect of fever and violence. He stands in the blind spot of indifference where everything is equivalent; Julien stands at the summit of a difference which owes its worth to a unique existence. And yet, in front of death, the two meet in a revolt born of their nostalgia for happiness. Julien rediscovers in Mme. de Rênal's love all the joy of which ambition had formerly robbed him. Meursault discovers at last the truth concerning his sordid life: he has been happy, he still is happy, and he is ready to relive everything. The same outburst of anger makes both heroes rise up against the priest who has come to offer them his consolations and his exhortations. But Julien's revolt has a limited purpose: against society it sets up the individual and his sovereign demands. Beyond the social mechanisms which have trapped him, Meursault directs his protest against the human lot. Amid the indifference of a world devoid of God, nothing has any importance or value, except the pure act of living.

To live is enough—there is no humility whatsoever in this assertion. Camus reached it through revolt. Like one of his heroes, Caligula, he had meditated on this "very simple and very clear and somewhat idiotic truth, but a truth difficult to discover and heavy to bear . . . men die and they are not happy." What they need, then, is the impossible, "something which is insane perhaps, but which is not of this world." For Camus, everything this need invents to sate itself is a lure. Is there any certainty one can set up in the place of hopes which betray and despair which debilitates? Again Camus answers: to live. Life as passion, challenge, obstinate refusal of all supernatural consolation, *amor fati*. Here again, Meursault and Julien meet; both think "that there is no destiny above which one cannot rise through contempt." One also sees where they part company: from one obstacle to the next, from one victory to another, Julien conquers his destiny. No sooner has he reached the summit, than he is hurled straight into the abyss. Imprisoned, then condemned, it occurs to him that he might escape, but he does not dwell on the idea. A great individual does not begin his adventure anew, does not consent to repeat himself. Enlightened by his failure, Meursault reaches very different conclusions, and his modern revolt becomes clearly differentiated from the romantic revolt of which it is the heir: at the juncture he has reached, Meursault must consider the question of beginning anew. A sure instinct guided Camus when he chose the myth of Sisyphus. He understood with Nietzsche that repetition, starting over again until death, is the supreme test of the absurd. Hence the curious impression *The Stranger* makes on the reader. A book without hope, or rather against hope, it ends on a promise. The Meursault who seems to us from the very beginning inhumanly stripped of illusions, who tries only to put the world in the wrong by bringing its hatred and disapproval down on himself, extracts from defeat a grim acceptance of life. Such as he lived it, he deems it worth reliving.

In the trajectory of revolt which links us to the Romantics, Julien is at the highest, Meursault at the lowest point, but at the exact spot where revolt can surge up again. We can see what has been lost during the period that separates Julien from Meursault: the ideal of the Great Personality (today Malraux and Montherlant are the only writers who carry on this tradition). But, if it is true that the great personality contained the germ of its own disintegration, that between Napoleon and Hitler—the frantic puppet who has disappeared under the myths he fanned to a white heat—there exists only the difference between an original and its caricature, one may wonder whether revolt is not a phenomenon of decadence.

We neither can nor want to renounce what is has brought us. We would not have wished to be spared the suffering it has brought upon us. The reward was too beautiful: a freedom of view never before attained; a really heroic lucidity; a new tenderness for the terrestrial; an unparalleled development of the passion for knowledge; an impetuous conquest of freedom under the multiple assaults of our will to justice; a renewal of philosophy through our questioning of philosophy itself; in poetry and in the arts, an era of experimentation in which discoveries are accumulating; a secularization of Biblical ideas and Christian concepts simultaneously reviving atheism and faith; the trial of morality leading to a study in depth of ethics—there would be no end to a list of these assets. But, if we consider the liabilities, how can we deny the bankruptcy of revolt: society, nations, the world cut in half; slavery, the like of which was hitherto unknown in history; contempt for man carried to heretofore unknown extremes; a rapid decadence of the love of truth, paradoxically combined with a perfecting of the techniques of lucidity. From revolt to revolt, from revolution to revolution, we were supposedly moving toward greater freedom and we end up with the

Empire. We have been alienated from the eternal by the very revolt which taught us to apprehend the eternal in the instant, and we have now been handed over to history, that is, to the will to power which is the law of history. We have lost our way in time, strangers to ourselves like Meursault—man without a past, accomplice of baseness, unwilling murderer—who lives at the edge of his own nothingness. We are one with him who is so close to the truth and yet without truth, because he is without illusions. Like him, we are carried away into a world which is nothing more than the stage on which the tragedy of power is acted out.

It was the lot of the Nietzschean generation to experience a disappointment compared to which the disillusionment of the Napoleonic generation seems mild. Raised on Marx and Nietzsche, it witnessed both the caricature of Nietzsche's ideas in the Hitlerian state, and the falsification of Marxism in the Stalinist dictatorship. It would be unjust to hold Marx and Nietzsche responsible for these frightful counterfeits, which they would have been the first to denounce. The fact remains that such a mishap would not have befallen them if their doctrines had not harbored some fundamental defect capable of causing these deviations. We can discern the defect today; it is the rationalization and, thereby, the justification of the will to power. What Marx must be reproached for is not for having urged a struggle unto death, but for having transformed it into a system. One may be driven to violence: who could maintain in good faith that without it the workers would have succeeded in convincing the bourgeoisie that they, too, are human beings? Who would deny that the proletariat owes its emancipation to Marx more than to any other theoretician? And would Nietzsche have taught us to think if he had not done us violence, if he had not knocked down our certainties, destroyed our security and unleashed the war among truths which is the condition of our progress? Evil appears only when reason intervenes in order to smother the plurality of freedoms by setting over them the will to power. That alone explains the tragic miscarriage of Marx's and Nietzsche's thought. The two great liberators who wanted to create the myth of the future, and so free men from "the tradition of dead generations which weighs like a nightmare on the brains of the living," have brought the past back to us: the empire and man deified. It is therefore not by chance that the aristocratic revolt of Nietzsche and the proletarian revolt of Marx both end in the setting up of a chosen class, of a dominant group, upon whom has devolved the right to make the rules for the rest of a humanity whose sole duty is to obey. But one cannot forget that Nietzsche transcends history by vigorously going beyond each partial truth, and through the dialectic of the contradictory myths of the superman and the eternal return; that Marx transcends dialectical materialism by means of his impassioned criticism of egoism. One needed only to eliminate their contradictions in order to falsifv their thought. It is not surprising that, for our contemporaries, the disappointment caused by their failure was far more severe than was the case with the romantic hero. Revolt certainly has not reached its end. But, this time, it will have to be a revolt against revolt, against the will to power. *The Plague* must be read in the context of this situation.

The Plague

What moves us straight away is the integrity of the novel, which wishes to be modest, and eventually succeeds in so being. It is not easy to be honest at a time when nothing else is. The style of honesty has its demands, and Camus could not satisfy them without seeking an answer to the aesthetic problem he had to solve within the limits of his talent. How can one bring into the field of art a reality which defies the means of art, and recapture through fiction an experience which eludes the poetization of recollection? Camus had to avoid fictionalizing too recent an experience which could be expressed only through the direct testimony of the patient. He therefore kept only the structure of the facts in the symbolic equivalent he substituted for them. The image of the plague, here, is a means of rethinking events, on which, with worn-out indifference, we are already turning our backs, a way of straightening up from under their weight, of gauging them. "War," wrote Saint-Exupery, "is not an adventure. War is a disease, like typhus." In order better to make us feel this, Camus painted disease, not war. Consequently, realistic techniques, which, applied to the historical event, would have been laughable, become legitimate and effective. The objectivity with which Camus describes the epidemic is dependent on the same cryptic and non-naturalistic realism he used in *The Stranger*. Perhaps the use of the term *cryptic* to define a style which is at times sententious and whose transparency appears without mystery, will seem debatable. The multiplicity of meanings and interpretations it suggests, the deciphering it necessitates, certainly seem to remove it from allegory, which always conceals some precise object. Nothing of the sort in *The Plague,* where the scourge sometimes designates the event, sometimes the human condition, sometimes sin, sometimes misfortune.

Camus did not attempt to convey the complexity of the events through the technique of simultaneity and juxtaposition of scenes. To the pulverization of time and space he preferred the concentration of a continuous narration which could keep the tone of a testimony. The difficulty lay in taking up, one by one, through symbolic transcription, the themes of life and death during the occupation, starting from both subjectivity and collectivity. Certainly, the theme of the successive manifestations of the scourge is developed in too linear a pattern, and there is something too schematic in the characters, who synthetize the manifold aspects of the ordeal. One should not forget, however, that the real hero is not the I but the *we* elevated to the dignity of the particular being. Those who went through the ordeal of occupation recognize those situations where, speaking of themselves, they were compelled to say *we* at a time when each lived the *we* in an abyss of isolation and exile. The precarious solidarity which had thus linked people as they faced the catastrophe, and which would not outlive this catastrophe, called for a testimony which would rescue it from history and restore it to ethics. This is the task of the poet. Camus answered this call. He tried to describe an experience which had taken place at the level of intersubjectivity, without using either Jules Romain's unanimist technique or an analytical technique. Giving the humiliated *we* a voice required a form of speech simple enough to reflect the banality of the atrocious, and yet closely knit enough to sustain an insurgent thought. The slightest lack of authenticity would immediately have reduced the *we* to the *they*. A poet-moralist and not a novelist-poet, Camus is not gifted with the visionary imagination which creates myths and worlds. He draws a diagram and leaves it up to us to decipher it.

In one respect *The Plague* seems to us to fall short of the reality it recalls: it has no symbolic equivalent for the humiliation of the suffering inflicted upon man by man. It may seem strange that Camus should have deliberately left aside torture and the demonic attempt to reduce man to the state of a superfluous puppet. But we should not forget that the sentence of death is the central theme of his work. It matters little here whether it is nature, fate, justice, or human cruelty which pronounces the sentence. We know that in his most diabolic inventions man only imitates the tortures of life. In principle, the act of inflicting death without accepting the risk of dying, insofar as it transforms a human being into a thing, lays the physical and metaphysical foundation of torture. Camus thought that, in a sense, the sadistic executioner was less exemplary than the mere executioner. The sentence of death which spurred Tarrou's vocation may seem mild in comparison with the horrors of the plague. Camus had to make us feel that there was no essential difference between the two. It is for the same reasons that Camus depicts man's complicity with the plague with great restraint. The "collaborator" who accepts and invites the plague is anything but a monster: he is a humbled individual, unhappy rather than despicable, who takes refuge in catastrophe in order to escape fear. Camus's attitude can be understood: by identifying war with the plague, evil with illness, he wanted to present a picture of sin without God; and in this perspective, the partisans of the plague are no longer "possessed," but sick. This leads him dangerously to dissolve individual responsibility in the diffuse guilt of life. "What is the plague?" says one of the characters, "it's life and that's all." Having undertaken to fight the will to power, Camus had first to cure himself, through a kind of purification, of the passion of contempt, and to serve his apprenticeship in the new discipline of humility—hence, a tendency to hide baseness from view in order to see misfortune alone. And it is certainly not easy to rid oneself of contempt for man, to resist the impulse which for a century and a half has urged the individual to deify himself or to exalt himself in the guise of humanity, because he can no longer stand himself. Guides and healers, the stubborn heroes of *The Plague* remain subjected to the precariousness which binds them to the *we,* of which they are and want to be a part. In short, attempting to be modest without God, they nurse the supreme ambition of doing without God, without aspiring to become gods.

On the way, they discover the three theological virtues. What is it that sustains Dr. Rieux in his fight against the plague, if not faith, that is to say, beyond reasons and proofs, the certainty that the battle is worth fighting unto death. Where does Tarrou draw the strength to die "a good death" if not from hope, the ultimate unforeseen resource which springs from the death of human hopes. And how does he propose to attain sainthood if not through charity, which he calls "sympathy"? But the three virtues have changed their countenance and bearing; they no longer claim they are daughters of heaven and they acknowledge no other origin for themselves than the passion for earthly life in revolt against death. If God does not answer, if he can no longer be made to answer, man is rich only in infinite patience toward himself. Henceforth, the three Virtues will have to rely on that patience alone.

Thus, in *The Plague,* Camus's answer to the fundamental question—What value can withstand the death sentence?—is no longer the same as in *The Stranger*. For the exiled *I* whose existence is literally nothing but fall—a fall into the past, into the sin of indifference—the often ignored happiness which wells up with memory, the happiness of being, is the only authentic value. But for the man who starts to struggle, living is not enough. Man regains control of himself in the revolt against death, and henceforth this recovery itself, the good will to begin anew without illusions as to the outcome of the struggle, becomes for him the primary value. To be a man condemned, with and among other men likewise condemned: therein lies our task. For Camus, this is the province of ethics—of the *we* engaged in a desperate venture, beneath a narrow sky darkened by the plague. But Camus wants to base the common effort on individual freedom. We have already noted that he defines freedom through revolt and lucidity—by means of what limits freedom, since revolt clashes with the irreparable and lucidity with the irrational. It is a strange freedom whose motto is: "as if." It has made so many concessions to necessity that it can only act "as if" it were freedom. Camus knows this only too well and admits it: "What freedom can there be in the fullest sense without assurance of eternity?" He has granted himself the only freedom compatible with the world of the man condemned to death. Does it bring nothing but a semblance? If we examine it more closely, we can recognize it as the freedom of Adam and Eve banished from paradise, at the moment when alone and unprotected they assume the burden of their earthly existence. The mutilated freedom of Adam and Eve after the fall is not devoid of love, since it begets the solidarity of this first *we* facing a hostile world. If we examine it even more closely, we recognize the frightening present-day freedom with which we face a future that must be created out of nothing. "The individual can do nothing, and yet he can do everything," said Camus in *The Myth of Sisyphus*. *The Plague* reaffirms the same thing on the level of the "we."

What does the ethic of rebellious acceptance bring to the man who rots in the concentration camps of life? It does not tell him, "You are free," or "Cease your complaints." But through the thickness of the walls surrounding him it hammers the same words into him: "*We* are not resigned to your pain; *we* do not accept your defeat. As long as we are lucky enough to escape the scourge, we shall begin anew; we shall commit our freedom in your stead, and we shall not rest until we have obtained your release." Christianity speaks differently: "Be infinitely resigned," it tells the plague-stricken, for beyond infinite resignation begins faith. "Be infinitely resigned, for in your agony begins the contact with God. You must will the agony which reveals to you the God of love. You must will the uprooting which thrusts you into the divine. This good is your freedom, and this freedom is grace."

We do not propose to pit these two ethics against each other. We do not choose an ethic as we choose a coat. It steals in on us, permeates us, and is already within the walls while we are still arguing about it. The de-Christianized ethic is heir to Christianity in more ways than one, if only because it gives primordial importance to the theme of the sentence of death, which is the theme of the Passion. It began with an act of defiance, and it still must bring about the paradoxical fusion of revolt (in time) and acceptance (in eternity). If this ethic implies, as Camus thinks—but does he really think it?—a renunciation of eternity, it would annul itself by destroying the paradox on which it rests. All the contradictions in Camus stem from the fact that he wants to reduce freedom to the liberty of action in history, while seeking to find "freedom in salvation" through history.

Camus had to find the original link between revolt and ethic. In this sense, *The Plague* makes the task easier, for it calls for united action at a time when danger itself is our last refuge. But, if we make revolt the supreme value, in the name of what shall we condemn the partisan of the plague? It is impossible to extract from revolt anything which would lead us to prefer sainthood to cruelty. Should we conclude that the violent revolt against love, while the saints revolt against evil? But then, beyond revolt, we must set up a value which qualifies and determines it. We then go beyond history, within the limits of which Camus wants to remain. . . .

Caligula and *The Misunderstanding*

In order to express the themes which obsess him, Camus made use of two complementary art forms, the *récit* and the drama. In his *récits,* Camus successfully fused the tradition of the purest French artists, particularly of Gide, with the influence of Kafka. As for the drama, I detect no teacher save himself. It must be said, however, that he belongs to a time where metaphysical problems assume such a concrete appearance that writers as different as Gabriel Marcel, Sartre and Camus himself, feel the need to resort simultaneously to the discursive and to the dramatic expression of their thought. Camus reserved the theme of the will to power for his theater, and, for his *récits,* the theme of the struggle of the oppressed to whom violent rebellion is forbidden. Not that violence and revolt are absent from the *récits,* but they either assume a mask of indifference, or else they give way to the liberating action they stirred up. Since tragedy is by definition the place where a revolted freedom is at work, Camus has turned to tragedy when he wished to treat the problem of the relationships between freedom and revolt. By a kind of predestination, the debate which was personal to Camus coincided exactly with the political tragedy of our time. Inside, outside, the pressure was the same; Camus wrote *Caligula* and *The Misunderstanding* both in order to gain control over his own personal situation and in order to resist the pressure of history. His heroes, like Camus himself, experience the common condition as an individual condition, at the point where history and subjectivity collide. They also join the procession of characters who have incarnated the Lucifer myth of the Occident. Sustaining their particular conflicts, we discern the din of a vaster drama which, in the realm of fiction, reproduces the drama of history: the drama of the Great Personality. Its rise and fall, the heights it attains in Stendhal and Dostoevski, the blows it is dealt by Flaubert and Tolstoy, its crises, its resurgence and its ultimate defeat make up a history which lives once more with Camus's rebels. They mime the passion and the agony of individuality; their cry is his cry, their violence prolongs the wave of cruelty which always accompanies the destruction of a great model, be it the Knight, the seventeenth-century "Honnête homme," or the Significant Personality.

Caligula suddenly understands, and not in an absent-minded and abstract fashion, that men die and are not happy. If death overcomes everything, it is because death is right, and this must be proclaimed. Like Achilles when Patrocles was killed, Caligula proclaims his hatred of all creation. He will make of himself a scourge and decimate it. At the instant of his discovery Caligula goes into absolute solitude, and this is the mark of his sovereignty. Interchangeable, depersonalized by the mere glance he casts over them, his victims are literally nothing but the food of solitude. Henceforth, he can justify his existence only by performing the tasks of death's Deputy. But the harsh joy which spurs his race into nothingness cannot conceal from him the fact that his power, which he would like to be infinite, somehow is always confronted by a world still to be destroyed, values still to be denied. The plot, which emanates from the central character, develops simultaneously on two levels; on the one hand, Caligula acts the histrion playing the role of Caligula; on the other hand, he reflects on his existence as the lucid witness of his own tragedy. Play-acting, as Camus so clearly saw, is by no means an accidental trait here; it is part of the very being of the tyrant. Insofar as Caligula is not equal to his scheme of total annihilation, and he knows it while not wishing to know it, he is in bad faith and therefore must play for himself and for others the comedy of absolute power. The staccato humor of the scenes of mockery alternates with the impassioned irony of the dialogues in which the ally of death confronts, first the defender of the sacred, then the advocate of reason. The struggle is all the more poignant as Camus turns against himself, being, in a sense, just as much on the side of Caligula as with Scipio, the poet, and Chereas, the wise man who refuses to acquiesce in the sacrilegious disorders of hatred. But Chereas' reply is insufficient: reason cannot by itself fill the void in which the will to power plunges. That is why Camus contrasts the spirit of destruction with the purity of the young poet, guardian of the sacred, who puts nature and sainthood on the same side and binds them together against their common enemy. The fear and the hatred of Caligula's victims, the breathless anguish of the Killer grow from act to act, until, at last, Caligula succumbs not to the revolt of his mediocre enemies, but to the blows of the two friends he has deemed worthy of delivering him from his fate. As he dies, he has the satisfaction of having driven the reasonable Chereas and Scipio the pure to that same violence which they condemned in him. Vanquished, but not punished, he recognizes his error: he demanded the infinite from that absolute finality which is death. What does he ask for? The impossible, the moon, "something which is mad perhaps, but which is not of this world," and which he cannot make an attribute of his power. Caligula must eradicate from his soul this desire which makes him dependent upon something he cannot put into words. And it is precisely the one thing he cannot do. Therein lies his limitation, therein his paradox.

He wants to be guilty; he needs the transgression of sacrilege in order to assert his freedom. And at the same time, with all his might, he denies his guilt, for indeed, what justice would there be under the rule of equivalence? He externalizes evil in order to liberate himself, and by doing so he clings to necessity and plays into its hands. The externalizing of evil is nothing but a way of shifting the responsibility for original sin on an absent god.

There is only one guilty party here, and that is life; or, more exactly, what is wrong is that there is no sin. But the more Caligula proclaims his innocence, the more his offense is projected before him as his future, transforming his freedom into fatality, and his revolt into impotence. As a result, every act he accomplishes is nothing but a deferred suicide to which he tries to make the universe a party. Having arrived at the end of his logic, he is forced to admit his failure: "My freedom is not the right one . . . I did not take the right road." Fascinated by nothingness, insurgent freedom has killed creative freedom by identifying itself with the will to power. When he equated freedom and revolt, Caligula forgot that it is always within the power of freedom to annihilate itself. To be sure, Camus is right in a sense: evil is outside; Sophocles is right: the gods have run the show. But the opposite is also true, as the myth of original sin recalls: freedom's attempt to destroy itself is consummated within.

Camus's art was never surer of itself than in *The Misunderstanding.* From an anonymous news clipping dealing with a chance event he drew a pure tragedy of high quality, achieving an architectural style which carries the play out of reality so that the sacrifice played out on stage becomes a kind of poetic celebration. Humanism, left to its own inclination, would easily fall into the "human all too human" if it did not preserve a sense of the sacred in profane tragedy. With *The Misunderstanding* all that was emphatic and too highly colored in *Caligula* has disappeared. Only that blending of nostalgia and violence peculiar to all of Camus's rebels remains. His vengeful heroine has a stature, a splendor which make her not unworthy of comparison with Electra. Nothing is further removed from the anemic, moreover, than Martha's obsessive yearning, mainspring of the will and passion of the mind. Thanks to the remarkable power of fusion which allows him to blend contrasts without blurring them, Camus combines an acute romanticism with the completely classic structure of his play. Romantic in its theme of discontent, in its demand for the absolute in earthly happiness, in its apotheosis of the body against a backdrop of absolute pessimism, *The Misunderstanding* is an austere work which harks back to ancient drama by way of Kafka. Everything begins and ends in an inn, which resembles the inn where Kafka's surveyor "K." appears, as it recalls the palace of Oedipus; all is consummated in the course of a night befogged by the thickening of the misunderstanding. Camus has returned to his themes—the conflict of sainthood and the will to power, of individual happiness and of action —and has narrowed them so as to make them converge on the central issue of the choice. Freedom surges up between chance and fate; nothing external limits it or forces its hand at the moment when it goes astray. It is freedom itself which begets the fate on which it runs aground. Therein lies the tragedy of *The Misunderstanding,* rather than in the consequences of the choice, however dreadful they be. The dramatic tension which one experiences here as a choking sensation derives less from the horror of the impending murder than from the contrast between the lucidity of the characters with respect to themselves and the blindness they display in their relations with one another. Everything takes place as if their lucidity were their prison. There is almost no sentence in the second act which does not have a different meaning for the one who speaks it and for the one who hears it. The entire play is built on ambiguity: one has to choose in the dark, without being recognized and without being able to make oneself known. Everyone is betrayed by everybody, including himself. Camus saw the heart of the matter: our modern tragedy is the tragedy of ambiguity touching all mankind. But Camus characteristically depicted ambiguity in the guise of misunderstanding rather than bad faith, just as elsewhere he reduces treason to a fear complex, and cruelty to the transgression of a man humiliated by death. All things being equal, his attitude recalls Corneille, always at ease in extreme violence, and whose vocabulary does not include the word for treason. In this light, the heroine of *The Misunderstanding* is indeed the sister of Corneille's heroines: she has the same tense nobility and the same wilful mind in the madness of her pride. It is not by chance, either, that Camus recreates the pathos of ambiguity, as found in the Greek tragic poets. His conception of evil as diffused guilt and the fatal mistake of a will to power quite naturally recalls the Greeks. But he is faced with a new problem which neither the Greek nor the French classical traditions can help him solve. Individual conflicts tend more and more to become equated with collective conflicts, not in order to lose themselves in the collective, but in order to embody it. Consequently, the work of the modern tragic poet has a double point of departure, in interiority and in the historical situation. It cannot move from the particular into the universal, it cannot speak to each conscience in particular, unless that conscience has first faced history. We are not, of course, describing an illusory mediation between the particular and the collective. What is in question is the regrouping, the reintegrating of discordant elements within the tragic order. The setting which surrounds the stage is no longer the ancient city or the court of Versailles, but the confusion of the world, and the tangling up of individual and collective destinies. The playwright must therefore simultaneously expand our field of vision and circumscribe the field of drama; he must rebuild a stage which spans the chaos and is ready to receive and transform the creatures which come to it out of chaos. If the poet thinks he can elude history by means of a short cut, he becomes a counterfeiter; if he lets himself be absorbed by history, he becomes superficial. Yet, the duality of his point of departure must lead him to heights where, beyond antagonisms, the tragic poem finds the balance and calm of beauty. Camus almost meets these conditions in *The Misunderstanding,* a personal drama if ever there was one, but one in which we discern the rumblings of a collective disaster.

Subjective anguish and the despotism of outer events have each had a part in the creation of the characters in the play. The fact that they are described through their reflections rather than their confessions does not mean that they lack psychological truth. What makes *The Misunderstanding* a classical play, even though it carries romantic recrimination to a paroxysm, is much less its observance of the three unities than the intimate collaboration of the moralist and the poet in its creation. Camus proves, moreover, that the controlled and taut language which his cryptic realism calls for can, if need be, take over the functions of poetry and adapt to the needs of tragedy. We are far from ideological melodrama.

The tragedy unfolds in triple perspective: on the level of the bodies, or of pure force, where the brief and brutal action carries everything off toward death; on the ethical level where the choice and failure of freedom is played out; lastly, on the metaphysical level suggested to us at the end by the "no" of the old servant representing on stage the silence, the absence, the nothingness of the God who answered neither Jan nor Maria. We should not be surprised again to meet Camus's inner contradiction. *The Misunderstanding* ends on an indignant denial, a total denial of God in view of the endlessness of human suffering. And, as always, Camus's outraged awareness of the injustice done to man is so intense that it leads him to an affirmation of the exteriority of evil. Yet, in contrast, Camus shows us the will to deification as logically fulfilled in the deicide, or murder of the Son. In spite of everything, the free individual is still responsible for the alienation of his freedom. Sin without God is nothing but the choice of the wrong freedom.

A Mediterranean romantic in his insatiable longing for the finite, the tangible, for contours which light does not erode and which even night respects, Camus is very close to the Latin elegists in his lyricism, and to the Greek tragic poets in his pathos. He is in his own element with the French classics. A skeptic by temperament, not through philosophic conviction, a skeptic in so far as he is an artist, his lineage goes back to Montaigne and Saint-Evremond. But he is passionate, too, in a serious, virile fashion, and can also claim Corneille and Pascal as his ancestors. Besides, there is nothing he need disavow in order to reconcile within himself the teachings of the classics and those of Kierkegaard, Dostoevski and Chestov. We have already pointed to the remarkable coexistence in Camus of the gift of fusion and of contradiction. I believe I have found in *The Myth of Sisyphus* some lines which suit him marvelously:

> It is possible to conceive of another type of creator who proceeds by juxtaposition. Their works may seem to be devoid of interrelation. To a certain degree, they are contradictory. But viewed all together, they resume their natural grouping. Thus it is from death they derive their definitive significance. They receive their brightest light from the very life of their author. At the moment of death, the succession of his works is but a collec-

tion of failures. But if these failures all have the same resonance, the creator has managed to repeat the image of his own condition, to make the air echo with the sterile secret he possesses.

If we strike out the word "sterile," we can do nothing better than to conclude with this "self-appraisal."

An Explication of *The Stranger*

by Jean-Paul Sartre

Camus's *The Stranger* was barely off the press when it began to arouse the widest interest. People told each other that it was "the best book since the end of the war." Amidst the literary productions of its time, this novel was, itself, a stranger. It came to us from the other side of the Equator, from across the sea. In that bitter spring of the coal shortage, it spoke to us of the sun, not as of an exotic marvel, but with the weary familiarity of those who have had too much of it. It was not concerned with re-burying the old regime with its own hands, nor with filling us with a sense of our own unworthiness.

We remembered, while reading this novel, that there had once been works which had not tried to prove anything, but had been content to stand on their own merits. But hand in hand with its gratuitousness went a certain ambiguity. How were we to interpret this character who, the day after his mother's death, "went swimming, started a liaison with a girl and went to see a comic film," who killed an Arab "because of the sun," who claimed, on the eve of his execution, that he "had been happy and still was," and hoped there would be a lot of spectators at the scaffold "to welcome him with cries of hate." "He's a poor fool, an idiot," some people said; others, with greater insight, said, "He's innocent." The meaning of this innocence still remained to be understood.

In *The Myth of Sisyphus,* which appeared a few months later, Camus provided us with a precise commentary upon his work. His hero was neither good nor bad, neither moral nor immoral. These categories do not apply to him. He belongs to a very particular species for which the author reserves the word "absurd." But in Camus's work this word takes on two very different meanings. The absurd is both a state of fact and the lucid awareness which certain people acquire of this state of fact. The

"An Explication of *The Stranger.*" (Originally titled "Camus's *The Outsider.*") First published in *Situations I* (Paris: Librairie Gallimard, 1947). From *Literary and Philosophical Essays of Jean-Paul Sartre* (New York, 1955). Translated by Annette Michelson.

"absurd" man is the man who does not hesitate to draw the inevitable conclusions from a fundamental absurdity.

There is the same displacement of meaning as when we give the name "swing" to the youthful generation that dances to "swing" music. What is meant by the absurd as a state of fact, as primary situation? It means nothing less than man's relation to the world. Primary absurdity manifests a cleavage, the cleavage between man's aspirations to unity and the insurmountable dualism of mind and nature, between man's drive toward the eternal and the *finite* character of his existence, between the "concern" which constitutes his very essence and the vanity of his efforts. Chance, death, the irreducible pluralism of life and of truth, the unintelligibility of the real—all these are extremes of the absurd.

These are not really very new themes, and Camus does not present them as such. They had been sounded as early as the seventeenth century by a certain kind of dry, plain, contemplative rationalism, which is typically French and they served as the commonplaces of classical pessimism.

Was it not Pascal who emphasized "the natural misfortune of our mortal and feeble condition, so wretched that when we consider it closely, nothing can console us"? Was it not he who put reason in its place? Would he not have wholeheartedly approved the following remark of Camus: "The world is neither (completely) rational, nor quite irrational either"? Does he not show us that "custom" and "diversion" conceal man's "nothingness, his forlornness, his inadequacy, his impotence and his emptiness" from himself? By virtue of the cool style of *The Myth of Sisyphus* and the subject of his essays, Albert Camus takes his place in the great tradition of those French moralists whom Andler has rightly termed the precursors of Nietzsche.

As to the doubts raised by Camus about the scope of our reasoning powers, these are in the most recent tradition of French epistemology. If we think of scientific nominalism, of Poincaré, Duhem and Meyerson, we are better able to understand the reproach our author addresses to modern science. "You tell me of an invisible planetary system in which electrons revolve about a nucleus. You explain the world to me by means of an image. I then realize that you have ended in poetry . . ." (*The Myth of Sisyphus*). This idea was likewise expressed, and at just about the same time, by another writer, Maurice Merleau-Ponty, who draws on the same material when he says, "Physics uses mechanical, dynamic and even psychological models without any preference, as if, freed of ontological aspirations, it were becoming indifferent to the classical antimonies of the mechanism or dynamism which presupposes a nature-in-itself" (*La Structure du Comportement*). Camus shows off a bit by quoting passages from Jaspers, Heidegger and Kierkegaard, whom, by the way, he does not always seem to have quite understood. But his real masters are to be found elsewhere.

The turn of his reasoning, the clarity of his ideas, the cut of his expository style and a certain kind of solar, ceremonious, and sad sombreness, all indicate a classic temperament, a man of the Mediterranean. His very method ("only through a balance of evidence and lyricism shall we attain a combination of emotion and lucidity.") recalls the old "passionate geometries" of Pascal and Rousseau and relate him, for example, not to a German phenomenologist or a Danish existentialist, but rather to Maurras, that other Mediterranean from whom, however, he differs in many respects.

But Camus would probably be willing to grant all this. To him, originality means pursuing one's ideas to the limit; it certainly does not mean making a collection of pessimistic maxims. The absurd, to be sure, resides neither in man nor in the world, if you consider each separately. But since man's dominant characteristic is "being-in-the-world," the absurd is, in the end, an inseparable part of the human condition. Thus, the absurd is not, to begin with, *the object of a mere idea; it is revealed to us in a doleful illumination.* "Getting up, tram, four hours of work, meal, sleep, and Monday, Tuesday, Wednesday, Thursday, Friday, Saturday, in the same routine" (*Sisyphus*), and then, suddenly, "the setting collapses," and we find ourselves in a state of hopeless lucidity.

If we are able to refuse the misleading aid of religion or of existential philosophies, we then possess certain basic, obvious facts: the world is chaos, a "divine equivalence born of anarchy"; tomorrow does not exist, since we all die. "In a universe suddenly deprived of light and illusions, man feels himself a stranger. This exile is irrevocable, since he has no memories of a lost homeland and no hope of a promised land." The reason is that man is *not* the world.

> If I were a tree among other trees . . . this life would have a meaning, or rather this problem would have none, for I would be part of this world. I *would be* this world against which I set myself with my entire mind. . . . It is preposterous reason which sets me against all creation.

This explains, in part, the title of our novel; the stranger is man confronting the world. Camus might as well have chosen the title of one of George Gissing's works, *Born in Exile*. The stranger is also man among men. "There are days when . . . you find that the person you've loved has become a stranger." The stranger is, finally, myself in relation to myself, that is, natural man in relation to mind: "The stranger who, at certain moments, confronts us in a mirror" (*The Myth of Sisyphus*).

But that is not all; there is a *passion* of the absurd. The absurd man will not commit suicide; he wants to live, without relinquishing any of his certainty, without a future, without hope, without illusion, and without resignation either. He stares at death with passionate attention and this fascination liberates him. He experiences the "divine irresponsibility" of the condemned man.

Since God does not exist and man dies, everything is permissible. One experience is as good as another; the important thing is simply to acquire as many as possible. "The ideal of the absurd man is the present and the succession of present moments before an ever-conscious spirit" (*Sisyphus*). Confronted with this "quantitative ethic" all values collapse; thrown into this world, the absurd man, rebellious and irresponsible, has "nothing to justify." He is *innocent,* innocent as Somerset Maugham's savages before the arrival of the clergyman who teaches them Good and Evil, what is lawful and what is forbidden. For this man, *everything* is lawful. He is as innocent as Prince Mishkin, who "lives in an everlasting present, lightly tinged with smiles and indifference." Innocent in every sense of the word, he, too, is, if you like, an "Idiot."

And now we fully understand the title of Camus's novel. The stranger he wants to portray is precisely one of those terrible innocents who shock society by not accepting the rules of its game. He lives among outsiders, but to them, too, he is a stranger. That is why some people like him—for example, his mistress, Marie, who is fond of him "because he's odd." Others, like the courtroom crowd whose hatred he suddenly feels mounting towards him, hate him for the same reason. And we ourselves, who, on opening the book are not yet familiar with the feeling of the absurd, vainly try to judge him according to our usual standards. For us, too, he is a stranger.

Thus, the shock you felt when you opened the book and read, "I thought that here was another Sunday over with, that Mama was buried now, that I would go back to work again and that, on the whole, nothing had changed," was deliberate. It was the result of your first encounter with the absurd. But you probably hoped that as you progressed your uneasiness would fade, that everything would be slowly clarified, would be given a reasonable justification and explained. Your hopes were disappointed. *The Stranger* is not an explanatory book. The absurd man does not explain; he describes. Nor is it a book which proves anything.

Camus is simply presenting something and is not concerned with a justification of what is fundamentally unjustifiable. *The Myth of Sisyphus* teaches us how to accept our author's novel. In it, we find the theory of the novel of absurdity. Although the absurdity of the human condition is its sole theme, it is not a novel with a message; it does not come out of a "satisfied" kind of thinking, intent on furnishing formal proofs. It is rather the product of a thinking which is "limited, rebellious, and mortal." It is a proof in itself of the futility of abstract reasoning. "The fact that certain great novelists have chosen to write in terms of images rather than of arguments reveals a great deal about a certain kind of thinking common to them all, a conviction of the futility of all explanatory principles, and of the instructive message of sensory impressions" (*The Myth of Sisyphus*).

Thus, the very fact that Camus delivers his message in the form of a novel reveals a proud humility. This is not resignation, but the rebellious recognition of the limitations of human thought. It is true that he felt obliged to make a philosophical translation of his fictional message. *The Myth of Sisyphus* is just that, and we shall see later on how we are to interpret this parallel commentary. But the existence of the translation does not, in any case, alter the gratuitousness of the novel.

The man who creates in absurdity has lost even the illusion of his work's necessity. He wants us, on the contrary, to be constantly aware of its contingent nature. He would like to see, inscribed below it, "might never have been," as Gide wanted "could be continued" written at the end of *The Counterfeiters*. This novel might not have been, like some stone or stream or face. It is a thing in the present that happens, quite simply, like all other happenings in the present. It has not even the subjective necessity that artists pretend to when, speaking of their works, they say, "I had to write it, I had to get it off my chest." In it we find one of the themes of surrealist terrorism sifted through the classic sun. The work of art is only a leaf torn from a life. It does, of course, express this life. But it need not express it. And besides, everything has the same value, whether it be writing *The Possessed* or drinking a cup of coffee.

Camus does not require that attentive solicitude that writers who "have sacrificed their lives to art" demand of the reader, *The Stranger* is a leaf from his life. And since the most absurd life is that which is most sterile, his novel aims at being magnificently sterile. Art is an act of unnecessary generosity. We need not be over-disturbed by this; I find, hidden beneath Camus's paradoxes, some of Kant's wise observations on the "endless end" of the beautiful. Such, in any case, is *The Stranger,* a work detached from a life, unjustified and unjustifiable, sterile, momentary, already forsaken by its author, abandoned for other present things. And that is how we must accept it, as a brief communion between two men, the author and the reader, beyond reason, in the realm of the absurd.

This will give us some idea as to how we are to regard the hero of *The Stranger*. If Camus had wanted to write a novel with a purpose, he would have had no difficulty in showing a civil servant lording it over his family, and then suddenly struck with the intuition of the absurd, struggling against it for a while and finally resolving to live out the fundamental absurdity of his condition. The reader would have been convinced along with the character, and for the same reasons.

Or else, he might have related the life of one of those saints of the Absurd, so dear to his heart, of whom he speaks in *The Myth of Sisyphus:* Don Juan, the Actor, the Conqueror, the Creator. But he has not done so, and Meursault, the hero of *The Stranger,* remains ambiguous, even to the reader who is familiar with theories of the absurd. We are, of course, assured that he is absurd, and his dominant characteristic is a pitiless clarity. Besides, he is, in more ways than one, constructed so as to furnish a concerted illustration of the theories expounded in *The Myth of Sisyphus.* For example, in the latter work, Camus writes, "A man's virility lies more in what he keeps to himself than in what he says." And Meursault in an example of this virile silence, of this refusal to indulge in words: "[He was asked] if he had noticed that I was withdrawn, and he admitted only that I didn't waste words." And two lines before this, the same witness has just declared that Meursault "was a man." "[He was asked] what he meant by that, and he said that everyone knew what he meant."

In like manner Camus expatiates on love in *The Myth of Sisyphus.* "It is only on the basis of a collective way of seeing, for which books and legends are responsible, that we give the name *love* to what binds us to certain human beings." And similarly, we read in *The Stranger:* "So she wanted to know whether I loved her. I answered . . . that it didn't mean anything, but that I probably didn't love her." From this point of view, the debate in the courtroom and in the reader's mind as to whether or not Meursault loved his mother is doubly absurd.

First of all, as the lawyer asks, "Is he accused of having buried his mother or of having killed a man?" But above all, the words "to love" are meaningless. Meursault probably put his mother into an old people's home because he hadn't enough money and because "they had nothing more to say to one another." And he probably did not go to see her often, "because it wasted [his] Sunday—not to speak of the effort involved in getting to the bus, buying tickets and taking a two-hour trip." But what does this mean? Isn't he living completely in the present, according to his present fancies? What we call a feeling is merely the abstract unity and the meaning of discontinuous impressions.

I am not constantly thinking about the people I love, but I claim to love them even when I am not thinking about them—and I am capable of compromising my well-being in the name of an abstract feeling, in the absence of any real and immediate emotion. Meursault thinks and acts in a different way; he has no desire to know these noble, continuous, completely identical feelings. For him, neither love nor individual loves exist. All that counts is the present and the concrete. He goes to see his mother when he feels like it, and that's that.

If the desire is there, it will be strong enough to make this sluggard run at full speed to jump into a moving truck. But he still calls his mother by the tender, childish name of "Mama," and he never misses a chance to understand her and identify himself with her. "All I know of love is that mixture of desire, tenderness and intelligence that binds me to someone" (*The Myth of Sisyphus*). Thus we see that the *theoretical* side of Meursault's character is not to be overlooked. In the same way, many of his adventures are intended chiefly to bring out some aspect or other of the basic absurdity of things. *The Myth of Sisyphus,* for example, extols, as we have seen, the "perfect freedom of the condemned prisoner to whom, some particular daybreak, the prison doors swing open," and it is in order to make us taste this daybreak and freedom that Camus has condemned his hero to capital punishment. "How could I have failed to see," says Meursault, "that nothing was more important than an execution . . . and that it was even, in a way, the only really interesting thing for a man!" One could multiply the examples and quotations.

Nevertheless, this lucid, indifferent, taciturn man is not entirely constructed to serve a cause. Once the character had been sketched in, he probably completed himself; he certainly had a real weight of his own. Still, his absurdity seems to have been given rather than achieved; that's how he is, and that's that. He does have his revelation on the last page, but he has always lived according to Camus's standards. If there were a grace of absurdity, we would have to say that he has grace. He does not seem to pose himself any of the questions explored in *The Myth of Sisyphus;* Meursault is not shown rebelling at his death sentence. He was happy, he has let himself live, and his happiness does not seem to have been marred by that hidden gnawing which Camus frequently mentions in his essay and which is due to the blinding presence of death. His very indifference often seems like indolence, as, for instance, that Sunday when he stays at home out of pure laziness, and when he admits to having been "slightly bored." The character thus retains a real opacity, even to the absurd-conscious observer. He is no Don Juan, no Don Quixote of the absurd; he often even seems like its Sancho Panza. He is there before us, he exists, and we can neither understand nor quite judge him. In a word, he is alive, and all that can justify him to us in his fictional density.

The Stranger is not, however, to be regarded as a completely gratuitous work. Camus distinguishes, as we have mentioned, between the *notion* and the *feeling* of the absurd. He says, in this connection, "Deep feelings, like great works, are always more meaningful than they are aware of being. . . . An intense feeling carries with it its own universe, magnificent or wretched, as the case may be" (*The Myth of Sisyphus*). And he adds, a bit further on, "The feeling of the absurd is not the same as the *idea* of the absurd. The idea is grounded in the feeling, that is all. It does not exhaust it." *The Myth of Sisyphus* might be said to aim at giving us this *idea,* and *The Stranger* at giving us the feeling.

The order in which the two works appeared seems to confirm this hypothesis. *The Stranger,* the first to appear, plunges us without comment into the "climate" of the absurd; the essay then comes and illumines the landscape. Now, absurdity means divorce, discrepancy. *The Stranger* is to be a novel of discrepancy, divorce and disorientation; hence its skillful construction.

We have, on the one hand, the amorphous, everyday flow of reality as it is experienced, and, on the other, the edifying reconstruction of this reality by speech and human reason. The reader, brought face to face with simple reality, must find it again, without being able to recognize it in its rational transposition. This is the source of the feeling of the absurd, that is, of our inability to *think,* with our words and concepts, what happens in the world. Meursault buries his mother, takes a mistress, and commits a crime.

These various facts will be related by witnesses at his trial, and they will be put in order and explained by the public prosecutor. Meursault will have the impression that they are talking of someone else. Everything is so arranged as to bring on the sudden outburst of Marie, who, after giving, in the witness box, an account composed according to human rules, bursts into sobs and says "that that wasn't it, that there was something else, that they were forcing her to say the opposite of what she really thought." These mirror tricks have been used frequently since *The Counterfeiters,* and they do not constitute Camus's originality. But the problem to be solved imposes an original form upon him.

In order to feel the divergence between the prosecutor's conclusions and the actual circumstances of the murder, in order, when we have finished the book, to retain the impression of an absurd justice, incapable of ever understanding or even of making contact with the deeds it intends to punish, we must first have been placed in contact with reality, or with one of these circumstances. But in order to establish this contact, Camus, like the prosecutor, has only words and concepts at his disposal. In assembling thoughts, he is forced to use words to describe a world that precedes words. The first part of *The Stranger* could have been given the same title as a recent book, *Translated from Silence.* Here we touch upon a disease common to many contemporary writers and whose first traces I find in Jules Renard. I shall call it "the obsession with silence." Jean Paulhan would certainly regard it as an effect of literary terrorism.

It has assumed a thousand forms, ranging from the surrealists' automatic writing to Jean-Jacques Bernard's "theatre of silence." The reason is that silence, as Heidegger says, is the authentic mode of speech. Only the man who knows how to talk can be silent. Camus talks a great deal; in *The Myth of Sisyphus* he is even garrulous. And yet, he reveals his love of silence. He quotes Kierkegaard: "The surest way of being mute is not to hold your tongue, but to talk." [1] And he himself adds that "a man is more of a man because of what he does not say than what he does say." Thus, in *The Stranger,* he has attempted *to be silent.* But how is one to be silent with words? How is one to convey through concepts the unthinkable and disorderly succession of present instants? This problem involves resorting to a new technique.

[1] Quoted in *The Myth of Sisyphus.* Note also Brice Parain's theory of language and his conception of silence.

What is this new technique? "It's Kafka written by Hemingway," I was told. I confess that I have found no trace of Kafka in it. Camus's views are entirely of this earth, and Kafka is the novelist of impossible transcendence; for him, the universe is full of signs that we cannot understand; there is a reverse side to the décor. For Camus, on the contrary, the tragedy of human existence lies in the absence of any transcendence

> I do not know whether this world has a meaning that is beyond me. But I do know that I am unaware of this meaning and that, for the time being, it is impossible for me to know it. What can a meaning beyond my condition mean to me? I can understand only in human terms. I understand the things I touch, things that offer me resistance.

He is not concerned, then, with so ordering words as to suggest an inhuman, undecipherable order; the inhuman is merely the disorderly, the mechanical. There is nothing ambiguous in his work, nothing disquieting, nothing hinted at. *The Stranger* gives us a succession of luminously clear views. If they bewilder us, it is only because of their number and the absence of any link between them. Camus likes bright mornings, clear evenings, and relentless afternoons. His favorite season is Algiers' eternal summer. Night has hardly any place in his universe. When he does talk of it, it is in the following terms: "I awakened with stars about my face. Country noises reached my ears. My temples were soothed by odors of night, earth, and salt. The wonderful peace of that sleepy summer invaded me like a tide" (*The Stranger*). The man who wrote these lines is as far removed as possible from the anguish of a Kafka. He is very much at peace within disorder. Nature's obstinate blindness probably irritates him, but it comforts him as well. Its irrationality is only a negative thing. The absurd man is a humanist; he knows only the good things of this world.

The comparison with Hemingway seems more fruitful. The relationship between the two styles is obvious. Both men write in the same short sentences. Each sentence refuses to exploit the momentum accumulated by preceding ones. Each is a new beginning. Each is like a snapshot of a gesture or object. For each new gesture and word there is a new and corresponding sentence. Nevertheless, I am not quite satisfied. The existence of an "American" narrative technique has certainly been of help to Camus. I doubt whether it has, strictly speaking, influenced him.

Even in *Death in the Afternoon,* which is not a novel, Hemingway retains that abrupt style of narration that shoots each separate sentence out of the void with a sort of respiratory spasm. His style is himself. We know that Camus has another style, a ceremonious one. But even in *The Stranger* he occasionally heightens the tone. His sentences then take on a larger, more continuous, movement.

> The cry of the news-vendors in the relaxed air, the last birds in the square, the calls of the sandwich-vendors, the wail of the trams on the high curves of the city and the distant murmur in the sky before night began to teeter over the port, all set before me a blind man's route with which I was familiar long before entering prison.

Through the transparency of Meursault's breathless account I catch a glimpse of a poetic prose underneath, which is probably Camus's personal mode of expression. If *The Stranger* exhibits such visible traces of the American technique, it was deliberate on Camus's part. He has chosen from among all the instruments at his disposal the one which seemed to serve his purpose best. I doubt whether he will use it again in future works.

Let us examine the plot a little more closely; we shall get a clearer notion of the author's methods. "Men also secrete the inhuman," writes Camus. "Sometimes, in moments of lucidity, the mechanical aspect of their gestures and their senseless pantomime make everything about them seem stupid" (*The Myth of Sisyphus*). This quality must be rendered at once. *The Stranger* must put us right from the start "into a state of uneasiness when confronted with man's inhumanity."

But what are the particular occasions that create this uneasiness in us? *The Myth of Sisyphus* gives us an example. "A man is talking on the telephone. We cannot hear him behind the glass partition, but we can see his senseless mimicry. We wonder why he is alive?" This answers the question almost too well, for the example reveals a certain bias in the author. The gesturing of a man who is telephoning and whom we cannot hear is really only *relatively* absurd, because it is part of an incomplete circuit. Listen in on an extension, however, and the circuit is completed; human activity recovers its meaning. Therefore, one would have, in all honesty, to admit that there are only relative absurdities and only in relation to "absolute rationalities."

However, we are not concerned with honesty, but with art. Camus has a method ready to hand. He is going to insert a glass partition between the reader and his characters. Is there really anything sillier than a man behind a glass window? Glass seems to let everything through. It stops only one thing: the meaning of his gestures. The glass remains to be chosen. It will be the Stranger's mind, which is really transparent, since we see everything it sees. However, it is so constructed as to be transparent to things and opaque to meanings.

> From then on, everything went very quickly. The men went up to the coffin with a sheet. The priest, his followers, the director and I, all went outside. In front of the door was a lady I didn't know. "Monsieur Meursault," said the director. I didn't hear the lady's name, and I gathered only that she was a nurse who'd been ordered to be present. Without smiling,

she nodded her long, bony face. Then we stood aside to make room for the body to pass. (*The Stranger*)

Some men are dancing behind a glass partition. Between them and the reader has been interposed a consciousness, something very slight, a translucent curtain, a pure passivity that merely records all the facts. But it has done the trick. Just because it is passive, this consciousness records only facts. The reader has not noticed this presence. But what is the assumption implied by this kind of narrative technique? To put it briefly, what had once been melodic structure has been transformed into a sum of invariant elements. This succession of *movements* is supposed to be rigorously identical with the *act* considered as a complete entity. Are we not dealing here with the analytic assumption that any reality is reducible to a sum total of elements? Now, though analysis may be the instrument of science, it is also the instrument of humor. If in describing a rugby match, I write, "I saw adults in shorts fighting and throwing themselves on the ground in order to send a leather ball between a pair of wooden posts," I have summed up what I have *seen,* but I have intentionally missed its meaning. I am merely trying to be humorous. Camus's story is analytic and humorous. Like all artists, he *invents,* because he pretends to be reconstituting raw experience and because he slyly eliminates all the significant links which are also part of the experience.

That is what Hume did when he stated that he could find nothing in experience but isolated impressions. That is what the American neo-realists still do when they deny the existence of any but external relations between phenomena. Contemporary philosophy has, however, established the fact that meanings are also part of the immediate data. But this would carry us too far afield. We shall simply indicate that the universe of the absurd man is the analytic world of the neo-realists. In literature, this method has proved its worth. It was Voltaire's method in *L'Ingénu* and *Micromégas,* and Swift's in *Gulliver's Travels.* For the eighteenth century also had its own outsiders, "noble savages," usually, who, transported to a strange civilization, perceived facts before being able to grasp their meaning. The effect of this discrepancy was to arouse in the reader the feeling of the absurd. Camus seems to have this in mind on several occasions, particularly when he shows his hero reflecting on the reasons for his imprisonment.

It is this analytic process that explains the use of the American technique in *The Stranger.* The presence of death at the end of our path has made our future go up in smoke; our life has "no future"; it is a series of present moments. What does this mean, if not that the absurd man is applying his analytical spirit to Time? Where Bergson saw an indestructible organization, he sees only a series of instants. It is the plurality of incommunicable moments that will finally account for the plurality of beings. What our author borrows from Hemingway is thus the discontinuity between the clipped phrases that imitate the discontinuity of time.

We are now in a better position to understand the form of his narrative. Each sentence is a present instant, but not an indecisive one that spreads like a stain to the following one. The sentence is sharp, distinct, and self-contained. It is separated by a void from the following one, just as Descartes's instant is separated from the one that follows it. The world is destroyed and reborn from sentence to sentence. When the word makes its appearance it is a creation *ex nihilo*. The sentences in *The Stranger* are islands. We bounce from sentence to sentence, from void to void. It was in order to emphasize the isolation of each sentence unit that Camus chose to tell his story in the present perfect tense.[2] The simple past is the tense of continuity: *"Il se promena longtemps."* These words refer us to a past perfect, to a future. The reality of the sentence is the verb, the act, with its transitive character and its transcendence. *"Il s'est promené longtemps"* conceals the verbality of the verb. The verb is split and broken in two.

On the one hand, we find a past participle which has lost all transcendence and which is as inert as a thing; and on the other, we find only the verb *être,* which has merely a copulative sense and which joins the participle to the substantive as the attribute to the subject. The transitive character of the verb has vanished; the sentence has frozen. Its present reality becomes the noun. Instead of acting as a bridge between past and future, it is merely a small, isolated, self-sufficient substance.

If, in addition, you are careful to reduce it as much as possible to the main proposition, its internal structure attains a perfect simplicity. It gains thereby in cohesiveness. It becomes truly indivisible, an atom of time. The sentences are not, of course, arranged in relation to each other; they are simply juxtaposed. In particular, all causal links are avoided lest they introduce the germ of an explanation and an order other than that of pure succession. Consider the following passage:

> She asked me, a moment later, if I loved her. *I answered that it didn't mean anything, but that I probably didn't love her. She seemed sad.* But while preparing lunch, for no reason at all she suddenly laughed in such a way that I kissed her. Just then, the noise of an argument broke out at Raymond's place.

I have cited two sentences which most carefully conceal the causal link under the simple appearance of succession.

[2] The following passage dealing with Camus's use of tenses is not intelligible in translation. The simple past tense in French is almost never used in conversation; it is limited almost exclusively to written narration; the usual French equivalent of the English past is the present perfect. (Translator's note)

When it is absolutely necessary to allude to a preceding sentence, the author uses words like "and," "but," "then," and "just then," which evoke only disjunction, opposition, or mere addition. The relations between these temporal units, like those established between objects by the neo-realists, are external. Reality appears on the scene without being introduced and then disappears without being destroyed. The world dissolves and is reborn with each pulsation of time. But we must not think it is self-generated. Any activity on its part would lead to a substitution by dangerous forces for the reassuring disorder of pure chance.

A nineteenth-century naturalist would have written, "A bridge spanned the river." Camus will have none of this anthropomorphism. He says "Over the river was a bridge." This object thus immediately betrays its passiveness. It *is there* before us, plain and undifferentiated. "There were four negro men in the room . . . in front of the door was a lady I didn't know. . . . Beside her was the director. . . ." People used to say that Jules Renard would end by writing things like "The hen lays." Camus and many other contemporary writers would write "There is the hen and she lays." The reason is that they like things for their own sake and do not want to dilute them in the flux of duration. "There is water." Here we have a bit of eternity—passive, impenetrable, incommunicable and gleaming! What sensual delight, if only we could touch it! To the absurd man, this is the one and only good. And that is why the novelist prefers these short-lived little sparkles, each of which gives a bit of pleasure, to an organized narrative.

This is what enables Camus to think that in writing *The Stranger* he remains silent. His sentence does not belong to the universe of discourse. It has neither ramifications nor extensions nor internal structure. It might be defined, like Valéry's sylph, as

> Neither seen nor known:
> The time of a bare breast
> Between two shifts.

It is very exactly measured by the time of a silent intution. If this is so, can we speak of Camus's novel as something whole? All the sentences of his book are equal to each other, just as all the absurd man's experiences are equal. Each one sets up for itself and sweeps the others into the void. But, as a result, no single one of them detaches itself from the background of the others, except for the rare moments in which the author, abandoning these principles, becomes poetic.

The very dialogues are integrated into the narrative. Dialogue is the moment of explanation, of meaning, and to give it a place of honor would be to admit that meanings exist. Camus irons out the dialogue, summarizes it, renders it frequently as indirect discourse. He denies it any typographic privileges, so that a spoken phrase seems like any other happening. It flashes for an instant and then disappears, like heat lightning. Thus, when you start reading the book you feel as if you were listening to a monotonous, nasal, Arab chant rather than reading a novel. You may think that the novel is going to be like one of those tunes of which Courteline remarked that "they disappear, never to return" and stop all of a sudden. But the work gradually organizes itself before the reader's eyes and reveals its solid substructure.

There is not a single unnecessary detail, not one that is not returned to later on and used in the argument. And when we close the book, we realize that it could not have had any other ending. In this world that has been stripped of its causality and presented as absurd, the smallest incident has weight. There is no single one which does not help to lead the hero to crime and capital punishment. *The Stranger* is a classical work, an orderly work, composed about the absurd and against the absurd. Is this quite what the author was aiming at? I do not know. I am simply presenting the reader's opinion.

How are we to classify this clear, dry work, so carefully composed beneath its seeming disorder, so "human," so open, too, once you have the key? It cannot be called a *récit,* for a *récit* explains and co-ordinates as it narrates. It substitutes the order of causality for chronological sequence Camus calls it a "novel." The novel, however, requires continuous duration, development and the manifest presence of the irreversibility of time. I would hesitate somewhat to use the term "novel" for this succession of inert present moments which allows us to see, from underneath, the mechanical economy of something deliberately staged. Or, if it is a novel, it is so in the sense that *Zadig* and *Candide* are novels. It might be regarded as a moralist's short novel, one with a discreet touch of satire and a series of ironic portraits (those of the pimp, the judge, the prosecuting attorney, etc.), a novel that, for all the influence of the German existentialists and the American novelists, remains, at bottom, very close to the tales of Voltaire.

Ethics and Aesthetics in *The Stranger*

by Robert Champigny

What is meant by "ethics" is to be explained in a preliminary analysis. What is meant by "aesthetics" will be elucidated in the course of the development.

Ethical values are concerned basically with activities, not things, not motions. Activities can be classified. We may isolate a class of "ethical" activities, that is to say, of activities on which judgments of the ethical type can bear with relevance. Thus we may decide to call "ethical" (ethically good, or bad, or both), the class of activities which are effectively designed to remove or produce pain, or both. We may also isolate an ethical aspect or element in activities which, globally, would not be classified under the heading of ethics. Thus it is customary to speak of the ethics of a game. The designation "ethics of activities" can be used to cover both cases.

Instead of being content to consider particular activities as members of classes of activities, we may also try to see them as constituent parts of a whole. The totality in question is not that of an object (a work of art, a machine); it is the totality of one existence, one life that is probably, though not necessarily, human: it depends on how far we are willing to extend the notion of activity. In this case, a positive ethical value is granted to a particular activity insofar as it contributes to the composition of a coherent existential whole. Such a totality I call an ethical or existential figure. According to this type of valuation, "ethical validity" and "existential coherence" are synonymous. The ethics of existence which is thus defined differs from the ethics of activities: a set of activities, each of which is ethically right in its class, may be devoid of existential coherence and fail to compose an ethical figure. Existential coherence must be distinguished from formal coherence. Temporality is involved, which requires a dialectical approach. The word "ethics" in the title refers primarily to the ethics of existence.

"Value" and "meaning" are partially synonymous. Something is given a value, or meaning, when it is comprehended. Comprehension may be formal, cognitive, aesthetic, ethical, philosophical. In a scheme of comprehension, the material to be comprehended is made intelligible with the help of tools of comprehension: relations, patterns, frames. These tools themselves are comprehended in action. Taken by themselves, they are not intelligible: a notion cannot make itself intelligible. Consider these questions: "What is there beyond space? When did time begin?" Such tools, in the scheme they help build, are basic, absolute. Taken by themselves, they are absurd. "Absolute" and "absurd" are partially synonymous.

The Platonic arsenal of ideas and the god of the theologians were invented to serve as tools of comprehension. Taken by themselves, they are absurd. I can make something intelligible by using a pattern of finality or the relation of causality. Taken by themselves, causality and finality are unintelligible. I can try to make finality cognitively intelligible by dissolving it in a causal network: this is the task of a physicalistic psychology. I can try to give a meaning to causality by fitting it into a pattern of finality; every informed activity accomplishes this implicitly. This paragraph should make clear the pointlessness of the traditional bouts between freedom and determinism. It also suggests what is philosophically wrong with certain psychological concepts: thus "motivation" is a mixture of "cause" and "intention" which discloses a confusion between finality and interiority on the one hand, causality and exteriority on the other.

In a perspective of interiority, this-life is an autonomous whole, an absolute. From the outside, this absolute appears unconnected, hence absurd. The concept of this-life is a totality concept in a scheme of comprehension. It is supposed to help give meaning, not to be given meaning. If you prefer, it has meaning insofar as it gives meaning. If I want to give an existential value, or meaning, to something, I have to see it as part of this-life and make it assume a constitutive function through the use of a pattern of comprehension which may be finality, which may also be destiny (but not causality). Destiny is the pattern which fits the figure of Meursault. What is meant by "destiny" will be explained.

Let us now suppose that a certain life appears too lacking in coherence for me to consider it as an autonomous whole. I may be content to salvage certain activities, I shall proceed according to the ethics of activities. I may also consider this life in a perspective of exteriority, as one life-unit, as a member of the class of lives, or human lives. In this case, the value, or meaning, is cognitive, not ethical. I provide an explanation, not a justification.

In order to bestow an ethical value on a life which is lacking in inner value, I have to see it as part of a whole. I can do so through a confusion of conceptual modalities: I confuse generality and totality; I mistake a class concept for a totality concept. This is made easier by the fact that names of class concepts are generally written in the singular. "Man, oh, not men," exclaimed Shelley, thus providing political totalitarianism with a motto. The phrase "desire to belong" reveals this attempt and this confusion, since the verb "to belong" may mean either "to be a member of a class" or "to be part of a whole." The image of a model individual may be involved in the process, so that the conceptual confusion extends to the mode of individuality—consider the ideas of communion and of the mystical body.

I call pseudo-ethics the theoretical or practical attempt to give meaning, value, to a life by viewing it as part of a whole. The totality in question is a pseudo-totality. The prefix "pseudo" indicates a contradiction between the end (understanding, valuation) and the means (confusion, hypnotism). Pseudo-ethics is distinct both from the ethics of activities and from the ethics of existence.

A team-activity may be considered as composing an objective totality; but it does not exhaust an existence. The actor plays a role; but he remains distinct from it. The pseudo-ethical goal is to transmute an existence into an essence (character, role) comprehended (saved) in a socio-religious pseudo-world. This attempt does not prevent the organism from continuing to live and die its own life and death: the transfiguration is a mask. But this is all that may be needed to set the mind at rest. Theoretically incorrect, the attempt may be reasonably successful in practice, as long as the mask is not disturbed. Meursault may appear to some as a disturbing factor.

In the second part of *The Stranger,* the ethos of Meursault is confronted with pseudo-ethics. From a philosophical standpoint, that is what the trial consists in. The following passage reports the word of the *juge d'instruction* (examining magistrate):

"He told me that it was impossible, that everybody believed in God, even those who turned away from his face. This was his conviction and if he should come to doubt it, his life would no longer have a meaning."

The question appears to be: "Is the class of believers-in-God identical with the class of human beings or a sub-class thereof?" To understand how the answer to this question can affect the meaning of the life of the magistrate, I have to assume that the said magistrate confuses generality and totality. Mankind is implicitly conceived as a whole constituted through communion. The life of the magistrate is supposed to be given a meaning, a value, through this magic participation. But Meursault is a man and he does not commune: "How can one be a Persian?" asked the Parisians of Montesquieu. If Meursault is taken seriously, the concept of mankind as a value-giving whole is shattered.

The jury decides that Meursault cannot be salvaged. He is a monster: on the one hand, he is a member of the human race (animals are not invited to courtroom festivals); on the other hand, he does not belong to the society-of-men (mystical body). His death will efface this discrepancy between generality and totality. Then the priest tries to salvage Meursault for the divine city.

The global effect of Meursault's retort to the priest is a rejection of pseudo-values and the affirmation of existential values. But the impassioned words of Meursault bear little resemblance to the elegant discourse of Socrates in the *Apology*. The affirmation of existential values is mostly implicit. As in the rest of the book, they are shown rather than told: the explicit rejection of pseudo-values is an implicit affirmation of values. Still, it is apparent that two kinds of valuation are involved. On the one hand, Meursault seems bent on leveling everything. On the other, he suggests differences in value: "I had been right, I was still right." Why does not Meursault say instead: "What difference does it make to be right or wrong?"

In a pseudo-ethical process, uniqueness is dissolved in a generality, then generality is misinterpreted as totality. Meursault's speech takes us explicitly one step back, implicitly two. He adopts the perspective of exteriority. He considers his life as one life-unit among others. In this way, instead of retiring within the subjective absolute, he can speak to the priest. But he refuses to smuggle a part-whole relation, a false interiority, under the individual-general relation. Thus pseudo-values are expelled. Each life is a member of the class of lives. All lives are mortal. All lives are equal before death: "Only one fate was to elect me and with me billions of privileged beings who, like him [the priest], said they were my brothers." It is under the cloak of such words as "brother" that the leap from generality to totality is often effected.

But if Meursault explicitly considers his life from the outside as a life-unit, he has to be alive to do so. He has to live a unique life in order to be able to speak about life in general. In this perspective of interiority there may be values, namely, whatever helps constitute the whole as a whole. The rightness which Meursault claims is apparently one of these values.

In a previous essay, I set out to analyze the ethos of Meursault.[1] Concerning the relation between ethics and pseudo-ethics, I tried to show how the trial brought the logic of the character into relief. Concerning the relation between ethics and aesthetics, I noted: "The book holds together because the character holds together and vice-versa." I am going to analyze what this formula indicates and conceals.

The aesthetic mode of apprehension has often been called a kind of "knowledge"; it has been said that aesthetical expression could establish a kind of "truth." It might be more judicious to dump these two harpies in the lap of the philosopher of science, who clamors for them. On the other hand, it would be a good opening move to consider the aesthetic

[1] See bibliography in this volume.

mode of apprehension and expression as a mode of comprehension. Aesthetic values (aesthetic meaning) have the same theoretical extension as cognitive values: they can be tried on any object. But the aesthetic mode of intelligibility is based on the part-whole relation; it uses a perspective of interiority. The cognitive mode of intelligibility, on the other hand, is based on the individual-general relation; it uses a perspective of exteriority. The aesthetic mode of comprehension has a basic similarity with the ethical (existential) mode. But aesthetic values bear on objects, ethical values on activities and existence.

In *The Stranger,* the relation between ethics and aesthetics can be studied on two levels: the aesthetic aspect and the ethical aspect will first be considered as elements of the fictional field; then they will be considered as informing, each in its own way, the whole fictional world.

The ethical element is provided by Meursault's account of his behavior and by his meditations; the aesthetic element is provided by his descriptions of the physical *ambiance.* The first chapters of the book, on the whole, depict a peaceful accord between Meursault's ethos and the physical conditions. A basic move in the aesthetic process is to turn thing into quality (poetry), or at least to subordinate thing to quality (novel). The descriptions in *The Stranger* emphasize pervasive qualities rather than limited things—air and light, sea and sky. Quick notations suffice to make the reader's imagination enjoy what is fluid, expansive, non-finite, sensuous. But there are intimations that the accord between the physical and ethical is threatened: the light and the heat tend at times to be overwhelming. Thus the episode of the murder on the beach is prepared. As far as the ethical element is concerned, the episode is a blank: there was no action, but an event, an accident. On the other hand, the aesthetic suggestions scattered so far in the narration converge and coalesce. The episode which is most unintelligible ethically is also the episode which is most intelligible aesthetically.

The physical elements which were emphasized are now fused together, mainly through metaphors: the "breath" of the heat is also that of the sea; light falls like a "rain." An aesthetic whole is obtained through the interpenetration of qualities. The events are taken out of their temporal context so as to become part of this whole: "It was two hours since the day had ceased to move, two hours since it had cast anchor in this ocean of boiling metal." A metaphysical experience is suggested. Meursalt is drawn into a domain which ethical values cannot penetrate, at least at the moment, but which is open to aesthetic values. This is marked by the abrupt rise of the metaphors.

Essentially, what the description attempts to evoke is power. Even as a scientific notion, power remains metaphysical: energy is the metaphysical concept kept by physics. Some of the metaphors tend to make the direction of the power appear as a purpose; they are the first steps in the composition of a god. The god whom the description does not quite bring out is Apollo Loxias, the sun-god and source of oracles who "fated" Orestes. Trying to account for his action, or rather for his motions, Meursault will say that it was "because of the sun." He does not try to justify himself, but to explain. In the context of the book, this explanation points to an aesthetic reason rather than to a scientific cause. In the murder episode, Meursault is a resistance and a conductor.

At the end of the book, we are presented again with a detached aesthetic tableau: that of the starry night. This time the aesthetic element does not eliminate the ethical element. The ethos of Meursalt has won its fight against pseudo-ethics. As in the beginning, but in a tragic key, there is a harmony between the ethical and the aesthetic elements. The "fraternity" which Meursalt says that he feels with the "universe" contrasts with the brotherhood which he has refused: communion in a socio-religious pseudo-world. An analogy can be drawn between the spectacle of the night and the speech of Meursault as I have analyzed it.

Let us consider each star as analogous to one life. We do not apprehend the spectacle in the manner of Pascal, trying to pass on his terror to an imaginary reader. We do not apprehend it in the manner of Valéry, or Pythagoras, who imagined a music of the spheres, that is to say, mathematical proportions. We consider the stars as members of a class, similar and unconnected. Each star, or life, taken by itself, is an absolute. This does not mean that there is no unity in the spectacle. But the unity is not the image of a human or divine city. It is purely aesthetic: the cosmic quality of the night is what unifies.

This final accord has been prepared. The aesthetic element almost disappears during the account of the trial. The human pseudo-world has closed upon Meursault and he has to reject it as he is rejected. Yet, halfway through this second part of the book, the aesthetic element is glimpsed. There is an evocation of the evening air and sky which serves as a transition between the afternoon on the beach and the vision of the starry night.

Let us, for a moment, allow images to unfold their fluid logic. Meursault kills the man who stands between him and the spring. The sun directs Meursault toward the spring. The day hastens toward night. Meursault goes to his death. The sun is the power of life. The work of life is death. Meursault kills because of the sun. The spring, death and night are superimposed. Meursault has to pierce through the human pseudo-world in order to reach the spring. The human obstacle into which he fires and this pseudo-world are superimposed. Thus there are signals between the ethical and the aesthetic elements as between two ships which are to meet.

If we now consider the book in its unity, the ethical and aesthetic elements become part of a composition which may itself be considered either as an aesthetic or as an ethical whole. The way in which I have presented the play between the two elements suggests an asthetic composition.

Beauty is harmony. This definition may appear less otiose if it is noted that harmony implies tension. What is to be avoided is flatness on the one hand, disparateness on the other. Harmony is a play of opposition and fusion. We are dealing with a narration. The pattern of harmony can be unfolded temporally. The global arrangement of the two elements can be represented as follows. A circle and its horizontal diameter are drawn. This diameter is oriented so as to represent the direction of time. The upper half of the circumference represents the aesthetic element, the lower half the ethical. There is a meeting of the two elements at both ends of the temporal line. It is notable that though the narration covers a much greater span of time, the passages which emphasize the aesthetic element are ordered in a one-day sequence: the funeral in the morning, the murder at the beginning of the afternoon, the glimpse of the evening, the starry night. The upper half of the circumference thus represents the solar revolution. The zenith of the aesthetic element (of cosmic power) corresponds to the nadir of the ethical element (its disappearance).

If the book as a whole is to be considered as composing an ethical figure, it will be viewed as a monologue, not as a novel. The descriptions (the aesthetic element) will be interpreted as expressions of the ethos of Meursault. Actually, it is as a monologue that the book is ostensibly presented. The story is told in the first person and this first person is not limited to the introduction of events: the narrator is also a commentator. He affirms his presence outside and above the human character caught in the flow of events. This is most obvious when a present tense is used: "Now I think that it was a false impression. . . . I still do not know why. . . . I can say that. . . . I think I slept. . . ." More globally, the use of the compound tense ("j'ai vu"; "il m'a dit") instead of the historic tense contributes to the distinction between the narrator and the character: the auxiliary, in the present tense, goes with the narrator; the past participle goes with the character.

Some commentators have expressed doubt as to the likelihood of certain passages: the metaphor-laden description of the murder episode, the speech to the priest. If we insist on likelihood, there is something more basically disturbing: when and to whom does Meursault tell the story that we have been reading? However, this is reasoning as if the subject matter preceded its treatment, whereas the contrary is true: the book creates its subject matter. We are thrown back on questions of likelihood only when the work is lacking in internal coherence, when we feel the need to account for the scattered pieces and we try the exterior criterion which is valid in the judgment of historical studies. In other words, art is artificial and great art is greatly artificial. The list might begin with *The Iliad*—which does not mean that what is greatly artificial is great art. What is to the point is whether the book is coherent esthetically and whether it composes a coherent existential figure. If it does, I am no more interested in the likelihood of *The Stranger* than in the likelihood of the Gospel. The consideration of ethical values involves no epistemological restrictions. The subject, whether it be Meursault, Joan of Arc, a friend, or myself, has to be imagined. No doubt, I do not have to imagine my own life in order to experience it; but as subject matter, it has to be imagined.

Actually, the situation is even more strange than I have suggested. The "now" of the narrator is mutable. On the first page I read: "I shall take the bus"; and in the next paragraph, without a transition: "I took the bus." Further on I read: "Today is Saturday"; yet the story of this Saturday is told in the past. The same shift in tenses occurs in the last chapter. My task is to show how the status of the narrator helps compose an existential figure.

I see two patterns of intelligibility which can befit such a composition. One is finality: this is the pattern recommended by Sartre. The other is destiny: this is the pattern which fits *The Stranger*. By destiny, I do not mean causality; I do not mean the general fate to which Meursault alludes; I do not mean the evil genius who seems personally attached to some character and who performs like a judo champion; i.e., whatever the character does boomerangs against him. All this takes place in a perspective of exteriority. The cause is exterior to the effect; fate is exterior to the one who is fated. Understood in this way, fate can be used in an aesthetic, not in an ethical, whole.

Destiny, in the sense here used, has to shape the ethical figure from the inside. What has happened must be internalized, so that the life in question no longer appears as fashioned by the events, but as identical with them; the haphazard series of events is transfigured into an existential whole. This operation I call an existential totalization, as distinct from an existential project (pattern of finality). It is as a narrator, not as a character moving with the events, that Meursault can effect this totalization. Finality and causality can appear before the fact; I plan and I make use of causality in my plans. Destiny can only appear after the fact. The compound past tense catches some of the flavor of the Greek perfect.

The study of the character can reveal a static and somewhat abstract ethos. We look for recurrences of the same type of behavior; they indicate certain virtues and we try to see whether these virtues help compose a coherent static figure. What is missing is the unique process, the existential dialectics, the temporal dynamics which the word "destiny" is here intended to imply.

As a narrator placed at the end of the series, Meursault can capture events which the ethical element did not penetrate: the courtroom comedy as well as the episode on the beach. But this recuperation is only a collection. A decisive move in the ethical transfiguration is the speech to the priest. It expresses mainly the negative side of the operation. Meursault as it were sterilizes, neutralizes, the sum of events. According to his own words, he purges himself of "evil," that is to say, of the temptation of pseudo-values. He refuses to repent, to deny what has happened, to be robbed of his material. On the other hand, however, it is interesting to note that he rejects the possibility of a pattern of finality: "What mattered to me . . . the lives that one chooses, the fates that one elects, since only one fate was to elect me . . . ?" The irony on "choice," a holy word for Sartre, shows that Meursault is not afflicted, or blessed, with sartritis. He does not say, "My life is such as I chose it"; he says, or implies, "My life is such as I see it and have always seen it."

The rightness which he claims is important to him. His philosophy will be "justified" on the morning of the execution. The wisdom of Meursault is the first unifying factor which contributes to the composition of an existential whole. The events now seem to have been accumulated by fate, or chance, in order to prove the soundness of Meursault's philosophy. But this is not enough. This comprehension is too purely intellectual, too negative, too superficial. It encloses the events in a philosophical skin.

Meursault intimates an affinity between his outlook and the "tender indifference" of the "universe." His indifference is the ataraxy of the sage. It lacks, but it permits, the penetration of tenderness—the alliance of the two words is paradoxical, but sound. It is Meursault's tenderness for what has happened that allows him to constitute his life as a destiny, to change contingency into existential necessity.

This tenderness, as well as this indifference, characterizes the tone of the narration. The narrator stands with the events, as well as above and after them. That is how I would justify the shifts to the present tense in the narration. Between the narrator and the narrated, there is a play of detachment and identification which echoes, and sometimes coincides with, the play between the aesthetic and the ethical elements. Thus the character catches up with the narrator in the final tableau: the confrontation with the starry night.

I have drawn an analogy between a star and a life seen in a perspective of exteriority. But Meursault says that he feels an affinity with the "universe," that is to say, with the spectacle as a whole. In this perspective, Meursault's life is not one life among others. His life is the ethical whole. The existential totalization which he effects finds its aesthetic analogue in the cosmic quality of the night. In this perspective of interiority, each star is analogous, not to one life, for instance Meursault's, but to one event in the life of Meursault.

To the priest who asks him how he would picture an after-life, Meursault answers: "A life in which I could remember this one." And on the last page I read: "I felt ready to live everything again." Is an "absurd" series of events worth remembering? Is it for the sake of proving his wisdom twice that Meursault feels ready to live this particular life again?

In life recollected, not in life lived moment after moment, totalization is possible and destiny may appear: this is the existential equivalent of a poem. In life lived again, not in life lived once, totalization would be possible from the start and destiny might appear: this would be the existential equivalent of a novel. As we read it, or perhaps reread it, the monologue of Meursault appears as the equivalent of a novel entitled *The Stranger*.

Image and Symbol

in the Work of Albert Camus

by S. Beynon John

In intellectual power, coherence, and originality Albert Camus may not be the equal of Jean-Paul Sartre—with whom he shares certain affinities—but he speaks of man's predicament in accents so humane and generous that he attracts the attention of all those who care for the quality of life in contemporary Europe. It is precisely the attention paid to the ideological content of Camus's writing—the sense of the absurd, the idea of revolt—that has tended to divert critics from the study of the creative process in his novels and plays. The great majority of essays and articles devoted to Camus have concentrated on the philosophical value or the political relevance of his ideas, while those critics who have addressed themselves to Camus as an imaginative writer have often done so in passing, restricting themselves to generalities about his style and indulging a robust appetite for literary affinities. The present essay is, therefore, an attempt to examine critically a specific, and admittedly limited, aspect of Camus's literary talent: his creation of symbols. The essay has no pretensions to being exhaustive even in this direction and will be confined to tracing the process by which two images—sun and sea —recur in this author's work and achieve symbolical force.

The range of Camus's imagery is fairly narrow and derives almost entirely from the central experience of his life, his encounter with nature along the North African littoral. This experience is described directly and personally in his formal essays: *L'Envers et l'endroit* (Betwixt and Between) (1937), *Noces* (Nuptials) (1938), and "Le Minotaure ou la Halte d'Oran" (1945). From these essays a distinct sensibility emerges, born of an essentially pagan experience of nature. One's awareness of this paganism does not have to wait upon an older Camus's confession of emotions "recollected in tranquility." The Algerian child was certainly father to the successful man of letters respectfully approached by the editors of reviews:

"Image and Symbol in the Work of Albert Camus." From *French Studies,* IX, No. 1 (January, 1955), 42-53.

> . . . je ne suis pas chrétien. Je suis né pauvre, sous un ciel heureux, dans une nature avec laquelle on sent un accord, non une hostilité. Je n'ai donc pas commencé par le déchirement, mais par la plénitude. Ensuite . . . Mais je me sens un cœur grec.[1]

> . . . I am not a Christian. I was born poor, beneath a happy sky, into a nature which inspires a feeling of harmony, not hostility. I did not begin in privation but in plenitude. Later . . . But I feel I have a Greek heart.

In fact, the paganism breathes through Camus's earliest pages. He confesses nostalgia for the lost Greek virtues, especially that "insolent candor" which characterized their enjoyment of the senses. He sees even the palpable symbols of Christianity threatened by more primitive and more potent forces:

> La basilique Saint-Salsa est chrétienne, mais chaque fois qu'on regarde par une ouverture, c'est la mélodie du monde qui parvient jusqu'à nous . . .

> The basilica of St. Salsa is Christian, but each time one looks out through some opening, the melody of the world reaches in to us.

For the youthful Camus nature is animated by the ancient divinities. He records the fact with an engaging, if somewhat self-conscious, directness when he refers, on the opening page of the same essay, to the "gods that speak in the sun." The mark of this paganism, naturally enough, is the intense life of the senses. If the incidence of his imagery is any guide, Camus's most sharply attuned senses are those of sight and smell. He conveys powerfully the acrid scent of wild herbs that catches at the throat and he distinguishes the cargoes of visting ships by their smell; timber in the Norwegian vessels, oil in the German, wine in the coasters. Auditory images are few and mainly concerned with the cry of birds and the sigh of the wind. These sounds usually serve to emphasize the surrounding silence and loneliness. It is, however, visual images that predominate, especially those connected with the blinding sun. In this Algerian landscape, light is crude and exorbitant. Camus amasses images of light, and the final effect, in some passages, is to produce that shimmering surface common to Impressionist painting. In the steady accretion of visual images, Camus suggests admirably that slight distortion of vision which intense light sometimes produces in extremely hot and dry climates. He contrives this by including, in a series of visual images, one image that combines both reflection of light and the sense of motion, as the following passages exemplify:

> . . . la mer cuirassée d'argent, le ciel bleu écru, les ruines couvertes de fleurs et *la lumière à gros bouillons* dans les amas de pierres.

[1] Interview originally published by Émile Simon in the *Reine du Caire* (1948) and reprinted in Albert Camus, *Actuelles. Chroniques 1944-1948* (Paris: Gallimard, 1950), p. 225.

> . . . the silver-plated sea, the raw blue sky, the flower-covered ruins and *the great swirls of light* upon the heaps of stone.

and again:

> Du haut des plateaux, les hirondelles plongent dans d'immenses *cuves où l'air bouillonne.*
>
> From atop the plateaus, the swallows plunge into huge *cauldrons of seething air.*

This device is symptomatic of the way in which Camus exploits his verbal resources in order to convey how powerful is the impact of natural phenomena. This is no more than an accurate reflection of his own reactions, for he experiences a sort of vertiginous identification with nature. He describes how he feels himself to be assimilated into nature, annihilated by the elements whose vibrating life is everywhere present:

> Ce bain violent de soleil et de vent épuisait toutes mes forces de vie . . . Bientôt, répandu aux quatre coins du monde, oublieux, oublié de moi-même, je suis ce vent et dans le vent, ces colonnes et cet arc, ces dalles, qui sentent chaud et ces montagnes pâles autour de la ville déserte. (*Noces*)
>
> The violent bath of sun and wind exhausted my life-strength. Now, spread out to the four corners of the world, forgetful, having forgotten myself, I have become the wind and, within the wind, the columns and arch here, the stone slabs smelling of the sun and the pale mountains set around the deserted city. (Nuptials)

There are even intense moments when he longs for this annihilation, for the cessation of conscious being. How enviable is the dense integrity of *things* when compared with the divided nature of man, with that "fissure of being" (to borrow from the existentialist vocabulary) which separates man from the rest of nature:

> Quelle tentation de s'identifier à ces pierres, de se confondre avec cet univers brûlant et impassible qui défie l'histoire et ses agitations. Cela, bien entendu, est vain. Mais il y a dans chaque homme un instinct profond qui n'est ni celui de la destruction, ni celui de la création. Il s'agit seulement de ne ressembler à rien. ("Le Minotaure")
>
> What a temptation to identify oneself with these stones, to mingle with this burning and impassive universe which defies history and its agitations. This, of course, is in vain. But there is in every man a deep instinct which is neither for destruction nor creation: wishing merely to be like nothing at all. ("The Minotaur")

It is within the context of this particular experience of nature that Camus's references to the sun and the sea need to be set. These images figure prominently in Camus's work because they are obviously the representative images of the type of landscape in which he was born and spent the formative years of his life. Moreover, in Camus's autobiographical essays "sun" and "sea" are frequently set in contexts which lend them emotional overtones that prefigure the symbolical significance they attain later, in his imaginative writing.

For example, in these essays, allusions to the sun constantly evoke a tonality of violence. Camus is assaulted and dazed by the sun, "abruti de soleil"; (stunned by the sun) he is permeated by it, a porous vessel receptive to its heat. The same sense of violence is suggested by Camus's use of the image "tourbillons de soleil" (swirls of sun), an image that recalls the characteristic whirling suns which dominate many of Van Gogh's paintings and refract something of the intensity of that artist's vision. Again, the author writes of ". . . la tête retentissante des cymbales du soleil" (his head reverberating from the cymbals of the sun) and thus fuses into one striking image the idea of a blinding reflection of light (as suggested by the metal of the cymbals), and the sense of a violent physical reaction like the pounding of blood in the ears, implied by the notion of "cymbals" as instruments of percussion. The area and significance of such an experience is extended by a comment that Camus makes in one of the essays:

> Mais être pur, c'est retrouver cette patrie de l'âme où devint sensible la parenté du monde, où les coups du sang rejoignent les pulsations violentes du soleil de deux heures. (*Noces*)
>
> But to be pure was to find once more that homeland of the soul where one's link with the world becomes perceptible, where the beating of the blood overtakes the violent pulsations of the two-o'clock sun. (Nuptials)

Nor are the images that define the sun restricted to those which suggest simple violence; occasionally, they reflect the sense of destruction. Hence, when the sun rains down its light on to the stony fields near Oran, it is described in a destructive image: ". . . le soleil allume d'aveuglants incendies" (the incendiary sun sets blinding fires). Then again, the sun is not infrequently associated with silence, that is to say, the absence or negation of specifically human activity. This is the case when Camus depicts the deserted sea off Algiers at midday, or the ruins at Djémila where the presence of the sun and the brooding silence of nature—intensified rather than broken by the passing wind—confirm the transience of man's achievement. The sun and the silence, in a sort of elemental union, preside over the empire of *things,* where man figures almost as an accident.

The sea features in these personal records as the constant solace, the source of refreshment in a burning climate. It is the arena of youth and hence, of life, in so far as life can be equated with youthful vigor and the beginnings of the sexual cycle. Each summer the sea welcomes "a fresh harvest of flower-like girls"; it is the scene of easy, animal joy, of the arrogant play of muscles. Even the fall of waves upon the shore evokes an erotic image, ". . . les premiers rochers que la mer suce avec un bruit de baisers" (the first rocks that the sea sucks with a kissing sound) and so, though more obliquely and remotely, suggests the sense of renewal. The waters of the sea, glimpsed at the turn of each street in Algiers, are a reminder of relief from the dust and the hot stone. The mineral landscape at Oran conveys the sense of the permanence of nature in its massive inertness ("une gangue pierreuse," [a stony paste]), but this permanence suggests death, as is evidenced in the image "ces ossements de la terre" (the earth's bony remains), whereas the sea ("une mer toujours égale," [an unchanging sea]) also conveys the notion of permanence but in the context of perpetual renewal.

In his personal narratives of his life in Algeria, therefore, Albert Camus gives to "sun" and "sea" respectively a distinct tonality and, if we now turn to his imaginative writing, we can examine the process by which they acquire a symbolical sense; achieve another dimension, in a word, while retaining marked affinities with that emotional experience with which they are associated in the essays. The importance that "sun" and "sea" achieve in this way can best be gauged, not from any mechanical count of the frequency with which they recur, but rather from the context in which they appear. Indeed, both images tend to emerge fully as symbols only in passages of great significance in the novels and plays. Situated in such passages, they represent the focal point of a symbolical event or situation. The overriding metaphysical intention of the author may also supply, in certain instances, a relevant criterion by which to judge the force of this imagery.

In general, one may say that physical relaxation and mental serenity are associated with evening and moonlight in Camus's work, while violent sensation and the impulse to destroy are related to the intense heat and light of a Mediterranean day.

Albert Camus's first novel, *The Stranger* (1942), crystallizes this tendency more precisely in a series of related acts and offers a striking example of the process by which the sun is transformed into a symbol. The decisive series of events in this novel begins when the central character, Meursault, accompanied by two acquaintances, Raymond and Masson, takes a walk along a beach near Algiers, after enjoying an early lunch. It is not quite midday but already the glare of the sun off the sea is described as unbearable. The three men walk steadily until they sight in the distance two Arabs with whom Raymond has already been involved on account of his maltreatment of a former Arab mistress. Raymond instructs his two companions on the roles they are to play in the event of an affray. The Arabs draw nearer, and it is at this point that Meursault observes: "Le sable surchauffé me semblait rouge maintenant" (The overheated sand now seemed red to me). In this phrase, an obvious physical reference to the intense light of the sun on the sand foreshadows, in a figurative sense, the violence that is to follow. The color of the sand under the sun's rays suggests the shedding of blood. A scuffle ensues with the Arabs in which Raymond and Masson are involved. Blows are exchanged and then Raymond's opponent produces a knife, wounding him in the arm and the mouth. Both Arabs then retreat cautiously behind the brandished knife, and, finally, take to their heels. While they retreat, the three Frenchmen remain stock-still, "cloués sous le soleil" (nailed to the spot by the sun). Masson and Meursault assist Raymond to return to the hut and Meursault agrees to explain what has happened to Masson's wife and his own mistress, Marie, both of whom had been left behind in the hut. In the meantime, Masson accompanies Raymond to a neighboring doctor where he receives treatment, returning to the hut shortly afterwards. On his return, Raymond insists upon "taking the air" and when Masson and Meursault, alarmed at the prospect of another fight, offer to accompany him, he flies into a rage. In spite of his outbursts, Meursault does in fact join him. They walk for some time along the beach, Meursault becoming increasingly aware of the overpowering sun which is reflected off the sand in dazzling splinters of light. The two men reach a tiny rivulet at the edge of the beach and find the two Arabs lying there, one absorbed in playing a monotonous tune on a reed pipe. The oppressiveness and fatality of the situation are suggested by references to the sun and the silence, while the faint sound of the stream and the notes of the pipe seem to express the potentialities, or at least the possibility, of life. Raymond, wishing to tackle his Arab antagonist on equal terms, hands his revolver to Meursault, who pockets it, but the Arabs scuttle away suddenly and a fight is averted. Raymond and Meursault return to the hut but Meursault, reluctant as ever to communicate with other human beings and dazed by the sun, does not enter the hut and returns along the beach for a solitary walk. In the course of this walk, the sun is described in terms of a hostile presence. It is as though the weight of the sun obstructs Meursault's progress, and the heat that emanates from it makes his body tense aggressively, as against a powerful assailant. The image employed here by Camus to describe the reflections of light, "chaque épée de lumière" (each rapier of light), suggests precisely the hostile nature of the sun. Meursault longs for shade and sees ahead of him the rock behind which the Arabs had disappeared. Striding towards it, he realizes with surprise that Raymond's attacker is lying there alone. The encounter between these two men now becomes the central point of a complex of images of light, so that the sun and the impulse to violence are invariably associated. The destructive act takes place under the aegis of the sun and seems to be a simple extension of its influence. The shape of the Arab dances before Meursault's eyes in the flaming air and the sea is like molten metal. It is at this point that the possibility of human initiative is suggested, but the sun overwhelms the human will:

> J'ai pensé que je n'avais qu'un demi-tour à faire et ce serait fini. Mais toute une plage vibrante de soleil se pressait derrière moi.

> I thought then that all I need do was to turn back and it would all be over. But behind me a whole beach vibrating with sun was pressing down upon me.

Such a sun recalls to Meursault the heat on the day of his mother's funeral and this allusion further emphasizes the association between death and the sun. The blood pounds in Meursault's veins. The foci of light multiply; first, a flash from the blade of the knife which the Arab has drawn ("La lumière a giclé sur l'acier et c'était comme une longue lame étincelante qui m'atteignait au front," [The light splashed out on the steel and it was like a long glittering blade striking me on the forehead]); next, the blur of light through the beads of sweat that tremble on Meursault's eyelashes and fall across his vision like a mist; and then again, the glitter of the blade, the reflection from which painfully probes the eyes. The world spins; fire seems to rain out of the sky. Meursault aims the fatal shots.

It will be seen how the sun, in its direct or indirect manifestations, provides a sort of baleful focus for these three related episodes and how the incidence of images of light increases as the events reach their destructive climax. The sun, experienced with such pagan receptivity in the early essays, again dominates these passages of *The Stranger* and unifies them insofar as it symbolizes violence and destruction. The key to this symbolical use of the sun lies in the metaphysical intention that animates Camus's work. The entire novel is an allegory of that absurd universe which Camus had described elsewhere—*The Myth of Sisyphus* (1942)—in philosophical terms. Meursault is the symbol of man perpetually estranged in the world and this conception is reinforced when Camus, lending the sun this potent destructive influence, absolves man from responsibility—and hence from guilt—by reducing him to something less than man, to the status of an irresponsible element in nature. In this way, the notion of the absurdity of life, which is the central and governing irony of so much of what Camus has written, is underlined and given dramatic color.

In Camus's play, *The Misunderstanding,* produced in 1944, the sun is again used, though more obliquely, as a symbol of destruction. The play is another extended allegory on the absurd universe, and its dramatic tension is derived from the same irony. A mother and daughter (Martha) who keep an inn in a remote corner of Czechoslovakia murder rich travellers who lodge with them. The son of the house (Jan), who had left home to seek his fortune, returns many years later as a wealthy man bringing with him his wife (Maria) and their child. He presents himself at the inn without disclosing his identity and his mother and sister fail to recognize him. He takes a room; he is drugged and his inert body dragged to the river and thrown in, at dead of night. His wife comes in search of him the following day and reveals his identity. Martha discloses the happenings of the night but, instead of offering contrition or consolation to the distraught widow, she gives expression to the tragic irony of the situation:

MARTHA . . . Mais je ne puis mourir en vous laissant l'idée que vous avez raison, que l'amour n'est pas vain et que ceci est un accident. Car c'est maintenant que nous sommes dans l'ordre. Il faut vous en persuader.
MARIA Quel ordre?
MARTHA Celui où personne n'est jamais reconnu.

MARTHA . . . But I cannot die leaving you with the illusion that you are right, that love is not futile and that this is an accident. It's now that we are in the normal order of things. Of this you must be persuaded.
MARIA What order?
MARTHA The one where no one is ever recognized.

This is a clear metaphysical irony, but the motive which impels the two women to murder—even if intended figuratively—is oddly banal. It is the need to amass enough money, out of the pockets of their victims, to escape to an easier and more carefree existence close to the sea, in a warmer climate. It is in relation to these aspirations that the sun again emerges as a symbol of fatality and destruction, for the land to which Martha longs to escape is represented only by the sun and the sea. These two symbols recur several times in her thinking and lure her on to new acts of murder. It is, however, significant that the goal of Martha's dreams is symbolized by the sea inasmuch as it holds out liberty (from toil, from the asperities of her native climate), but by the sun in the degree to which it offers dark oblivion for her past activities. Hence, the Mother, when referring to this distant haven, suggests that there ". . . le soleil dévorait tout" (the sun devoured everything). Martha ardently approves:

MARTHA J'ai lu dans un livre qu'il mangeait jusqu'aux âmes et qu'il faisait des corps resplendissants, mais vidés par l'intérieur.
LA MÈRE Et c'est cela, Martha, qui te fait rêver?
MARTHA Oui, car j'en ai assez de porter toujours mon âme et j'ai hâte de trouver ce pays où le soleil tue les questions. Ma demeure n'est pas ici.

MARTHA I read in a book that it devours even people's souls and gives them bodies that glow but have nothing left inside.
THE MOTHER And is that what you long for, Martha?
MARTHA Yes, I'm tired of always carrying around my soul and I'm in a great hurry to find that country where the sun silences all questions. I don't belong here.

The sun, in a word, burns in Martha's mind, lighting the way to destruction. It is doubly destructive: first, in that it can only be enjoyed over the corpses of Martha's victims, and next, in that the coveted power it radiates annihilates conscience and thought and so voids man of his humanity.

There occurs in Camus's work a disparity, or at least an unresolved tension, between his literary sensibility and his philosophical ambitions, especially as crystallized in *The Rebel* (1951), a study which integrates and develops a number of themes previously introduced into Camus's work. *The Rebel* attempts to create a sort of classical point of equilibrium to which it will be relevant to refer problems of action and change in the contemporary world. It seems to be dedicated to an aphorism that occurs in the play, *State of Siege:* "there is no justice, but there are limits." In fact, in its insistence upon restraint, limit and moderation, the spirit of *The Rebel* is at variance with Camus's normal mode of feeling, which is impassioned and intensely subjective. Camus's most natural manner of expression (already evident in his early essays) is lyrical, by which I mean highly personal and emotive, and this feeling passes over into his prose-technique, creating poetic overtones that derive, partly from the richness of his imagery, partly from his feeling for the rhythm and music of a phrase. It is true that what I conceive of as Camus's authentic manner is sometimes deliberately concealed. Thus, the prose style of *The Stranger* which is clipped and laconic, reflects the deliberate subordination of Camus's natural lyricism to the exigencies of his theme, that of conveying the sense of the absurd. In the same way, much of his novel, *The Plague,* is written in a rather dry and meticulous prose, admirably suited to the ironical intentions of the author. Even so, in both these novels a distinct lyricism continues to vibrate below the surface, often erupting in passages of genuine poetic force, especially when Camus introduces an elegiac note. The language of the plays, on the other hand, is often unrestrainedly lyrical. Indeed, there are moments, particularly in *State of Siege* and *The Just Assassins,* where lyricism passes into an inflated rhetoric which weakens the author's achievement. If I have dealt with this at some length, it is to suggest the element of neo-Romanticism that exists in Camus's writing and which is underlined by the recurrence of the figure of the Romantic rebel in his plays—Caligula and Ivan Kaliayev, for example—and by his tendency to exalt the life of the senses. It is in the light of this literary sensibility that Camus's use of sea symbolism needs to be considered. At this point it will be useful to recall what a distinguished contemporary poet recently wrote about the imagery of the sea and the desert in Romantic literature:

> As places of freedom and solitude the sea and the desert are symbolically the same. In other respects, however, they are opposites. For example the

> desert is the dried-up place, i.e., the place where life has ended, the Omega of temporal existence . . . The sea, on the other hand, is the Alpha of existence, the symbol of potentiality.[2]

Camus therefore approaches conventional Romantic usage of the sea in the symbolism of freedom which he associates with it, but he differs from many of the Romantic writers who used it as a literary symbol divorced from their own experience. Camus turns to the sea for a symbol because it is for him an intensely lived experience.

In *The Stranger* sea-bathing is one of the main delights of the clerk, Meursault. The sea is the scene of his first tentative caresses of Marie; it is a source of intense physical pleasure. As the action of the novel unfolds, however, the sea ceases to be merely a place where physical restraint disappears. To Meursault, awaiting trial in prison, the sea is identified with his longing for freedom. He associates the condition of being free with the sea, and the pleasures it offers—the motion of running down to the sea, the sound of the waves, the sensation of his body slipping into the water. The sea thus becomes the symbol of freedom as contrasted with the confining walls of his prison-cell.

In *The Plague* one of the consequences of the epidemic is the closing of the beaches and bathing pools of Oran. Maritime traffic ceases completely and the port is deserted, cordoned-off by military pickets. Hence, although the sea is there, it exists in the background and, as the plague increases in severity, the presence of the sea becomes less and less real in the minds of the inhabitants of the town. In the early weeks, the sea continues to have a real existence for them since it serves as a palpable reminder of a link with that outside world with which they are confident of resuming contact in the near future. But, as the plague establishes itself in all its terrifying permanence, the sea recedes from minds that no longer dare to dwell on freedom and are simply concerned to survive within the imprisoning walls of the town. As a symbol of freedom, the sea diminishes in reality as the action of the novel proceeds. That is why one of the later episodes of *The Plague* seems peculiarly significant. Dr. Rieux, accompanied by one of his voluntary assistants, Tarrou, concludes an exhausting day by a visit to one of his regular patients, an old man suffering from chronic asthma. They pass from the sick-room up to a terrace on the roof. It is November; the evening air is mild, the sky clear and brilliant with stars. In this atmosphere of serenity, Tarrou is moved to give Rieux an explanation of his motives for joining the voluntary organization created to combat the epidemic and, further, to reveal something of his personality, his principles and his aspirations, which he defines as the attempt to become a saint without God. This long personal confession creates new bonds of intimacy, mutual sympathy and respect

[2] W. H. Auden, *The Enchafèd Flood or The Romantic Iconography of the Sea* (London: Faber and Faber, 1951), p. 27.

between the two men and, at this point, Tarrou suggests that a bath in the sea would be a fitting pledge of their friendship. Rieux instantly agrees and they make for the port, gaining access to the quayside by virtue of their special passes. Here, for the first time in many months, they become really aware of the shifting presence of the sea. They plunge into the water and strike out together with regular, matching strokes. They feel themselves to be at last ". . . solitaires, loin du monde, libérés enfin de la ville et de la peste" (alone, far from the world, at last free of the city and the plague). The swim ended, they return to the town, full of a strange and secret happiness and ready to resume the fight against the epidemic. It is impossible not to feel that this episode has the character of a symbolical ritual. The plunge into the sea is at once an act of purification from the plague (insofar as the epidemic represents suffering, evil and death), a rite of friendship, and a means of recovering freedom or, at least, of being recalled to it. In this last sense, the sea might be said to reassert itself as a symbol of freedom for these two men, to imbue them again with the need to be free. The sea that has been hidden, remote and ineffectual, suddenly becomes actual and effective as a symbol of freedom in the heart of a city subjected to the arbitrariness and the brute determinism of the plague.

In no work of Camus's is the symbolical nature of the sea made more explicit than in his play, *State of Siege* (1948). In spite of the author's cautionary preface, this play has obvious and striking affinities with the novel, *The Plague,* and, like the novel, it can be interpreted at more than one level. It is a metaphysical play whose symbols relate to the eternal predicament of man in the face of evil and death. It may be read as a symbolical account of an enemy occupation in time of war or as a more general protest against totalitarian systems. The arrival of the plague in the town of Cadiz is presaged by the alarming passage of a comet which temporarily disturbs a people ridden with habit and inertia, and represented by a Chorus. The inhabitants quickly recover their composure and the Chorus expresses its jubilation for the sensual joy of living and for the bounty of the earth. In this genial atmosphere, the lovers, Diégo and Victoria, are revealed sharing a moment of blissful happiness. To crown the festive spirit, a troupe of actors begins its performance of a comedy in the main square. The Governor of the city arrives and addresses the citizens in terms that condemn the spirit of change and eloquently defend the principle of total stagnation. It is at this juncture that the plague strikes down its first victim, one of the actors. Doctors diagnose the plague and provoke panic in all classes. The Governor, after feeble attempts to mask the reality of the situation and to maintain the status quo, concludes a dishonorable bargain with the plague itself, incarnated in a sort of barrack-square martinet who demands the surrender of the city. Aided by a chilling female Secretary and by some members of the existing order, the Plague issues his edicts. These impose a series of totalitarian measures upon the people of Cadiz and, as their scope becomes clear to the citizens, they attempt to quit the city before all the gates are closed. It is at this critical stage in the action that the Chorus gives expression to the people's urgent desire for freedom in words which unmistakeably envisage the sea as the source and symbol of freedom:

> Nous sommes les fils de la mer. C'est là-bas, c'est là-bas qu'il nous faut arriver . . . Courons à la rencontre du vent. A la mer! La mer enfin, la mer libre, l'eau qui lave, le vent qui affranchit!

> We are the sons of the sea. It's out there, out there that we must go . . . We must run to meet the wind. To the sea! The sea at last, the open sea, the water that cleanses, the wind that liberates!

This symbolism recurs in the second part of *State of Siege*. This section of the play is dominated, first by a mordant satire on totalitarian bureaucracy, and next, by the fate of Diégo who is defeated by fear in his first challenge to the power of the plague but returns to the attack. In his second encounter, Diégo discovers that the plague is powerless against men who have lost their fear and accepted their "sacred duty" of revolt. He turns to one of the townsfolk who has been gagged as part of the policy of the plague and removes his gag. There is a moment of tense silence before the released man speaks, turning his head skywards in an attitude of interrogation. The sky gradually grows lighter and a breath of wind stirs the curtains of a windless city. It is the wind from the sea and, because it comes off the sea, the harbinger of freedom. This symbolical event supplies the dramatic climax of the play's second part. The final section of *State of Siege* records the desperate tactics employed by the Plague to undermine Diégo's initial victory. The issue remains in doubt for some time, but, when Diégo agrees to forfeit his own life so as to revive the stricken Victoria, his act of abnegation accomplishes the final defeat of the Plague. Not even the ironical entry of the Governor and his clique, symbolizing the return of a corrupt and reactionary order, quite invalidates Diégo's sacrifice. Their return, however, provokes a final spasm of hatred and contempt from Nada, a curious figure who represents—as is suggested by the punning Spanish name he bears—the spirit of nihilism. In a last spasm of negation, he throws himself into the sea and his mortal struggle there is reported by a fisherman in the play's concluding passage. It is surely significant that in these closing lines the sea should be depicted as a sort of live, raging creature devouring an enemy of human freedom, and that it should be apostrophized as the symbol of men in revolt—"O vague, ô mer, patrie des insurgés, voici ton peuple qui ne cédra jamais" (Oh tide, oh sea, home of rebels, these are your people who never yield)—men, that is, exercising their freedom.

In conclusion, we may say that when Camus particularizes, when he has his eye fixed *on the object* with a sort of innocent stare, then his images are fresh and telling—for instance, the imagery of fruit he employs to suggest the passing seasons in a choral speech of the play *State of Siege*. When, however, he reaches beyond the level of sense experience, he is less successful in bringing about that fusion of "disparate elements" which so often distinguishes new and memorable imagery. There is nothing remarkable about the choice of "sun" and "sea" as the respective symbols of destruction and freedom; indeed, in the case of "sea," I have suggested the exact contrary. Yet, both symbols grow so naturally out of a personal and vividly felt experience of nature that they remain free of the deliberate and rather artificial air they sometimes wear in the work of other writers. They retain an afterglow, as it were, of the intense pantheism which informed Camus's first physical encounter with them, and this lends them a relevance, an inevitability and an impressiveness they might otherwise have lacked.

Notes on *The Plague*

by Gaëtan Picon

The Plague has scarcely met with anything but eulogy, and it would be easy for me to add my plaudits to so unanimous a criticism. It is all too evident that the novel is important and of great value. If I were asked which French novels published since 1940 are worthy of being called masterpieces, I would answer without hesitation that I see just four: Malraux's *The Walnut Trees of Altenburg,* Bernanos's *Monsieur Ouine,* Sartre's *The Reprieve,* and Camus's *The Plague*. Books which stand out from the ordinary as these do impose an unaccustomed severity upon us. I shall go so far as to say that the unreserved praise that Camus's novel has met with is in my view a questionable homage. To see *The Plague* exclusively as a subject for eulogies is, I fear, to contrast it with contemporary literary productions from which it is not difficult for it to stand out. On the other hand, if we consider the novel's many exceptional and admirable qualities, we are led to compare it with the greatest works of literature. It is at this point that it seems to me difficult to remain insensitive to the book's limits and imperfections.

Some novels are spellbinding and enslave the reader from the very first moment; others only reveal their power slowly. Obviously *The Plague* belongs in the second category. And Camus intended it to. One must be careful not to find fault with the book for somehow lacking persuasive force. Certainly one doesn't become involved in Oran's plague in the way one lives through the London plague described in Daniel DeFoe's unforgettable journal. Nor does one see or know Rieux or Tarrou as one would a Balzacian or Tolstoian character, or live through the dying moments of the plague-stricken child as one does through the dying moments of Bernanos's country priest. In *The Plague* one should neither look for something stronger and more real than real life nor should one expect the hallucinating presence of an imaginary world that sometimes seems more effective and convincing than reality. Yet how

"Notes on *The Plague*." From *L'Usage de la lechire* (Paris: Mercure de France, 1960), pp. 79-87. Translated by Ellen Conroy Kennedy. Reprinted by permission of the author and Mercure de France.

numerous are the books inferior to *The Plague,* in spite of just that ability to shock and that persuasive power! Camus never wanted to ensnare his readers in this fashion. He never intended to play what one might call the "realistic" game, if for the sake of clarity we agree to call "realistic" the kind of realism Balzac and Maupassant, Dostoevsky and Zola have in common, i.e., any literary effort whose success is measured by its power to create an illusion. Albert Camus wanted his novel to be first of all a work of art, carefully composed and written, and secondly, an expression of wisdom. The seductions and persuasiveness of realism conceal the writer's art along with the moralist's values: Camus therefore had to limit that portion of illusion which is a necessary part of all novels. If everything remains at a certain distance from us in *The Plague,* if the characters are more than anything else voices in a dialogue, and the events hint of a reality merely suggested, it is because Camus wanted it so. And from this point of view the novel is a success. For at no moment does the story become so obsessive as to make us overlook the dramatic, fervent, bare prose that sustains it, the moral maxims that mark its course. Nor do we ever lose the sense of an art which blends conflicting riches, an order born of disorder, that is never so striking as in the book's many and characteristic transitions: the transition from the pure and simple narrative (*récit*) to the chronicle, from realism to allegory, from the individual perspective to the collective perspective, from spareness to lyricism, from the dramatic to the humorous.

The Plague is one of those books which far from confining us to the outer appearances which it builds up around us attempts rather to free us from these appearances. This it does by keeping the apparent within a perspective such that we suspect it is not sufficient unto itself. It is one of those books which represents more than it presents, which consists less in what it gives than in what it conceals. To simplify things, one can say that *The Plague* is an allegorical novel. The quotation from DeFoe at the very beginning of the book is a first proof of this allegorical intention: "It is as reasonable to represent one kind of imprisonment by another as it is to represent anything that really exists by that which exists not." Very soon, we know without any doubt what significance to give to the allegory. The epidemic of the plague which breaks out in Oran in the 1940's is very plainly the symbol of a historical reality which we know only too well. How can one fail to recognize this city, taken by surprise by the abrupt apparition of tragedy, a city soon its own prisoner, no longer able to communicate with the free world except through memory, imagination and the vaguest of messages; a city shut in upon a universe of exile and separation, of suffering and brotherhood; a people of whom it is said that "a number of them piled into the maw of a crematory, evaporated into oily fumes, while the rest, chained down by fear and impotence awaited their turn." But if this city fallen prey to the plague evokes wartime France under the German occupation, it is also any human city struck by any of the thousand plagues that destiny reserves for us. It gives us an image of that human condition for which Pascal long ago said that imprisonment was the best symbol. The importance of the book stems from the fact that it unites a metaphysical message whose sense soon becomes apparent with the specific emotional state that arises from its historical reference.

The story of the plague at Oran is not presented as a legend, but as a true story, as an historical fiction, if one may call it such. Consequently, how can it totally avoid the basic exigencies of truth? Actually the author presents his story both as reality and as symbol, as *Dichtung* (poetry) and *Wahrheit* (truth). From this stems the alliance, or more precisely, the juxtaposition of the symbolical and the realistic. Sometimes the author sought the immediate shock, the illusive power of realism: for example, when he evokes the apparition of the dead rats in the houses and streets of the city; Dr. Rieux's separation from his wife; the death agony of Judge Othon's son; the panic that ends a presentation of Gluck's *Orpheus and Eurydice* when the plague overwhelms a singer on the stage. In contrast, the pages written in chronicle style inform us of the events indirectly by means of the narrator's reflections about them, rather than directly. They give an impression of material distance: the narrator interposes himself between us and the events, and judges them after they have happened; also of spiritual distance: the plot seems to take on perspective, achieving a symbolical character.

I do not reproach the book for the contrast between these two "registers"; the transitions from one to the other are effected remarkably well. But I think that the division of the work into these two levels, and these two tones, keeps it from reaching its full stature in either direction, and is an obstacle to the attainment of that living and formal unity which alone could move us and satisfy us completely. The allegorical elements break the latent power of the real, and the reality dissipates the legendary aura as it forms. Thus, *The Plague* is neither deeply rooted in the real stuff of life nor in the poetical matter of myth. Allegory leaves reality too small a chance to catch us in its net—and the realistic elements lend allegory merely the value of an intellectual gesture. Thus, at every moment, and in whatever way one looks at it, the novel is paralyzed by its own form. Of all our contemporary writers, Camus was without doubt the most anxious to achieve the mythic; but the incapacity of allegory to become myth in *The Plague* is evident and reveals perhaps the real source of Camus's failure. One need only think of Kafka's *The Trial,* Melville's *Benito Cereno,* or Hawthorne's *The Scarlet Letter* to measure the distance that separates *The Plague* from those few mythic novels truly animated by a sense of the poetic.

On another level, the dialogues are troublesome in the same way. It is plain that their "register" is one of intellectual stylization. The voices answer one another like voices in a play-reading, when, unmindful of décor and characters, we are attentive only to the alternating brilliance of the language. But Camus seems suddenly to remember that his characters are not eloquent abstractions, and to want to remind us of their deep involvement in the tragic reality of the plague-ridden city. He then separates the voices and introduces moments of dramatic orchestration into these short silences. But the voices tend to come together again, and the orchestrations seem artificial. Plague-ridden Oran does not manage to live in these dialogues in the way bombarded Madrid lives through the dialogues of Malraux's *Man's Hope*. And very often the sentences which separate the voices and the dialogue seem like so much dramatic padding:

> "Who taught you all this, doctor?"
> The answer came promptly:
> "Suffering."

or

> "Do you really imagine you know everything about life?"
> The answer came through the darkness, in the same cool, confident tone.
> "Yes." [1]

It is tempting to see in Albert Camus a great writer who has not managed to discover where to apply his efforts. Neither the story, the novel, nor the theater have thus far provided him a medium that measures up to his gifts. A moralist in the tradition of the seventeenth century, or perhaps one of those sagacious travelers who flourished in the nineteenth century, he is face to face with a literature divided into definite genres which challenge the writer to prove definitely his worth in one of them. Perhaps the hesitation one senses in Camus's polyvalent work, which tends simultaneously toward the Voltairian *conte,* the Kafkian myth, the pitiless light of Hemingway, the gestures of melodrama, and the spareness of abstraction is the sign of a wealth of possibilities. Or is it rather a certain shortness of breath, which, lacking the power to make a single torch flame high, kindles many smaller fires at one and the same time? The same ambiguity is implicit in Camus's very style, a style whose peerless qualities we immediately recognize but whose inner division often has a paralyzing effect. Torn between reality and myth, Camus is also torn between a classical spareness of style, continually and admirably exemplified in his writing, and the lyrical and dramatic impulse which is also deeply his. I believe that his two stylistic veins extinguish each other more often than they nourish each other, when they are mixed together. I prefer in Camus either the extreme of classical spareness—as in the apparition of the rats or Rieux's separation from his wife in

[1] *The Plague,* trans. Gilbert Stuart (New York: Alfred A. Knopf, Inc., 1948), pp. 118, 119.

The Plague—or those pages in which Camus gives full expression to an interior lyricism, as he does in *Noces* (Nuptials), "The Minotaur," or "Prometheus in Hell." When Camus follows his bent and expresses himself in images, his lyricism, in spite of his distrust of the poetic, is surprisingly effective. In *The Plague* this lyricism often seems ashamed to show itself, strangling itself with its own hands, so to speak, as soon as it becomes conscious. It is there nonetheless, but we feel an inner constraint and a tendency to replace images with an abstract rhetoric rather than a reaching toward the poetic: "The spiteful winds of the sky," "the waters of the plague," "the panting night."

A will to impose order and unity in conflict with deep inner tensions, in the form of his work as well as in its meaning, such is Albert Camus as he appears to us. And we like him because of the battle he wages with himself, and not for the victory or the defeat that ends it. For the artistic balance and the moral wisdom he offers us betray the passionate ardor from which they spring, bringing us peace where we expected fervor.

With Camus there is always a surge upward and wings stopped in midflight. And it is here that this wisdom reaches its deepest expression, one might say—and I would add, its most irremediable expression, because it is a wisdom which knows what it opposes. It need not fear that one day it will discover its opponent and find itself unprepared. Camus knows what disturbs him, but he does not wish to be disturbed. Violence is at the source—calm has the last word. This is clearly manifest in the manner he has of triumphing over the absurd. He knows the bite of the absurd, but its violence in him is not so strong that he cannot escape it, or that he has no recourse but some other form of violence. To the intensity of the absurd, Camus opposes, not the intensity of human values, the passion for man and his actions, but the wise consciousness that it is impossible to live in the absurd and that values really do exist. This explains the quite rational way in which he moves. As Descartes moves syllogistically from doubt to certainty, Camus moves through reflection and reasoning from the absurd to the sense of value. Living is not enough for him; he must think. And doubtless he must think in order to be able to live. Against Bernanos who cries: "The arguments of honor do not stand up, but men hold up instead," Camus affirms that one must not act in terms of *ivresses* (intoxication), but in terms of thought. And what attitudes have a value to set against the absurd? Revolt, answers Camus. But the term is equivocal, as is clearly apparent when one reads *The Plague* after *The Myth of Sisyphus*. Revolt in *The Plague* has lost its Promethean halo; far from justifying man's triumphant undertakings, it merely nourishes his desire for protection. This is a defensive and not an offensive position. What Camus really retains from the notion of revolt is that there exists one part of man which does not tolerate humiliation. What shall we do for the sake of dignity? That is above all what we should like to know.

To Camus, who started with a total and unqualified demand it now seems to be enough that, in the long run, suffering and injustice be spared man, and that man's right to achieve happiness be respected. Does this not seem a rather modest request? When Camus declares that heroism ranks below the will to be happy, doubtless one is tempted to agree with him. It would still be necessary for happiness to put us in touch with some supreme force, to be a positive and passionate affirmation. But it seems to me that Camus never gives anything but a negative definition of happiness. If happiness consists merely in escaping from the plague, this cannot be enough. We want happiness to be the possibility of reaching something outside the realm of the plague, we want to find in it a use and justification of our freedom. That one must fight against the plagues that enslave man: this is the sole conclusion which, according to Albert Camus, is not open to doubt. But it can only be the first principle of morality; the essential thing we must discover is what we should do with the liberty rescued from plagues.

It is not enough to protect man from scourges. Still less is it enough to feel one might be exempt from reproach simply by virtue of not being on the side of scourges. One character in *The Plague,* Tarrou, thinks that our only moral duty, or rather our unique moral possibility, is not to be oneself a carrier of germs. It is true that for Dr. Rieux morality is first of all a question of curing people. But the two men share the same basic moral attitude, certainly not a passive one, since they both fight and sacrifice themselves to the same degree—Tarrou just as much as Rieux, more than Rieux even, since he pays the sacrifice. But it is basically a defensive attitude, and at bottom, an attitude of nonintervention. There are wounds to dress, crimes to understand and forgive: this is the sum of what one can do. Medicine and understanding: this is the ethic proposed.

And this is certainly the only ethic which is free from danger, the only one which leaves us with perfectly clean hands, which frees us of all responsibility in catastrophes. But the insufficiency and the inefficacity of any attitude is defined precisely by the fact that it holds no dangers. How can one fail to recognize and admit this is Camus's major obsession? But how can one not want to go beyond it? When we fear that our will to obtain something better may lead to something worse, refusing to intervene because we are concerned about future consequences, content to look after the victims so as not to add to the scourges, we shirk what has been the mission of certain men destined to bring us examples and revelation, and we exchange risk for security, responsibility for peace.

The notion of risk does not exist in *The Plague*. Everything happens as if the author were seeking to confine himself to a wisdom so sure that it contains no element he might be apprehensive about. And with the notion of risk goes the notion of choice. For in the last analysis, who can fail to see that his duty is to fight against the plague, and if he is a doctor, to do his job? The plague is an indisputable scourge, which leaves no room for hesitation. A natural catastrophe, it does not call forth any human justification, and there is nothing to risk in combatting it except one's life. But there are other scourges. Those which come from the will of men—war, social oppression, spiritual oppression—these are more ambiguous. Here, in order to take sides, we obviously need values other than those of defense and nonintervention, and, in order to vanquish, much more powerful forces. Certainly nonintervention is better than intervention that is criminal. But when the time comes to repel and challenge murderous passions, the tranquil commitment to nonviolence is ineffectual: it is as inoperative in the realm of value as it is as a weapon in the realm of force. If we are to make humiliation and suffering lose face, rather than merely to denounce them, we must show what meaning may be given to a human life freed from pain and humiliation. And we shall not crush our monsters in the name of an understanding that would transform us into accomplices, but in the name of some more powerful passion. In the voice of the author of *The Plague* one comes upon more than an echo of the great rationalist voices of the past: precisely those which failed to forestall the tragic events of our time. But in art as in existence, what is baffling to wisdom may not be so to the passions.

Exile and the Kingdom

by Gaëtan Picon

I do not think that any of the six tales contained in *Exile and the Kingdom* can be ranked with Albert Camus's most accomplished writings; but no other book by Camus has made me more keenly aware of the profound nature and actual status of his work. The quest, the intensity, the distribution of this work; what it has attempted and still is attempting to do; what new horizons open up before it: all seem to me to be more clearly visible here than anywhere else.

None of these tales are able to strike us, to hold our attention, to inscribe themselves in our memory with the force of *The Stranger, The Plague,* or even *The Fall.* The reason for this is evident. All of Camus's previous books carry through to conclusion a particular line of thought, which finds its form in the simplification and enlargement of a mythical image. These extremes of perspective, the massive writing have an imperious eloquence. Here we are brought back to a state of in-betweens, of confusion, to the careful fusing of the characteristics of everyday existence. Even when it is dramatic, this existence is composed of humble, day-to-day details. "The Silent Men," "The Guest," "The Adulterous Woman" are presented as realistic accounts: that is the way things actually happened, and there is always some detail, attesting to the brutish thoughtlessness of reality, which prevents the narrative from disappearing into the pure and inflexible line of myth. There is always some detail which describes an existing situation without any mental reservation. "The Artist at Work" and "The Growing Stone," on the other hand, have somewhat the appearance of fables. In "The Artist at Work" the irony of the narrator is directed visibly toward the narrative, dispelling the dust of insignificant facts. In "The Growing Stone" the tone is that of legend, but there is also amusement in this irony: the pleasure of recounting in a legendary tone. At any rate, it seems to me that these tales are the first in which Camus takes into consideration the actual subject

"Exile and the Kingdom." From *Mercure de France,* May, 1957, pp. 127-131. Translated by Josephine Valenza. Reprinted by permission of the author and *Mercure de France.*

matter of his narrative and dwells upon the details. Whereas previously he had sought the most exact and most simplified coincidence between a thought impulse and a dramatic action, here he is observing, imagining —caught in the web of reality.

It is possible that these tales will disappoint the admirers of Camus. As for myself, whom he has never quite satisfied, I feel that they announce a very salutary reappraisal. The author's impress is not as visible as usual: we no longer entirely recognize his austerity, his haughty abstraction, his willful reduction to bare essentials. The discordancy of tone may be perplexing because legend succeeds parody, interior monologue succeeds behaviorist narrative. Even the value accorded to geographical location is such as to surprise us. The Algeria of *The Stranger* and of *The Plague* was scarcely less allegorical than the Holland of *The Fall*. Here the setting is more than a conventional situation, or an allegorical agreement between space and mind: the Brazilian forest of "The Growing Stone," the North Africa of the other narratives—it is a fact, a reality which attracts to itself a large portion of that attention which had previously been fixed upon the moral and the symbol.

Each tale has a presence, a sort of material weightiness which, one might fear, could entail a weakening in meaning. But it suffices to go from one to the other to perceive that the collection of tales is animated by a significance which is scattered, flowing, diffuse, hence all the more active. Certainly Camus did not write the book for the purpose of amusement—or as an exercise in narration and observation after so many moral treatises. He has dispersed his secrets; he has simply set them down and let them live instead of giving them the too-evident appearance of allegory. Until this work, Camus had clung to an attitude which, although temporary, had been pushed to its extreme limit, thus imparting to each book a character both excessive and incomplete. Now, at last, he abandons himself to the fluctuations of life. In the place of abstractions we have here the agitation of waters at their dividing line. His preceding work was indeed in search of something, but, in regard to this quest, it only blocked out certain main perspectives. *The Stranger* and *The Fall* immobilize the quest at its limit in the trajectory, which goes beyond the existentialist surface of the story. *The Plague* fixes the quest in a circular kind of composition and compromise. For the first time, in *Exile and the Kingdom,* one feels a certain movement—a movement which allows the author to say everything without betraying anything.

Camus's problem is to relate the unity of artistic expression with a vibrant inner experience, torn apart so that it may live. How can one gather into unity of expression that which escapes all unity? Sometimes in his linear narrative the unity of myth achieves artistic efficacy only by belying the truth of the experience: the *roman-hypothèse* achieves unity solely because it is false; it has the air of a dangerous abstraction. Sometimes, notably in *The Plague*. Camus tried to integrate his inner diversity with the unity of a form by composing, in mid-stream, a somewhat disappointing fusion. To go in one direction only, but to its extreme limit—or to bring into balance opposing tendencies: Camus hesitates between Descartes and Gide, between utmost rigor and infinite comprehension. But the true path lies beyond this hesitation. The present work, rather than being entrapped by the author's fame is still in the process of defining itself, of seeking out its rightful place. I have always thought this, and I find a moving and comforting confirmation of this idea in these lines which Camus wrote for an edition of *L'Envers et l'endroit* (Betwixt and Between): "The day when a balance shall be struck between what I am and what I do; on that day perhaps, I scarcely dare write it, I shall be able to give substance to the work of which I have always dreamed."

The work he dreamed of is not *Exile and the Kingdom,* but this collection of stories allows him to envision it somewhat better. *Exile and the Kingdom* and, as I can imagine solely from the nature of the title, *L'Envers et l'endroit* are faithful to the author's concept of truth because they are based on a constant coming and going, on a particular tempo. *The Stranger, The Plague, The Fall* all contain effective myths, rigorous thoughts, but because of that unity which is reflected by the single word in their titles, they destroy the rhythmical truth of a life seeking to know itself. It is the image of tension which, one should recall, charged the concluding pages of *The Rebel* with the violence of experience, thus coloring the drabness of conciliatory dialectic:

> In this hour when each one of us must arch his bow in readiness to prove himself, to conquer within the bounds of history—and in spite of it—those things which he already possesses: the meager harvest of his fields, the fleeting love of the land; at the moment when, at last, we are born into manhood, we must leave behind us the frenzied agitation of adolescence. The bow strains, the wood screeches. At the utmost peak of tension an arrow flies out, straight and true, the result of the firmest and freest of shots.

Only strict adherence to this experience will reconcile Camus's writings with his personal being.

The drama—the theater—with its bold, conflicting characters would have been ideal for expressing "this dialogue which we are." Camus has a passion for the theater; but he does not seem to have the necessary genius. He wrote one theatrical masterpiece: *Requiem for a Nun,* but only by drawing upon Faulkner. His plays grow weaker as their structure becomes more dramatic. The finest one, *Caligula,* is simply a monologue. The best of Camus's writings up to the present have not touched upon this element of dialogue which is inherent in Camus. To be more precise, they suppressed or mitigated it; but here, in the succession of stories in *Exile and the Kingdom,* the tempo which myth destroyed, and which the theater reflected but feebly, imposes its rhythmical beat.

Only this tempo can simultaneously express and overcome the inner fluctuation. Only this tempo can retrieve what is destroyed by the various alternatives of thought. The preceding books show us first the right then the wrong side of the cloth: this one begins by placing the fabric in our hands. We must not separate the absurd from the joy of living, revolt from love, inner nobility from the militant refutation of evil. Each of Camus's books conformed to the other because each one brought forth only one word in its title instead of emitting the rhythm of an entire phrase. Thus *The Fall* corresponded to *The Plague* as *The Plague* corresponded to *The Stranger*. *Exile and the Kingdom* does not in the least correspond to *The Fall;* it does not add another segment in the formation of a line; but in contrast to the successes of abstraction, it poses an attempt at completeness.

The Fall was to have been included in this collection; but the author took it out because of its unforeseen bulk. It is important to note that the two books are not alike. *The Fall* fully explores one path, leaving us suspended on the verge of an answer which it cannot possibly give, because to do so it would have to return to the point of departure. Like all the preceding books, *The Fall* corresponds to a point in progression (which could, as is the case in this instance, assume a regressive pace), while *Exile and the Kingdom* contains a definite movement. In *The Fall* there is only an exile without a kingdom. There is no answer to the discovery made by Clamence (good itself is evil)—at least no answer which does not oblige us to start afresh from nothing. Here the answer is always given with the question, the right with the wrong side, the kingdom with the exile.

This book is not based upon a contradiction, and herein lies its success. The exile and the kingdom are not two continents separated by an ocean: they are two aspects of the same breath and heartbeat. The kingdom is in the exile, the exile is a path toward the kingdom—in fact, exile could actually be the kingdom. "The Artist at Work," with swift, ironical verve, evokes the life of an artist separated from his work by his family and friends. He finally isolates himself in his workshop by constructing a sort of cage—in which he dies. One word, in very small characters, is written in the center of the white canvas he leaves behind him. We do not know whether the word is *solitary* or *solidarity*. These two words are enough alike so that we need not oppose them too brutally. Without a doubt, Jonas dwelt in exile among his own circle of family and friends. He found his true home in the solitude of his work, but his circle remains the same. The cage wherein he dies is a mock kingdom. For the workers who are on strike in "The Silent Men," exile is the hostility of society—the kingdom is their silent revolt. They experience a feeling of fraternity which they could not have known without undergoing exile. In "The Adulterous Woman" the opposing elements seem particularly clear: exiled both in her marital life and in her daily work.

Janine has but to cast a glance upon the desert to discover the free, untrammeled existence of the kingdom:

> From the dawn of time, upon the dry, barren soil of this immeasurable land, a small band of men had trod relentlessly, owning nothing, serving no one; the wretched but free lords of a strange kingdom. Janine did not know why this idea filled her with a sadness so sweet and so vast that it obliged her to close her eyes. She knew only that this eternal kingdom had been promised her, and that, except for this fleeting moment, it would never again be hers. . . .

Drab as it may be, does it not yield possibilities of tenderness, of depth? In the very last lines she joins her sleeping husband and whispers, "my darling."

In "The Guest," which is perhaps the most effective story in the collection, we see clearly that the conflict is not between solitude and fellowship, or liberty and submission. The hero does not oscillate between two forms of solitude: one, the cruelest of exiles, is a solitude in which the gestures of fraternity turn against us—the solitude of incomprehension; the other, which constitutes the sole portrayal of the kingdom, is the solitude in which we are aware of what we have done, and realize that it was necessary to do what we did. Is this the opposing of two attitudes: building up a good point and tracking down a bad one? Not at all. The book invites us to probe the very pulse of existence—which unfolds, then shuts up tight; reveals itself in a flash of light, then veils itself in obscurity; waxes and then wanes. The moralist who isolates and dissects is succeeded by the poet who puts together and restores the one complex throb of life.

An Ambiguous World

by Roger Quilliot

"I see myself and ask myself: am I a monster more twisted and fuming with pride than Typhon?"

Socrates

"My whole work lies ahead of me." How scornful the hero of *The Fall* would have been of this short statement! What? Camus repudiating his work, considering it a failure? One can hear the famous laughter of the Pont des Arts break out and grow louder at Camus's back. False modesty, Camus! Unless of course you spoke the truth about never having said anything worthwhile . . . Unless like Jonas before his empty canvas you were dreaming of the impossible. How about it? But now no one laughs any longer, neither the scandal mongers nor the professional sarcastics. . . .

Besides, had anyone really laughed? Camus had a stubborn way of saying things that shook even the most skeptical. Yes, five long years had gone by between *The Rebel* and *The Fall,* broken only by a single short volume of essays, *L'Eté* (Summer)—years during which one might usefully have wondered about Camus's silence and questioned the possibility that he had exhausted his inspiration. But those who knew his patience and his obstinacy never doubted that Camus's work was maturing within. As early as 1952, almost before the controversy over *The Rebel* had died down, and as if in reaction to it, he had drawn up for himself a plan of his projected works: an adaptation of Dostoevsky's *The Possessed,* the creation of a sort of crossbreed Don Juan-Faust, experiments with short stories on the theme of exile, and a recreation of the "first man" in novelistic form.

Doubtless these plans were mere notes that he might dream over for years. "Then one day comes the idea, the conception that draws these scattered fragments together," as Camus said in a 1959 interview with Jean-Claude Brisville. "Then the long and arduous task of putting them

"An Ambiguous World." From *Preuves,* April, 1960, pp. 28-39. Translated by Ellen Conroy Kennedy. Reprinted by permission of the author and *Preuves.*

in order begins, all the longer because my mental anarchy goes deep and knows no limits." In November, 1954 "The Adulterous Woman" was published in Algiers; Camus had made rough drafts of other stories to appear later together in one volume as *Exile and the Kingdom. The Fall,* which was to have been one of these, soon achieved its autonomy and was published in 1956 as a separate novel.

Even then Camus thought of his fortieth birthday as marking if not a break at least a new stage in his work and in his life. It was then, in 1957, that he wrote the preface to a new edition of his *L'Envers et l'endroit* (Betwixt and Between), first published in Algeria in 1937, in which, as in his story "The Artist at Work," he declares his intention to begin everything all over again. He confesses his ambition to go all the way back to his first work, which in spite of its defects, contained all the contradictions, the fertile ambiguities with which he was resolved to live and create: the two facets of the world, its light and its shadow, innocence and a vague feeling of guilt. He was then only at the first stages of his pilgrimage.

If Camus felt for the first time the need to express himself directly, it was because he had certain doubts. So many people had commented on a lack of development in his work, on his meager output. His successes had been derided, as if failure were the only guarantee of talent and integrity. And later even the Nobel Prize was reproached him as if it were an insult. Camus, people whispered, was getting bogged down in moralizing and conformism. We were shown a man sure of himself and of his beautiful soul—in a word: complacent,—whereas in fact Camus was anxious and felt that he needed others to bolster what Roger Martin du Gard called "the hesitant confidence a writer has in himself which always needs to be reassured—because true greatness does not go without a background of self-doubt and modesty." Camus's short story, "The Artist at Work," bears witness to this anxiety success gives rise to, an anxiety sharpened by the ever-watchful critics. Jonas, too, is devoured by the twin leviathans of acclaim and envy and needs to be loved and reassured. And Clamence (of *The Fall*) echoes him: "How we admire those of our masters who speak no more, their mouths full of earth! That homage comes naturally, an homage perhaps that they had waited for all their lives."

But even those who reassure him—friends, disciples—are leviathans swallowing up his leisure. It seems to Jonas that he owes himself to them, must let them have a few minutes more, yield them a bit more time or space. Yet, what if the obligations he plunges into be but a way of masking his impotence? What if eventually, having withdrawn to an obscure corner of the house, almost to its very ceiling, to reconquer there a kingdom in the depths of exile, he should do no more than write one desperate word: "Solitary" unless perhaps it be "solidary"? There is a neccessary and tragic solitude, a Spanish solitude, Camus used to call it, whose misfortune consists both in being alone and in being unable to be alone. . . .

Camus questions himself with bitter humor. . . . In his distrust of the romanticism and disorderly passion that are so deeply his, has he not killed all spontaneity, all love? So he dreams of softening his style. In this perspective, *The Fall, Exile and the Kingdom* and the dramatic adaptations are so many exercises, variations on a common theme. Like a beginner, he is practicing his scales for a new departure.

But perhaps the severity of the style reflects a deeper withering? One might have asked if *The Plague* does not owe its militant greyness to the fight it describes, to the ethics it secretes. Shut off behind barbed wire in order to defend itself, Oran has recourse to the concentration camp. Similarly, *The Rebel,* in protest against abstract philosophies and historical fetishism, borrows abstraction's weapons. . . .

The Fall marks the end of an illusion. Camus had thought he was if not loved, at least respected. And suddenly anger, spite and hate broke over him like a wave. He was indignant, he protested, and the accusations multiplied. Was he then to protest more to keep up these pedantic dialogues? How ridiculous and painful for so reserved a man! His cries of pain—the cries of a man being flayed—these were to come only in one of those powerful ambiguous works to which he held the secret.

"It's very hard to disentangle the true from the false in what I'm saying," he wrote in *The Fall.* But "don't lies eventually lead to the truth?" Again and again we recognize in *The Fall* the sound of Camus's voice, his hatred of a Paris peopled by "four million silhouettes" with its taste for sports and the theatre, its instinctive scorn for the structures of society that consume the individual—"job, family, organized leisure activities."

The Fall is therefore a confession—an indirect confession, the only sort Camus could ever make; a falsified confession, as if he were replying to his accusers: a fraud? that's what I am at heart, so thoroughly that I don't see through the fraud myself. You never realized how right you were. Then he roars with laughter at the joke. *The Fall* might have been merely a long, drawn-out complaint, a lengthy plea for pity. Camus preferred to make it humorous. He had been called scornful, uncommitted, and a pharisee. Very well. He agrees. And he un-masks himself, tears himself to pieces with a somber gaiety. You wished, gentlemen, to knock the statue off its pedestal? He joins you. And he pushes harder than anyone else, stamping on the idol, breaking it into a thousand pieces. Arrogant? And how! "As a matter of fact, by dint of being so complete a man, I found myself rather a superman." Vain to boot and rotted with self-conceit. "Half Cerdan, half de Gaulle, if you please . . . Yes, I have never felt comfortable except in lofty places . . . I preferred the bus to the subway, open carriages to taxis, terraces to closed-in places." Generous? Come now!

> I also liked, and this is harder to say, I liked to give alms. A very Christian friend of mine admitted that one's initial feeling on seeing a beggar ap-

> proach one's house is unpleasant. Well, with me it was worse: I used to exult . . . To kiss the hand of a poor woman and break away, believe me, dear sir, this is achieving more than the vulgar ambitious man, rising to that supreme summit where virtue is its own reward.

As if by bravado, Camus intends to be the first at this deadly game in which his head is at stake. Then he can laugh a semi-distressed, semi-triumphant laugh and dominate the snickers or the murmurs of pity that had not failed to accompany him in his fall. . . .

But pain is not far away. The cry of the drowning woman echoes unceasingly in *The Fall* and interferes with Clamence's rhetoric. It sums up all the little acts of cowardice of which a man is capable, all the little failings, the moments of hard-heartedness. Who has not lied sometimes if only by omission? Who has not let fall a hand outstretched? Who has not, either from indifference or laziness turned away from some desperate young woman who wanted to die. "I make strict rules for myself, to correct my nature. And in the end it's my nature that I obey. The result is not brilliant." For there is almost no "nature," however generous it may be, which does not hesitate some day before icy water.

It is at this point that Camus lies in wait for us. His confession is ours. Let him who has never sinned throw the first stone. Those who reproached him for playing judge and public prosecutor, what were they themselves if not so many Fourquier-Tinvilles? So many manifestoes, so many signatures collected for the world's victims, and to what end? To give a clear conscience to the signers, the "professional humanists." All of them guilty, all, and wretched about it. All condemned to discomfort, to the spittle of passers-by.

The Fall is therefore a descent into Hell. "Are you familiar with Dante?" Clamence asks. Holland and her people ("I like these people . . . they're double") symbolize the modern hell of bad faith: merchants and Puritans, the Dutch dream of gold and of smoke. Here with "stagnant waters, the smell of dead leaves rotting in that canal," the odor of decay, we are at the heart of universal ambiguity. The isle of Marken is the most beautiful of "negative" landscapes, the "nether" side *par excellence;* the Zuider Zee is a dead sea ("No one knows where it begins or ends"), an absurd sea. Amsterdam, finally, takes shelter behind its canals like Pluto's kingdom behind the River Styx with its three times three excitement.

Ambiguity weighs on men as on things. All men claim they are innocent, but they all yield to the irresistible urge to judge. "We are all exceptional cases. We all want to make some kind of an appeal! Everyone insists on being innocent, even if in order to be so he must accuse the human race and all men." Camus came close here to a Pascalian analysis of man's powers of self-deception, self-love, and imagination: "I have brought to the light of day the profound duplicity of [all] creatures . . ." A few sentences suffice to dismiss any other recourse. The Greek idea of "balance" is lost: "The order of the world, too, is ambiguous." Beneath its serious façades, humanism is frivolous. Nietzschean power leads to delirium. Faith itself is equivocal, like the faith of Peter, the three-time renegade "on whom the Church is built." As to Christ, is he not the symbol of innocent guilt, he who benefited from the massacre of the Judean children? If religion once represented "a great washing clean," that was only at most during the three years preceding the crucifixion. Since then "the judges have multiplied, judges of every race, the race of Christ and of anti-Christs, which incidentally are the same."

For the great revolutionary movement which delivered the nineteenth century from God liberated it neither from judgment nor from necessity. Courts of justice are everywhere; the innocent accuse themselves publicly. "There are no more friends, there are only accomplices," victims and executioners, and, as before, masters and slaves. Power is no longer sought after as a remedy for boredom as Pascal suggested, but because it saves one from being judged. And henceforth the judgment itself has no foundation. Like Camus himself, the modern world has "the sense of the sacred" but no faith in a future life. One ought to conclude from this that sentences are relative, since "a day will come when the guilty person, too quickly executed, will not seem quite so black," since our civilization "has lost the only values which justify in a certain way the suppression of human life." But our world, deservingly represented by Clamence and by Verkovensky, hardly knows how to write anything besides "odes to the police and deifications of the guillotine."

For years Camus had done his utmost to preserve a certain innocence. Yet he had not escaped misfortune, that punishment without judgment, and his whole work protested against this form of injustice suffered by man. With war and a succession of trials, he was forced to discover the human beast, the beast which accuses, tortures and kills, which he had predicted in *Caligula* and later unmasked in *The Rebel.* But at least he had always hoped to escape "from the worst human torment, to be judged without law." In vain. Now it was his turn to confess; what, he did not know exactly. But own up he must, to escape from solitude, to recover solidarity, even if it had to be in an act of semi-collusion.

"I took the fellow by surprise," wrote J. P. Sartre in *The Prisoner of Altona,* as if in echo to *The Fall,* whose significance and purpose he understood:

> I struck; a man fell; in his dying eyes I saw the beast still alive—myself. One and one make one. What a misunderstanding! This rank and flavorless taste in my mouth—does it come from man, from myself? It's *le goût du siècle,* the flavor of the times. Happy ages gone by, you know nothing of our

hates; how would you understand the atrocious power of our deadly loves? Love, hate, one and one . . . Acquit us!

It would take another article to show how much Frantz von Gerlach (hero of Sartre's play) echoes Clamence, and how much, perhaps, in their respective solitude, Camus and Sartre came to understand each other better without being able to stand each other any longer. "An estrangement is nothing . . . just a way of living together," Sartre wrote at the time of Camus's death. One plus one make one . . . There is salvation neither outside this world nor within it: one plus one, this world is a lie and still the only truth; the man who kills and betrays dreams of innocence; but his dream itself is a lie. "My reflection in the mirror was smiling, but it seemed to be a double smile" (*The Fall*).

The honest judges are in the cupboard, the house of Descartes gives shelter to madmen. The doves, who are grace itself, wait in vain for a head to light upon. And the ballet master of this *danse macabre* among the ruins is Jean-Baptiste Clamence, "the empty prophet for a second-rate time," the very reverse of that other prophet, the harbinger. Clamence, "our scurvy kind of Christ," is the opposite of Meursault, "the only Christ we deserve." *The Stranger* owed its rhythm to its indirect style, to the intentional difficulties in its language. *The Fall* is nothing if not direct in style; it demonstrates a dizzying verbal facility. By turns lyrical, mocking, insinuating, sententious, the penitent judge imposes on everyone—on the critic as well—his caprices, his feigned friendliness, his syncopated style, grinding sarcasm, careless manner, aggressiveness, the poetry of his foggy hell, his feverish need to dominate, his whisperings and sudden outbursts—everything that can throw off the track. Meursault was simplicity, nudity, innocence incarnate; Clamence is duplicity, grimace, and mask. The one can be reduced to a thick transparency, the other toys with mirrors, finding a face for himself reflected in the face or faces of his interlocutor, be they singular or plural. He chatters on, protected behind a stream of words as if behind thick dark glasses, a third-rate ham like Cocteau's Liar, but so much more human in his anonymity.

Each one of his phrases is either a question or a challenge—and what is irony if not the challenge of an interrogation without any answer. Clamence's derisive, ferocious laugh tears him apart and tears us apart. This compulsive talker is of the same species as the "possessed," the terrorist who indulges in calculated, experimental explosions. Summing up in his person centuries of Manichaean dualism, of confessional and inquisition—whether Christian or revolutionary—he exhales his fetid breath over everything; he corrupts, he disintegrates, reasonably and with elegance.

In other words, for the praise of ambiguity which *The Fall* is essentially, Camus needed an ambiguous character whose every remark was questionable. He alone could smile while suffering, be brilliantly modest, fraternally domineering, and courteously cruel. Only he could become an abstract of all doubt and pain and make of failure not only revenge, but victory. "It is when a writer gives proof of an admirable mastery of the means of expression," Camus said in 1943, "that his failure becomes instructive." Discomfort certainly seems to have increased Camus's facility at writing—as if suffering, reawakening a long-absent cruelty, made him more alert, less stiff, freer already.

For he freed himself in part. He proved that neither Meursault nor Sisyphus had been murdered. He revived and brought to light all the anxieties which—in order better to cure them—he had formerly repressed and was accused of having snuffed out. *The Fall* is an act of purification. Camus settled an account not only with the scoffers but with himself. The author, like the fictitious narrator, like Faulkner's Temple Drake, like Dostoevsky's Nicolai Stavrogin, has let himself slide to the depths of confession, self-disgust and despair. To be born anew, he has cleansed the abcess. His wisecracks are like the grin of a patient projecting forth his pain. Camus knew that in the depths of despair he would somehow be able to give the kick that would make him rebound to the surface, there to rediscover the other, "right" side up of things. He accepted his responsibility so as to regain his innocence. He had to do away with bad faith and complacency along with "the fear of not being sincere and of lying in the face of death," so that he might regain that multiplicity of being as dear to the actor as to the "absurd" Don Juan, the equilibrium between Apollo and Dionysus.

So the "mentor" has disappeared, the guide to thought and action. "In order to teach, one must know. In order to guide others one must guide oneself." Once more Camus grappled with "nostalgia for the deep unity of the universe . . . the leaning toward ontology," which had never ceased to haunt him. He moved back again—and we along with him—to the relative. "We enter the world heavy with an infinite necessity . . . total responsibility never existed, nor consequently any absolute punishment or reward." Sometimes we shall have to defend the individual against the community and sometimes the community against the individual. Whether this be relativism in method or moral opportunism is entirely a question of proportion. We keep running back and forth with the marker on the scale, toward more solitude or toward more solidarity.

In Stockholm Camus spoke of his writing in similar terms. Discussing the artist and his time, he rejected the evasions and diversions of Parisian style just as firmly as the black and white concept of social realism. "The greatest work will always be, as in Greek tragedy, in Melville, Tolstoy or Molière, work that strikes a balance between the real and man's opposition to the real . . . The world is nothing, and the world is everything; this is the double and untiring cry of every true artist." Ambiguous by vocation, the artist "absolves rather than condemns. He is not judge but justifier; . . . the great work of art always finally confounds all judges." Camus no longer wishes to see the black and the white superposed one over the other, each concealing the other, to the great delight of every sort of prosecution. He wants to put them side by side, and more or less mingle them. There is no right side without its reverse, no exile without a kingdom and, vice-versa, no realism without dream.

Relieved of the dualism he was accused of, Camus could breathe freely. Nothing certainly is pure; nothing and no one is innocent; but neither is anyone completely guilty. Innocent *and* guilty: that is man; this conjunction re-establishes the balance and reconciles us with ourselves. What do they matter, the multiple faces people attribute to us or discover in us? Ambiguity is no longer a lie, complexity is no longer complicity. The adulterous woman has not betrayed anyone: she is double—both called by the desert and yet linked to her shopkeeper husband by all the force of habit. Lying close against the sleeping man, she is alone, but would she be less alone confronting the desert? Who can call it adultery when what is in question is a long exile and a kingdom half-glimpsed? With this slightly dumpy little housewife—nonetheless a creature of space, and a nomad at the bottom of her heart—we are a long way away from the abstract and anonymous judge—penitent reduced to his own sly laughter. Perhaps the tears of an aging woman may save us finally from judgment.

Childless and without a future, Janine is forty. Solitude and the cold of the approaching winter lie in wait for her. "She dreamed of the straight and flexible palm trees and of the young girl she had been." The years have slowly worn Janine down, she is heavier. "She really couldn't bend over without gasping a bit for breath . . . She stood there feeling heavy, her arms hanging, slightly stooped . . ." Too thick and too white. What do we know about Meursault's Marie, Rieux's wife, or Rambert's mistress? A beautiful figure, a silhouette seen through the window of a train, a head of hair snuggled in the hollow of a shoulder. But the adulterous woman "breathes with difficulty . . . fears the heat, the swarms of flies, the dirty hotels full of seedy smells." She carries a bag; wine makes her sleepy. Camus's characters are no longer seen from behind, like Rieux, or in silhouette like Tarrou; they have bodies—or rather Camus noticeably gives their physical form and feelings a place in the story. Symbols—formerly carefully introduced by observed details and emphasized through incidents and commentaries—are buried now under a mass of details and appear only at the very end of the stories. The very weight of the characters protects them from abstraction.

The same deep-rootedness, which accompanies a certain slowness in the narration, characterizes two robust short stories, "The Guest" and "The Silent Men." If Camus wanted to prove that he, too, was capable of not going beyond the story, and, as he told me jokingly one day, of writing in the vein of "socialist realism," he certainly won his bet. There is nothing to say about "The Silent Men" except that it reads in one sitting, that the characters impose on the reader their presence, their meager joys, their artisans' pride, their anger and their impotence—a rough, virile, hard world where every word has its weight. In "The Guest" the schoolmaster Daru, the policeman, and the Arab murderer are scarcely less silent—as if to set off the renegade priest's unstemmable flow of words. Behind all these silences one comes right up against a terror of death and poverty, a host of unexpressed sufferings, like those Camus had described in *L'Envers et l'endroit* (Betwixt and Between). All the misery of Algeria is suggested in a single comment: "This is the way the region was, cruel to live in, even without men—who didn't help matters either. But Daru had been born here. Everywhere else, he felt exiled." ("The Guest" in *Exile and the Kingdom.*) Daru, Balducci, the coopers, Ballesta, Esposito, Marcou, Yvars, Janine, and Marcel are Algerians and belong to the petty working class of whites that Albert Camus had known in his youth. His Belcourt pals have all grown older. They have become teachers, policemen, shopowners, workers not much richer than before—modest people, sturdy as vines, like Céleste, the bistro-owner in *The Stranger*. They have their worries, their narrow lives, holding no other promise for their old age; like them all, Yvars has "nothing to do but to wait quietly without quite knowing for what." But something in them rebels, and the call of the desert that once had set their ancestors in motion sounds again: "You're from hereabouts, and you are a man." ("The Guest") A man is what Céleste in *The Stranger* says about Meursault: not a condensation of honesty, conscience, humanity—ah, you know the modern bromides—but a certain sense of honor, physical courage, boredom, and dreams, a prince on the beach and an exile in the city.

The whole of Camus's adolescence comes out again in gusts, along with his "present," and shows him a deeply torn Algerian. As if Camus feared he might be misunderstood, that the luxuriance of his *Noces* (Nuptials) might have smothered our memories of the cold Algeria of the Kabyl and the Aurès mountains, he brings to life in counterpoint a whole stark and silent world, worn down by the wind like the stones of Djemila. Greeted by the raucous cries of the shepherds, shocked by the rugged, proud and disquieting faces of the Arabs, among the red and black rugs, the odors of wool, mint and spices, our Algerians feel like strangers and yet like relatives. Impoverished princes, reduced to indignation, "they think they can get away with anything now"—they console themselves with little—but they are in business too! ("The Adulterous Woman") We are far here from the proud adolescence of Camus's "Summer in Algiers," far, too, from the tea-roses of his Tipasa. Algeria is the country of exile as well as of the kingdom. As if by contrast, the desert indefinably virgin and sterile like the sea reddens under the fires of the setting sun. "Since the beginning of time, on the dry earth of this limitless land scraped to the bone, a few men had been ceaselessly trudging along, possessing nothing but serving no one, poverty-stricken but free lords of a strange kingdom" —supremely absurd beings dedicated to space, not to time; knights of adventure and of the undefined renewing of experience, in emptiness; nomads living at the margin of our civilizations, like the last witnesses of our nostalgia, like a reproach and a temptation. Janine, their sister and secret spouse, face to face with the desert:

> Breathing deeply, she forgot the cold, the dead weight of living persons, the madness and choking of the long anguish of living or dying. . . . The last stars of the constellations dropped their clusters a bit lower along the horizon of the desert and became immobile. Then, with an unbearable sweetness, the water of the night began to fill Janine, submerging the cold, and rising little by little from the hidden core of her being overflowing in wave after wave. . . .

For a short instant Daru gives in to the same dazzling vision on the bare plateaus of South Algeria. "Daru breathed in deeply the fresh morning light. He felt a sort of rapture before the vast, familiar expanse, now almost entirely yellow under its dome of blue sky." ("The Guest") The renegade priest himself, for whom faith was a sun, what had he come to seek in the city of salt if not its burn?

> Fierce sun! It is rising; the desert is changing; it has lost its mountain cyclamen color. Oh my mountain, and the snow, the soft enveloping snow—no, it is rather a greyish yellow, the ugly moment before the great resplendence. Nothing, still nothing from here to the horizon over yonder where the plateau disappears in a circle of still soft colors. . . . I feel the sun on the stone above me; it is striking, striking like a hammer on all the stones and it is the music, the vast music of noon, air, and stones vibrating over hundreds of kilometers. . . . ("The Renegade")

This is strange poetry which praises only sterility or delirium and whose barbaric accents echo to the heart of South America during the heavy, warm night when black girls in a state of trance celebrate the feast of St. George: "The intensified beat of the drums provided her with a sort of invisible support around which to entwine her languid arabesques until, stopping again, together with the music tottering on the edge of equilibrium, she uttered a strange bird cry, shrill and yet melodious" ("The Growing Stone"). Fascinating black Diana, grimacing fetishes, haunting images of a barbaric age in the process of disappearance, you drifted in Camus's memory like some dark Greece. There was innocence here, too, in "the long collective, colorless cries, without apparent respiration, without modulation" of bodies abandoned to convulsions, in the interminable march of nomads without problems or illusions. But our heroes, like our author, resemble Janine, "too thick, too white for the world she had just entered." The color of their skin, the heaviness of their limbs which reveals a surfeit of worldly goods excludes them from the community of simple people.

> D'Arrast, bewitched by the slow dance, was watching the black Diana when the cook suddenly loomed up before him, his smooth face now distorted. The kindness had disappeared from his eyes, revealing nothing but a sort of unsuspected avidity. Coldly, as if speaking to a stranger, he said: "It is late, Captain, they are going to dance all night long, but they don't want you to stay now."

Too late for d'Arrast, for Janine, for Daru; too late for a mechanized mercantile Europe, wholly launched in Promethean conquest. Tourists, ethnologists, perhaps. But never again hosts. The abandon of the adulterous woman, the loyalty of the schoolmaster, the servility of the renegade will not prevent their being suspect. Sunrise over the plateaus, a glimpse of the immensity of the desert, the hallucinating memory of a city black with light or of a ritual dance is all they can take away: "It is too late, captain." It is midnight in our era. Their "kingdom" they will bury in their secret hearts until a time when they can sleep in a valley of olive trees.

It is true that d'Arrast carries the stone to the man's hut, and there hears the words "Sit down with us," spoken by a native who mistrusted him the day before. But to gain the confidence of the few he has had to disappoint the expectations of the many who shouted: "To the church, to the church." Can the friendship of a few console him for not being loved by all?

There is misunderstanding everywhere: for Jonas, torn between the exigencies of his art and the obligations of fame; for Janine aspiring to dream and love, held back by habit and the need to be two; for the host, prisoner of a double fidelity, crushed between two recently born fanaticisms; for the silent men, caught between the logic of the working class struggle and the deep sympathy inspired by the suffering of a child; for d'Arrast, tempted for a short while by the mystique of a community, then brought back to individual men; for the cook himself, torn between pleasure and a promise made. Is no one either innocent or guilty any longer? The husband or the wife; the boss or the workman; the artist or his disciples; the murderer or the policeman; or more particularly, the schoolmaster with "clean hands?"

If this were so, if, endowed with a life of his own but incarnating one of Camus's temptations, each of these characters escaped judgment, then we should have returned to that stage in *l'Envers et l'endroit,* where nothing is justified, to be sure, but where all is explicable. An "adulterous" woman, a renegade missionary, workers reduced to silence, a guest who is suspect, a half-breed who is a perjurer—"what does it matter if all is accepted? After all, the sun warms our bones just the same." Camus shrugs his shoulders. Yet perhaps he forced his work in a certain direction, purposely introducing the "idea of a kingdom" into these stories of *Exile;* betting on life, on men? Just one stone, in the center of the hearth, but a stone which grows and which Camus threw there, before leaving, in a last great effort. Was this a gesture of consolation or was it the stone around which the first man might rebuild his hut? If they crowded together a bit, all our exiles could come there to warm their old age.

All? No, just the same. The "confused mind" would not obtain his grace. The missionary whose passion for the absolute makes him bow before fetishes, whose ardor to serve throws him into servitude—it is only too evident Camus will not forgive him, nor those penitent judges, beating in accusation on the breasts of others. Between its first publication in the *Nouvelle Revue Française* and the final edition, "The Confused Mind" became "The Renegade." To live, alas, is to judge. And the remainder of guilt on the rebound unexpectedly hits the schoolmaster in his mountains: "You handed over our brother. You will pay for this." An anonymous hand turns the innocent man into a traitor and makes of the host a stranger in the only land he loves, makes an adulteress of the little Algerian woman guilty of dreaming, and a perjurer of the cook. The step from equilibrium to equivocation is quickly taken. Except for the renegade, stifled by a handful of salt, all our heroes are condemned to *malconfort,* condemned to live in love and despair. Clamence's sirupy voice still whispers in our ears and floats over the holy water fount our age bathes in. The mists of the Zuyder Zee float over the Cherona and the forests of the Amazon. Is there no land free of sin? Where is the innocence and the serenity of the pristine heart? But did they ever exist?

Twenty years of a writer's life and, at the end as at the beginning, the Algerian bareness, the bitter odor of human lives, a few quickly subdued movements of lyricism and irony. The brilliant volubility of the renegade, the discretion of the adulterous woman, the realism of the silent men, and the schoolmaster host: everything is good that "renews forms, untiringly." But the artist is saying the same thing nonetheless, obsessed by "the two or three simple and great images" inherited from his childhood.

"*All* my work lies ahead of me." When he said this Camus repudiated nothing in his past; he was speaking like Sisyphus, determined to smile at his own doubts and to continue on his way—still the same way. After Oedipus, after Montaigne, he stubbornly repeated "all is well, all is in order, the failure and the hatreds, the triumphs and the defeats." It was only that he did not advance in quite the same way. *The Fall* had left behind something less assured in his step, a bitter crease at the corner of his mouth, and a slight trembling in his voice.

"One can be sure of nothing, you see." Neither of what one says, nor of what one writes. There are two ways we can be betrayed. "In order to cease doubting, one must simply cease being." Supreme irony! We have not finished questioning his work and answering his questions. Camus is as uncertain today as he was yesterday. This, doubtless, is why he has not ceased to exist.

Camus as Dramatist

by Henry Popkin

So honest a man as Camus is obviously at a disadvantage in so dishonest an institution as the theater. His sincerity has become a legend, but it has prevented him from becoming a successful dramatist. The Nobel Committee commended his "clear-sighted earnestness," and Harold Clurman called him "a moment in the conscience of mankind." Obviously, this is not a man who can easily lend himself to the subterfuges of the stage, who can say of his playwriting, as Henry James did: "Oh, how it must not be too good and how very bad it must be!" I can not think of a better application of the term "defect of his virtue"; Camus's strenuous virtue is the key to his plays and to his defective sense of the theater. Explicitly forswearing "psychology, ingenious plot-devices, and spicy situations," he requires that we take him in the full intensity of his earnestness or not at all.

Simple in plot, direct in argument, oratorically eloquent, his dramas are like few other modern plays. They remind us of Gide and of the early Sartre (in *No Exit* and *The Flies*), before Sartre mastered the deceptions of politics and of the stage. But even these comparisons are inadequate because Camus differs significantly from his many French contemporaries who have put ancient myths on the modern stage. The others have turned conventional myths—at least their antiquity has made them seem conventional—into instruments of iconoclasm. Obviously stimulated by French neo-classical drama, Cocteau, Giraudoux, and Sartre became the debunking inside-dopesters of ancient mythology; they made Oedipus into a young man on the make, Electra into a rather addled termagant, Zeus into a tyrant. They overturned or exposed the classical stories. But what Camus does is to begin with a sufficiently cynical legend—the history of Caligula or the murder of the prodigal son (the basis of Robert Penn Warren's "Ballad of Billie Potts")—and to dramatize it as forthrightly as possible, with no tricks, no sneers, no "modernization."

Both circumstances and characters are very carefully selected to per-

"Camus as Dramatist." From *Partisan Review, Summer,* 1959, pp. 499-503.

form only what the play requires. Nothing is ever thrown in for good measure or for any incidental purpose. We never encounter in these plays the casual bystanders whom a Broadway dramatist might permit to wander in. What characters there are have strict requirements imposed upon them. Camus primarily demands that his protagonists possess freedom, the capacity for exercising free choice. He has to go far to find his free men. His preference sets Camus off from his contemporaries in the theater; some of this difference is implicit in the contrast Eric Bentley once drew between "Strindbergian" and "Ibsenite" actors. The Strindbergian actor is less restrained: "His emotions come right out of him with no interference whatsoever and fly like bullets at the enemy." But Ibsen, not Strindberg, is the father of modern drama, and, consequently, modern stage characters keep their neuroses in check—or at least in balance. Camus's characters tend to be Strindbergian. Some of Strindberg's unbalanced heroes earn their freedom at the expense of their sanity; one of Camus's heroes, Caligula, pays just this price for freedom. Criminal purposes inspire the principal motivation of *The Misunderstanding* and so liberate the characters from ordinary scruples. The protagonists of *The Just Assassins* are also on the far side of the law, revolutionaries who have put aside the usual inhibitions and are in the act of measuring their freedom. The most dynamic figure in *State of Siege* is, like Caligula, in possession of supreme political power and subject to no regulation by sanity. Camus's characters tear right into the issues, and they ignore small details. Just as Lear's "Pray you, undo this button," could not have occurred in Racine, it also would be an unlikely line in Camus. Everyone in these plays is ready for action—or, more often, for argument. Nothing may intervene to distract, irritate, or enchant us, to explain the characters or to provide context for the events.

The characters are free so that they may best contribute to the simple patterns which the plays work out. Of the four plays at hand, two are constructed to the very simplest formulas—*The Misunderstanding* and *The Just Assassins.* The former play requires to be read as an equation. The prodigal son returns wealthy and incognito, to be killed by his desperate mother and sister. Most have seen in this play a perfect paradigm of the absurdity of hoping to escape from poverty or exile. Camus has become more optimistic about man's fate, but, in squeezing a new interpretation out of the play, he still, inevitably, reduces it to a formula.

> It can be reconciled with a relative optimism as to man. For, after all, it amounts to saying that in an unjust or indifferent world man can save himself, and save others, by practicing the most basic sincerity and pronouncing the most appropriate word.

In other words, don't play jokes on Mother. This is what Meursault, of *The Stranger,* saw in the same story, but even this authority is not conclusive. Surely it is more exact to say that the slightest weakness, the most innocent facetious impulse, will release an absurd and implacable destiny. Still, relatively optimistic or not, the play is flesh fitted to the bare bones of an equation.

Caligula is something else again. It has more life and irony than any of the other plays, and it comes closer than any of the others to a balanced, qualified statement of a complex theme. Caligula compels us to admire his comic talents; in one unconnected episode after another, this tyrant and mass-murderer engages our interest and even our sympathy with his ingenious exposures of patrician banality and the illogic of daily life. In his defense, this engaging monster is permitted to point out that he has caused far fewer casualties than a major war. A successful revolt fortunately reminds us that, all kidding aside, we need to find some compromise between banality and the loss of freedom.

The language of these plays is lofty and pure. It reflects the complaint Camus once lodged against our time: "For the dialogue we have substituted the communique." The dramatist sets out to remedy this situation, but his dialogue tends to become, especially in *The Just Assassins* and *State of Siege,* a formal exchange of weighty remarks which too clearly expose the dramatist's designs on us. Hardly anyone else in the modern theater lectures us quite so directly. If Arthur Miller conceives of the dramatist as a public speaker, he indicates some embarrassment at this role. In *The Crucible,* he conceals his public speaking in the awkwardness of his adaptation of seventeenth-century speech. Elsewhere, his tongue-tied orators salt their remarks with reminders of their semi-literacy: "Nobody dast blame this man." But Camus addresses us in the most elevated language he can write. The result has its merits as oratory and as dialectic, but it is deficient as drama.

The defect of Camus's plays bring to mind the virtues of his fiction, in which the method of narration always keeps us from colliding too abruptly with his themes and, above all, his ideas. This rationale surely underlies the impersonality of *The Stranger* and *The Plague,* as well as the highly subjective narration of *The Fall* and "The Renegade." The danger of becoming a pamphleteer in fiction must have been clear to Camus and must have compelled him to use technique as a shield for his ideas. But, in his plays, collisions are head-on; except in *Caligula,* we miss the theater's equivalents for the sophisticated method of his fiction.

Tribute to Albert Camus

by Jean-Paul Sartre

Six months ago, even yesterday, people wondered: "What is he going to do?" Temporarily, torn by contradictions that must be respected, he had chosen silence. But he was one of those rare men we can well afford to wait for, because they are slow to choose and remain faithful to their choice. Some day he would speak out. We could not even have dared hazard a guess as to what he might say. But we thought that he had changed with the world as we all do; that was enough for us to be aware of his presence.

He and I had quarreled. A quarrel doesn't matter—even if those who quarrel never see each other again—just another way of living together without losing sight of one another in the narrow little world that is allotted us. It didn't keep me from thinking of him, from feeling that his eyes were on the book or newspaper I was reading and wondering: "What does he think of it? What does he think of it *at this moment?*"

His silence, which according to events and my mood I considered sometimes too cautious and sometimes painful, was a quality of every day like heat or light, but it was human. We lived with or against his thought as it was revealed to us in his books—especially *The Fall,* perhaps the finest and least understood—but always in relation to it. It was an exceptional adventure of our culture, a movement of which we tried to guess the phases and the final outcome.

He represented in our time the latest example of that long line of *moralistes* whose works constitute perhaps the most original element in French letters. His obstinate humanism, narrow and pure, austere and sensual, waged an uncertain war against the massive and formless events of the time. But on the other hand through his dogged rejections he reaffirmed, at the heart of our epoch, against the Machiavellians and against the Idol of realism, the existence of the moral issue.

In a way, he *was* that resolute affirmation. Anyone who read or re-

"Tribute to Albert Camus." From *The Reporter Magazine,* February 4, 1960, p. 34.
 Translated by Justin O'Brien.

flected encountered the human values he held in his fist; he questioned the political act. One had to avoid him or fight him—he was indispensable to that tension which makes intellectual life what it is. His very silence, these last few years, had something positive about it: This Descartes of the Absurd refused to leave the safe ground of morality and venture on the uncertain paths of practicality. We sensed this and we also sensed the conflicts he kept hidden, for ethics, taken alone, both requires and condemns revolt.

We were waiting; we had to wait; we had to know. Whatever he did or decided subsequently, Camus would never have ceased to be one of the chief forces of our cultural activity or to represent in his way the history of France and of this century. But we should probably have known and understood his itinerary. He said so himself: *"My work lies ahead."* Now it is over. The particular scandal of his death is the abolition of the human order by the inhuman.

The human order is still but a disorder: it is unjust and precarious; it involves killing, and dying of hunger; but at least it is founded, maintained, or resisted by men. In that order Camus had to live. That man on the move questioned us, was himself a question seeking its reply; he lived *in the middle of a long life;* for us, for him, for the men who maintain order and for those who reject it, it was important for him to break his silence, for him to decide, for him to conclude. Some die in old age while others, forever on reprieve, may die at any minute without the meaning of their life, of life itself, being changed. But for us, uncertain without a compass, our best men *had* to reach the end of the tunnel. Rarely have the nature of a man's work and the conditions of the historical moment so clearly demanded that a writer go on living.

I call the accident that killed Camus a scandal because it suddenly projects into the center of our human world the absurdity of our most fundamental needs. At the age of twenty, Camus, suddenly afflicted with a malady that upset his whole life, discovered the Absurd—the senseless negation of man. He became accustomed to it, he *thought out* his unbearable condition, he came through. And yet one is tempted to think that only his first works tell the truth about his life, since that invalid once cured is annihilated by an unexpected death from the outside.

The Absurd might be that question that no one will ask him now, that he will ask no one, that silence that is not even a silence now, that is absolutely *nothing* now.

I don't think so. The moment it appears, the inhuman becomes a part of the human. Every life that is cut off—even the life of so young a man—is at one and the same time a phonograph record that is broken and a complete life. For all those who loved him, there is an unbearable absurdity in that death. But we shall have to learn to see that mutilated work as a total work. Insofar as Camus's humanism contains a *human* attitude toward the death that was to take him by surprise, insofar as his proud and pure quest for happiness implied and called for the *in-human* necessity of dying, we shall recognize in that work and in the life that is inseparable from it the pure and victorious attempt of one man to snatch every instant of his existence from his future death.

Chronology of Important Dates

1913 (November 7)	Albert Camus's birth in Mondovi, Algeria
1914	Father killed in Battle of the Marne, World War I
1918-23	Attends grade school at Belcourt in Algiers
1923-30	Scholarship student at the Lycée of Algiers
1930	Student of philosophy at University of Algiers; first serious attack of tuberculosis interrupts his preparation for career in college teaching; for next several years supports himself with a series of odd jobs
1933	A brief first marriage ending in divorce a year later
1934-35	Brief membership in Communist Party, with which he is soon disenchanted
1935	Actor-director-playwright in *Théâtre du Travail,* which he founds; production of *La Révolte dans les Asturies* (The Revolt in Asturia), of which he is part author
1936	Receives the *diplôme d'études supérieures* in philosophy
1937-39	Camus's *Théâtre du Travail* becomes the *Théâtre de l'Equipe*
1937	Publication of *L'Envers et l'endroit* (Betwixt and Between)
1938	Reporter for the *Alger Républicain,* publication of *Noces* (Nuptials)
1940	Second marriage, to Francine Faure, in Lyon; returns to Algeria in January, 1941
1942	Publication of *The Stranger* (*L'Etranger*); having left Algeria toward the close of 1942 to join French Resistance movement, becomes editor of clandestine newspaper *Combat*
1942-44	Recurrent attacks of tuberculosis

1943	Publication of *The Myth of Sisyphus* (*Le Mythe de Sisyphe*); becomes an editor at the Gallimard publishing house in Paris, a job he held until his death
1944	After Liberation continues as editor of *Combat;* production of *The Misunderstanding* (*Le Malentendu*) in Paris; meets Jean-Paul Sartre.
1945	Birth of the Camus twins, Jean and Catherine, in Paris; production of *Caligula*
1946-47	Lecture tour of United States
1947	Publication of *The Plague* (*La Peste*)
1948	Production of *State of Siege* (*L'Etat de siège*)
1949	Lecture tour of South America; production of *The Just Assasins* (*Les Justes*)
1949-51	New attacks of tuberculosis
1951	Publication of *The Rebel* (*L'Homme révolté*); controversy with Sartre
1952	Break with Jean-Paul Sartre
1956	Publication of *The Fall* (*La Chute*); production of Camus's adaptation of William Faulkner's *Requiem for a Nun* (*Requiem pour une nonne*)
1957	Receives Nobel Prize for "his important literary production, which with clearsighted earnestness illuminates the problem of the human conscience of our time"; publication of *Exile and the Kingdom* (*L'Exil et le royaume*)
1958	Production of Camus's adaptation of Dostoevsky's *The Possessed* (*Les Possédés*)
1959	Appointed by André Malraux, minister for cultural affairs of the French government, as director of the new state-supported experimental theater
1960 (January 4)	Camus's death in an automobile accident

Notes on the Editor and Contributors

GERMAINE BRÉE, editor of the anthology, is the author of *Camus, Marcel Proust and the Deliverance from Time, André Gide,* and, together with Margaret Guiton, *The Age of Fiction*. She is currently teaching at the Institute for Research in the Humanities of the University of Wisconsin.

The late RACHEL BESPALOFF, teacher and literary critic, taught at Smith College during the Second World War, and died soon after writing the article that appears in this volume.

ROBERT CHAMPIGNY, French critic, philosopher, and poet, is now teaching at the University of Indiana and has written studies of both Camus, *Sur un héros paiën* (A Pagan Hero), and Sartre, *Stages on Sartre's Way.*

NICOLA CHIAROMONTE, author, critic, and director of the Italian review *Tempo Presente,* was a close friend of Albert Camus.

SERGE DOUBROVSKY, French writer and critic, contributes frequently to French periodicals. He is a member of the department of modern languages at Smith College.

THOMAS HANNA, author of *The Thought and Art of Albert Camus,* received his Ph.D. at the Divinity School of the University of Chicago; at present he is teaching in the department of religion and philosophy at Hollins College.

S. BEYNON JOHN, since 1954 lecturer in French at the University of London, has recently completed a book on Sartre's literary art, *Sartre and the Moral Imagination.*

BERNARD G. MURCHLAND, C.S.C., a Holy Cross father, has taught at Notre Dame University and is a former editor of *Fides* magazine.

JUSTIN O'BRIEN has translated most of Camus's work, in particular, the stage version of *Caligula* presented on Broadway in 1960. Well-known for his biography of André Gide and for his many penetrating articles on contemporary French literature, he is chairman of the French department at Columbia University.

HENRY POPKIN is a frequent contributor to the *Partisan Review.*

ROGER QUILLIOT'S *La Mer et les prisons* (The Sea and the Prisons) is the best book-length study of Camus that has appeared in France.

GAËTAN PICON, outstanding French critic in the field of contemporary French literature, holds a position in the ministry for cultural affairs of the French government. Among his many books are critical studies of André Malraux and Georges Bernanos, as well as the *Panorama de la nouvelle littérature française*.

JEAN-PAUL SARTRE has achieved world-wide fame as philosopher, critic, playwright, and novelist, and as the chief exponent of French existentialism. Among his works are the two monumental treatises *Being and Nothingness* and *The Critique of Dialectical Reason,* the novel *Nausea,* the book of short stories translated as *Intimacy,* and such plays as *The Flies, No Exit, The Devil and the Good Lord,* and *The Prisoners of Altona.*

WILFRID SHEED, whose articles and short stories have appeared in *Vogue* and *The New Yorker,* is an associate editor of the Catholic periodical *Jubilee* and author of the novel *A Middle Class Education.*

Bibliography

Works by Camus

NOVELS:

La Chute. Paris: Librairie Gallimard, 1956. (*The Fall*. Translated by Justin O'Brien. New York: Alfred A. Knopf, Inc., 1957.)

L'Etranger. Paris: Librairie Gallimard, 1942. (*The Stranger*. Translated by Stuart Gilbert. New York: Alfred A. Knopf, Inc., 1946; Vintage Books, Inc., 1954. Translation published in England under the title of *The Outsider*.)

L'Exil et le royaume (Short Stories). Paris: Librairie Gallimard, 1957. (*Exile and the Kingdom*. Translated by Justin O'Brien. New York: Alfred A. Knopf, Inc., 1957.)

La Peste. Paris: Librairie Gallimard, 1947. (*The Plague*. Translated by Stuart Gilbert. New York: Alfred A. Knopf, Inc., 1948.)

PLAYS:

Caligula and Three Other Plays. Translated by Stuart Gilbert. Preface by Camus translated by Justin O'Brien. New York: Alfred A. Knopf, Inc., 1958.

L'Etat de siège. Paris: Librairie Gallimard, 1948.

Les Justes. Paris: Librairie Gallimard, 1950. (*The Just Assassins*. Translated by Elizabeth Sprigge and Philip Warner.

Le Malentendu suivi de *Caligula*. Paris: Librairie Gallimard, 1944.

La Révolte dans les Asturies: Essai de création collective. Algiers: Charlot, 1936.

TRANSLATIONS AND ADAPTATIONS:

Un Cas intéressant (Dino Buzzati). Paris: L'Avant-scène, 1955.

Le Chevalier d'Olmédo (Lope de Vega Carpio). Paris: Librairie Gallimard, 1957.

La dernière fleur (James Thurber). Paris: Librairie Gallimard, 1952.

La Dévotion à la croix (Pedro Calderón de la Barca). Paris: Librairie Gallimard, 1953.

Les Esprits (Pierre de Larivey). Paris: Librairie Gallimard, 1953.

Les Possédés (Dostoevsky). Paris: Librairie Gallimard, 1959. (*The Possessed*. Translated by Justin O'Brien with a foreword by Camus. New York: Alfred A. Knopf, Inc., 1960.)

Requiem pour une nonne (William Faulkner). Paris: Librairie Gallimard, 1957.

ESSAYS:

Actuelles I, II, III. Paris: Librairie Gallimard, 1950, 1953, 1958. (*Resistance, Rebellion and Death*. Selections from *Actuelles I, II* and *III*. Translated with an introduction by Justin O'Brien. New York: Alfred A. Knopf, Inc., 1961.)

L'Envers et l'endroit. Algiers: Charlot, 1937. Reprinted Paris: Librairie Gallimard, 1957 and 1958, with preface by Camus.

L'Eté. Paris: Librairie Gallimard, 1954.

L'Homme révolté. Paris: Librairie Gallimard, 1951. (*The Rebel*. Translated by Anthony Bower with a preface by Sir Herbert Read. New York: Alfred A. Knopf, Inc., 1954; Vintage Books, Inc., 1956.)

Lettres à un ami allemand. Paris: Librairie Gallimard, 1945.

Le Mythe de Sisyphe. Paris: Librairie Gallimard, 1943. (*The Myth of Sisyphus*. Translated by Justin O'Brien. New York: Alfred A. Knopf, Inc., 1955.)

Noces. Algiers: Charlot, 1938. Reprinted Paris: Librairie Gallimard, 1947.

Speech of Acceptance upon the Award of the Nobel Prize for Literature. Translated by Justin O'Brien. New York: Alfred A. Knopf, Inc., 1958; *Atlantic Monthly*, May, 1958, pp. 33-34.

Works on Camus

IN ENGLISH:

Brée, Germaine. *Camus* (includes bibliography). New Brunswick: Rutgers University Press, 1959; revised 1961.

Cruickshank, John. *Albert Camus*. London: Oxford University Press, 1959; New York: Galaxy Books, 1960.

Hanna, Thomas. *The Thought and Art of Albert Camus*. Chicago: Henry Regnery Co., 1958.

Maquet, Albert. *Albert Camus: The Invincible Summer*. Translated by Herma Brissault. New York: George Braziller, Inc., 1958.

Thody, Philip. *Albert Camus: A Study of His Work*. London: Hamish Hamilton Ltd., 1957. Distributed by Macmillan Co., New York.

IN FRENCH:

Brisville, Jean-Claude. *Camus*. Paris: Librairie Gallimard, 1959.

Champigny, Robert. *Sur un héros païen*. Paris: Librairie Gallimard, 1959.

Luppé, Robert de. *Albert Camus*. Paris: Editions Universitaires, 1958.

Maquet, Albert. *Albert Camus ou l'invincible été*. Paris: Editions Debresse, 1955.

Quilliot, Roger. *La Mer et les prisons: Essai sur Albert Camus* (with an extensive bibliography of Camus's work). Paris: Librairie Gallimard, 1956.

Thorens, Léon. *A la rencontre d'Albert Camus*. Brussels-Paris: La Sixaine, 1946.